Classroom Observation

Classroom Observation explores the pivotal role of lesson observation in the training, assessment and development of new and experienced teachers. Offering practical guidance and detailed insight on an aspect of training that is a source of anxiety for many teachers, this thought-provoking book provides a critical analysis of the place, role and nature of lesson observation in the lives of education professionals.

Illustrated throughout with practical examples from a range of education settings, it considers observation as a means of assessing teaching and learning and also as a way of developing teachers' skills and knowledge. Key topics include:

- the purposes and uses of lesson observation
- the socio-political and historical context in which lesson observation has developed
- practical guidance on a range of observation models and methods
- teacher autonomy and professional identity
- performance management, professional standards and accountability
- peer observation, self-observation and critical reflection
- using video in lesson observation.

Written for all student and practising teachers as well as teacher educators and those engaged in educational research, *Classroom Observation* is an essential introduction to how we observe, why we observe and how it can be best used to improve teaching and learning.

Matt O'Leary is Principal Lecturer and Research Fellow in Post-Compulsory Education at the Centre for Research and Development in Lifelong Education, University of Wolverhampton, UK.

Classroom Observation

A guide to the effective observation
of teaching and learning

Matt O'Leary

Routledge
Taylor & Francis Group

LONDON AND NEW YORK

14 - 891809 - 2

First published 2014
by Routledge
2 Park Square, Milton Park, Abingdon, Oxon OX14 4RN

and by Routledge
711 Third Avenue, New York, NY 10017

Routledge is an imprint of the Taylor & Francis Group, an informa business

British Library Cataloguing in Publication Data
A catalogue record for this book is available from the British Library

Library of Congress Cataloging in Publication Data
A catalog record for this book has been requested

ISBN: 978-0-415-52578-7 (hbk)
ISBN: 978-0-415-52579-4 (pbk)
ISBN: 978-0-203-11973-0 (ebk)

Typeset in Galliard
by Keystroke, Station Road, Codsall, Wolverhampton

Printed and bound in Great Britain by
TJ International Ltd, Padstow, Cornwall

Contents

Figures, tables and boxes

Figures

Tables

Boxes

Foreword

Denis Gleeson

Quality in education is high on the policy agenda, but what constitutes quality and how it is achieved and understood in practice is hotly contested. In addressing these questions, classroom observation has become an integral part of the way in which the quality of teaching and learning is assessed and measured. In an increasingly audit and inspection driven education system, classroom observation has become something of an omnipresent mechanism that permeates the working lives of teachers and lecturers throughout their careers. It is both a form of surveillance, which constitutes a technology of control, as well as an enhancement of teachers' professional learning and development. Given its dual purpose and central role in education improvement, it is somewhat surprising that classroom observation remains a largely under-researched field, until now.

This timely book explores the rich cultures of teaching and learning practice, which classroom observation visits and inhabits. It draws on a multi-method approach to educational research that makes evidence and data readily accessible to the reader, without pulling back on criticality. This is achieved through 'live' case studies and vignettes located in the contexts and cultures of teachers' work, which challenge market measures. A unique feature of the book is its ability to draw on a range of theories that intersect key areas of education, policy and practice. This is best exemplified in various sections that transcend conventional classroom observation models, entering realms of digital technology, lesson study and unseen observation, as ways of introducing more formative approaches of teacher development. Running through the book is the author's desire to develop a critical awareness and understanding among readers of the ideologies that underpin observation, as well as understanding its limits and possibilities in the current climate of educational positivism. *Classroom Observation: A Guide to the Effective Observation of Teaching and Learning* goes beyond its title in addressing both imposters. This is an authoritative and illuminative account of how democratic professionalism can unify the interests of students, tutors and institutions, in bringing education back in.

Denis Gleeson
University of Warwick and University of Wolverhampton

Acknowledgements

This book is dedicated to all those learners and teachers with whom I have worked throughout my career and have been a constant source of inspiration and motivation to me. In particular, I would like to thank my colleagues in the post-compulsory education (PCE) team at the School for Education Futures at the University of Wolverhampton, who have contributed to this book through on-going discussions, ideas, resources and, in the case of Dr Rob Smith, constructive feedback on the book itself. A big thank you also goes out to my many colleagues in the Further Education sector and the Trinity College London CertTESOL course providers who generously gave their time and shared ideas and resources around the topic of lesson observation with me.

I would also like to thank the editorial support I have received from Helen Pritt and Rhiannon Findlay at Routledge.

Finally, a special thank you to my wonderful wife and girls, Kate, Lola and Ella, for your continuing love and support.

Dr Matt O'Leary
Principal Lecturer in Post-Compulsory Education
Centre for Research and Development in Lifelong Education (CRADLE)
School for Education Futures
University of Wolverhampton

February 2013

Part I

Exploring the role of classroom observation in teaching and learning

Chapter 1

Introducing the book
Focus, content and structure

Introduction

This book explores the phenomenon of classroom observation and its role in the training, evaluation and continuing professional development (CPD) of pre-service and in-service teachers in the English education system. Whether it is in the context of an initial teacher training (ITT) course, a collaborative CPD programme, appraisal or an external inspection, classroom observation is a ubiquitous mechanism that permeates the working lives of all teachers from the beginning to the end of their careers. This book covers how observation is used in each of these contexts and discusses the associated purposes and processes involved.

Classroom observation has occupied a long-standing role in ITT and CPD, where it has commonly been used as a method of assessment and an important tool for nurturing key pedagogic skills and teacher learning. In recent years the use of observation has increased as governmental agencies such as the Office for Standards in Education (Ofsted) and colleges and schools, in particular, have come to rely on it as an important means of collecting evidence about what goes on in classrooms. Such evidence has invariably been used to inform current conceptualizations of what makes for effective teaching and learning along with providing the basis on which judgements about the performance and competence of teachers are made. This elevated profile makes it all the more surprising that it remains such an under-researched area of empirical inquiry with very few specialist books available. In drawing on data recently collected in a range of educational institutions in England, this book presents a detailed picture of the role(s) of observation and in so doing examines it through a critically informed lens that situates its use(s) in the varying contexts and cultures in which they appear.

Who is this book for?

The book is targeted at readers who require a broad and yet specialist coverage of the topic of classroom observation. It is designed to interest and serve the needs of all those involved in the observation process, i.e. those being observed (observees), those carrying out observations (observers) and those responsible for managing observation schemes on an institutional level. This far-reaching appeal means that it is likely to interest and be relevant to the following readers:

- Undergraduate and postgraduate students on ITT, in-service teacher training (INSET) and CPD courses in the compulsory schools' sector and post-compulsory sector

- Teacher educators and trainers involved in the field of professional learning/ development in schools, colleges and universities
- Middle and senior managers responsible for assessing and improving the quality of teaching and learning in schools, colleges and universities
- Academics and students engaged in educational research with a focus on the use of classroom observation.

What are the aims of this book?

This book is underpinned by two overarching aims. The first seeks to enable the reader to acquire a comprehensive and situated insight into the role(s) of classroom observation in the educational arena, leading to a greater understanding of how observation is used, in what contexts and for what purposes. The second aims to promote a critically informed awareness among readers of the underpinning ideologies and conceptual frameworks associated with the uses of observation, as well as its potential value as a tool for enhancing teacher learning and development.

How is this book different from others?

Previous publications have tended to take the form of textbooks whose focus has been on the *practice* or *pedagogy* of classroom observation with limited discussion of the wider socio-political contexts and cultures in which it is situated. In my opinion, such books have lacked a theoretical underpinning to them, which has resulted in a narrow and often apolitical conceptualization of observation. One of the unique strengths of this book is its ability to draw on a range of theories to synthesize elements of policy, practice and context when discussing observation. It argues that developing a critical awareness of the ideologies that underpin observation as a form of intervention in teaching and learning is fundamental to the reader acquiring a thorough understanding of it and its place in the educational arena. The notion of *critical reflection* therefore undergirds the analysis throughout the book. In short, at the centre of the book's original contribution is a critical approach to examining the ideologies that underpin extant models of observation, informed by a rich and recent set of empirical data collected from a range of educational institutions (colleges) in England.

This is not a toolkit or a 'how to' book but more of a 'why?' and 'how about?' book. All too often when practitioners are tasked with mediating and operationalizing government policies and initiatives, there is a pressure to come up with a 'quick fix'. This book is not interested in or designed to offer quick fixes but is more about getting practitioners to engage critically and reflexively with the mechanism of classroom observation and its role in their professional lives. Over the past twenty years or so a whole industry of 'education consultancy' has developed in England offering its services, most of which are targeted at improving the quality of educational provision. More often than not these services are reactive as they take their lead from the latest government and/or Ofsted agenda. In the case of classroom observation, this has typically consisted of consultants offering advice on what makes an observation system 'robust' and 'rigorous', or providing insights into what makes an outstanding teacher or lesson. It is not the intention of this book to go down the consultancy path, but to develop an informed awareness of current practices and future possibilities with a view to empowering practitioners to understand how they can use observation to be the best that they can be in their chosen profession.

What is the theoretical framework of this book?

Conceptualizing classroom observation is not an easy task given it is a topic that crosses over into several disciplines such as educational management, professional development, teacher assessment and teacher identity to name but a few. This multi-disciplinary nature of classroom observation means that it makes it very difficult to rely on a single theory or conceptual framework in order to make sense of it. What this book therefore attempts to do is to draw on a range of theories and ideas from different disciplines so as to provide a broad and varied insight into the topic. For instance, the book draws on the work of the French sociologist, Michel Foucault (1977, 1980, 2002) as its theoretical backbone, along with aspects of critical pedagogy (e.g. Brookfield 1995, 2005; Freire 1972, 2005) and concepts relating to theories of new managerialism (e.g. Clarke *et al* 1994; Clarke and Newman 1994; Randle and Brady 1997) and performativity (Ball 2001, 2003, 2012), discussed in detail in Chapter 2. At the same time, it also makes use of concepts from the fields of assessment and teacher development, particularly in relation to the use of observation in assessing teachers' classroom performance (see Chapters 4 and 5) and how best it might be applied to encourage teachers to develop and learn from each other (see Chapters 7 and 8).

Foucault's work, for example, provides a suitable framework for analyzing the phenomenon of classroom observation from a sociological perspective. Some of the key concepts he explored in his work, i.e. power–knowledge, surveillance, discourse and normalization, resonate with the related literature on observation and underlying themes to emerge from the empirical data informing the book. They also provide a useful lens through which to examine relationships of individual agency (i.e. practitioner level) and structure (i.e. institutional level), as well as an appropriate language with which to describe and discuss the phenomenon of classroom observation.

Foucault's ideas about the paradoxical and complex nature of power link well with classroom observation in an applied context and the book's overarching critique of how it currently operates largely as a performance measurement within a regime of surveillance and regulation in schools and colleges in England. For Foucault, power was capable of being both repressive and liberatory in the same situation. This dichotomous conceptualization provides a useful framework for understanding the different contexts and cultures that impact on the way in which teachers make sense of observation. It also links to the contradictory notion of professionalism, i.e. that it can be used both to control and to empower teachers.

In Foucault's eyes, power and knowledge are inextricably linked. This has particular resonance for classroom observation given that it is regarded by many as the most important means of collecting knowledge about what happens in classrooms and what it can reveal about teaching and learning. Thus, viewing classroom observation through a Foucauldian lens inevitably connects its use to power, which means that if we are to construct a detailed understanding of it then we must also understand the mechanisms of power that underpin it. This discussion is developed further in subsequent chapters (e.g. Chapters 2, 3 and 5) when examining the socio-political background to its emergence and the key themes and issues surrounding its use in the English education system.

What are the main themes and topics covered in the book?

Some of the main themes and topics explored in the book include:

• Educational assessment and evaluation
• Knowledge and power
• Normalization
• Observation methods and models
• Professional autonomy
• Professional identity
• Professional learning and development
• Professional standards
• Teacher effectiveness.

How is the book organized?

The book is divided into three main parts, each of which explores classroom observation from a particular angle and comprises a series of interrelated chapters. Part I seeks to contextualize the topic against the wider socio-political and educational backdrop in which observation emerged as a key mechanism in teacher learning and assessment. I believe that an understanding of this wider context is essential for the reader to fully appreciate the way in which observation operates in the English education system and thus be able to critically reflect on it. Part II is likely to be of most interest to those who wish to explore the use of classroom observation as a method of assessment, whereas Part III shifts its focus onto the use of observation for professional development purposes.

At the end of each chapter there is a section that includes discussion topics/tasks that are aimed at encouraging the reader to develop their understanding and thinking around some of the key areas covered throughout that chapter. These are primarily designed to be done in pairs or small groups, though they can also be done individually if the reader does not have regular contact with other colleagues.

Part I – 'Exploring the role of classroom observation in teaching and learning' sets the scene for understanding how and why classroom observation emerged as a pivotal tool in the domain of teaching and learning. In focusing on the English education system as an exemplar case study, Chapter 2 situates its emergence against the socio-political, historical and educational contexts in which this took place. It provides a critical analysis of the wider socio-political developments underpinning the educational reforms that were responsible for the implementation of classroom observation as a key mechanism in the training and appraisal of teachers, many of which occurred in the wake of the introduction of a performance management-driven culture in schools and colleges. This analysis draws principally on theories and ideas most closely associated with the discipline of educational sociology in order to interpret some of these changes. The chapter also discusses what the implications have been and continue to be for new and experienced teachers in terms of what it means to be a 'professional' in the field of teaching in the 21st century.

Chapter 3 reviews a range of related literature across the three education sectors in England [i.e. schools, Further Education (FE) and Higher Education (HE)] in order to compare and contrast the role of observation. In doing so it discusses the key themes and issues surrounding its use in each sector and identifies both common and contrasting patterns. It argues that in schools and FE observation has become entrenched as a mechanism of performance management over the last two decades, from which a dominant yet contested model has emerged that has come to rely on a simplified rating scale to grade professional competence and performance. In contrast, in HE there is limited evidence of it being linked to the summative assessment of staff, with preferred models being peer-directed and less prescribed, allowing lecturers greater autonomy and control over the use of observation and the opportunity to explore its potential as a means of stimulating critical reflection and professional dialogue about practice among peers. The chapter concludes with a synopsis that draws together the recurring themes and issues to emerge across all three sectors, as well as highlighting areas that are discussed in more depth in later chapters.

Part II – 'Classroom observation as a means of assessing teaching and learning' concentrates on the application of observation as a form of assessment and is made up of three chapters. Chapter 4 examines the use of observation as a research method for collecting data about what goes on in classrooms. As part of the discussion, quantitative and qualitative approaches to observation are compared and situated in an applied classroom context with the aim of developing awareness of some of the pros and cons of each approach. Examples from previous studies and current models in use are presented in order to illustrate how quantitative and qualitative approaches differ in practice and what they can tell us about the process of teaching and learning. Validity and reliability, fundamental cornerstones of any research method, are considered and discussed in relation to the use of observation as a means of data collection along with the repercussions for subsequent judgements made about the quality of teaching and learning.

Chapter 5 explores differing typologies of classroom observation in the context of assessing teaching and learning. The first half of the chapter examines the links between observation models and their underlying purposes by discussing the interrelated questions of what models exist, in what contexts do they occur, what are their purported aims and to what extent are these achieved? In order to answer these questions, the discussion draws on empirical data from a range of studies carried out in different educational settings. Among topics discussed in the first half of this chapter is the use of observation for performance management purposes, with particular attention given to the 'Ofsted model' of graded observation and the effects of grading on teacher identity and notions of self. The second half of the chapter outlines some of the protocols and procedures associated with assessed observations and includes practical guidelines for observers and observees on their respective roles in the feedback discussion.

Chapter 6 discusses the topic of 'teacher effectiveness' and what it means to be an effective teacher. When it comes to assessing the quality and effectiveness of teaching and learning through observation, most models have tended to rely on competency-based approaches. This chapter critically evaluates the underpinning principles and constituents of such models as well as discussing what the implications are for teachers in the workplace and how best to make sense of them. A key part of the discussion in this chapter centres on teacher standards, including analysis of the 2012 Teacher Standards in England. Mindful of the practical needs and interests of teachers, the chapter provides a set of ten key principles for 'good' or 'effective' teaching that could be applied to any context.

Part III – 'Classroom observation as a means of promoting teacher learning and development' explores a range of collaborative approaches to observation, each of which is underpinned by its use as a mechanism for stimulating teacher growth. Chapter 7 focuses its discussion on examining the value of observation as a tool for developing expansive professional learning among practitioners. It starts by outlining the importance of critical reflection in teacher development, along with the perceived benefits of observation as a collaborative and reciprocal tool. Peer-based approaches to observation are discussed in detail, drawing on theories of expansive professionalism and democratic notions of professional learning (e.g. Avis 2003). This discussion is also linked to the wider concepts of autonomy and ownership in professional development. There is a separate section that includes a range of targeted observation tasks where the focus and structure is varied, enabling both observer and observee to maximize the developmental benefits of observation and to use these observations as a springboard for collaborative, professional dialogue and learning.

Chapter 8 explores some alternatives to conventional models of observation through three separate case studies. A description of how each of these alternative models work in practice is provided, along with discussion and analysis of their potential contribution to the way in which classroom observation might best be harnessed as a tool for enhancing teacher awareness and understanding of pedagogic skills and knowledge. The first case study focuses on a model or process known as 'lesson study', originating from Japan but recently employed in the USA and countries in the Pacific Rim. Lesson study is based on an action research model of classroom investigation where a group of teachers work collaboratively to study specific features of their subject curriculum and pedagogy, with a particular emphasis on improving student learning. Lesson study involves teachers working together to plan, teach and observe a lesson(s). While one teacher implements the lesson in the classroom, others observe and take notes on student questions and understanding, which is then discussed and analyzed in a post-lesson focus group. In theory, lesson study appears to offer a more democratic approach to professional development as it is the teachers themselves who shape the focus and direction of the study.

The second case study explores a radical model of observation known as 'unseen observation' in which the observer or 'supervisor' does not actually visit the class, but relies on the teacher's account of it after it has happened. It might therefore seem contradictory to use the term 'observation' as no observation takes place, but the teacher and supervisor meet before and after the lesson for a professional dialogue as is the norm in many models of observation. In order to illustrate how this model works in practice, this case study draws on data from a small-scale qualitative research project. Within this model the teacher is allowed the freedom to choose their own areas of development, as the supervisor acts as both an active listener and a facilitator in assisting the teacher's development. One of the distinctive qualities of unseen observation is its potential for a role reversal in the power dynamics between the observer and observee, or, in this case, the supervisor and teacher.

The third case study examines the use of state-of-the-art remote, mobile video technology as an alternative and/or replacement to a 'live observer' present in the classroom. It discusses the opportunities that this technology has to offer for innovative professional learning and development and explores some of the practicalities of its use. Although video recording has been used for several decades in classrooms, particular features that are unique about recent advances in remote, digital video technology include the ability for non-intrusive observer–observee interaction to occur remotely and for 'live' coaching to be transmitted through the use of an earpiece.

The final chapter, Chapter 9, draws together discussion from the previous chapters. It provides a critical synopsis of the key themes/issues and concludes with a list of recommendations about how classroom observation might best be used along with the possibilities for future areas of research.

Author's note

I am aware that in recent years there has been an increase in the use of the phrase 'Teaching, learning **and assessment**' in some educational circles. As such, some readers may be wondering why the word 'assessment' has not been included in the book's title. The answer to this question is quite straightforward. I see it as an integral part of the teaching and learning process and as such do not believe that it needs to be named separately.

Chapter 2

Classroom observation in context

Understanding the background to its emergence and use in the teaching profession

Introduction

Classroom observation has emerged as a pivotal tool for measuring, assuring and improving the professional skills and knowledge base of teachers in colleges and schools in recent years. Understanding why and how observation emerged as a key instrument requires an insight into the socio-political and historical contexts in which this occurred. As James and Biesta (2007: 11) remark:

> Teaching and learning cannot be decontextualized from broader social, economic and political forces, both current and historic, and that addressing this complexity directly is the most likely route to acquiring an understanding that will be most useful to policy and practice.

So if we are to appreciate fully why observation has become such an important mechanism then we need to examine the wider backdrop and how it fits in to this. Focusing on the English education system as an exemplar case study, this chapter situates the emergence of observation against the wider socio-political forces underpinning the educational reforms responsible for its implementation as a tool in the education sector. In drawing on aspects of Foucauldian theory as well as the twin phenomena of new managerialism and performativity (discussed in detail on p. 16), it provides a critical analysis of these wider socio-political developments and elucidates their role in contributing to the prominent position that observation currently holds in the training and assessment of teachers' classroom competence and performance and what it means to be a 'professional' in the field of teaching in the 21st century.

The policy backdrop to the emergence of classroom observation: an overview

The origins of classroom observation in England can be traced back to the middle of the 19th century where its emergence in state schools coincided with the government's introduction of Her Majesty's Inspectorate (HMI), whose remit was to assess whether public money was being well spent in the newly created 'schools for the poor' and to identify ways in which the then governmental office of education could help to further improve provision (Grubb 2000). Since then it has come to be largely associated with teacher education/training and appraisal. As Lawson (2011: 3) comments, 'it was first associated with pre-service training, then with initial training in a first job, then with competency procedures, and only more latterly with inspection and quality assurance measures'. Despite this long-standing history, it is only during the last twenty years, in particular, that schools and colleges in England have witnessed the widespread use of observation on a regular basis outside of the ITT context. In this short space of time it has become the cornerstone of quality assurance (QA) and quality improvement (QI) systems for teaching and learning (Armitage *et al* 2003; Wragg 1999).

Understanding the context and rationale for the emergence of observation requires the sewing together of a patchwork quilt of governmental policies and initiatives produced as part of the on-going reform agenda that has characterized the English education system in recent times. As this chapter discusses, one of the key drivers of these reforms has been the heightened emphasis placed on teaching and learning in spearheading the drive for *continuous improvement* in educational provision. This policy focus subsequently resulted in the development of a package of reforms and initiatives aimed at measuring attainment, raising standards and ultimately improving the quality of teaching and learning. It was in light of this that classroom observation emerged as an important multi-purpose vehicle for policymakers and practitioners alike.

These initiatives were themselves linked to a wider neo-liberal reform agenda intent on transforming the working cultures of public sector institutions by introducing new systems of management from the private sector that were designed to improve levels of performance, productivity and accountability. This approach to management is commonly referred to as 'new managerialism' or 'new public management' and has become associated with the way in which schools and colleges have operated since the early 1990s in England (e.g. Ball 2001). It is a subject that will be discussed in detail (see p. 16), but before moving on to this it is important to chart some of the key milestones that paved the way for such change.

Over four decades ago, Paulo Freire, one of the most prominent educational thinkers and theorists of 'critical pedagogy' during the last century, argued that education and politics were inextricably linked. Freire viewed all educational activity as a political act, particularly emphasizing the strong bond between education and power. Thus, for Freire, the decisions teachers make concerning their approach to the curriculum and the teaching and learning experience per se are ultimately political. In other words, there can be no such thing as a 'neutral' pedagogy. Although Freire's reference to the 'politics' of education was meant in the wider rather than the party political sense, his work coincided with a period in which government intervention in the educational curriculum was on the increase.

Roughly around the time of the publication of Freire's seminal text, *Pedagogy of the Oppressed* in the 1970s, the OPEC international oil crisis occurred, which was to have far-reaching and damaging financial reverberations for many of the world's leading economies. One of the neo-liberal responses to this crisis was to hold the educational establishment responsible for the subsequent economic downturn. 'Under achievement' and 'poor teaching' were blamed and the need for a greater reliance on market forces was emphasized (Maguire 2010). The OPEC oil crisis was thus to become the catalyst for a 'new context for governments', which was to result in a reconfigured globalization as Mahony and Hextall (2000: 5–6) describe:

> The 1970s and 1980s [w]as a significant period in which a number of material and political factors came together to provide a new context for governments. The power

of Western governments to deliver prosperity, security and opportunity to their citizens within 'walled' economies controlling the movement of capital, goods and services was undermined by a world recession created by escalating fuel prices following oil crises in the 1970s (Halsey *et al* 1997). Falling profits motivated multinational corporations to seek new markets, with increasing deregulation of the world economy and financial markets in the 1980s and 1990s making it easier for them to do so. This was sustained by the increasing political influence of the New Right and their mobilization of reaction against Keynesian economic and welfare policies. In this context the 'competition state' was born, pressuring governments to seek reductions in public expenditure (in order to attract inward investment) and to secure maximum returns from public-sector resources.

During the 1970s the political landscape of England was beginning to change. The links between education and politics were about to become more apparent as the government embarked on a more active and interventionist role in defining and shaping the curriculum and the educational agenda than it had done previously. This change was triggered by the so-called 'Great Debate' speech.

The 'Great Debate' and the politicization of the curriculum

In 1976, the then Prime Minister, James Callaghan delivered his now famous 'Great Debate' speech at Ruskin College. The speech is commonly acknowledged as a major turning point in the history of the English education system and considered the catalyst for greater central government involvement in the curriculum and ensuing educational reform.

A major theme in Callaghan's speech was the need to close the perceived gap between the skills and knowledge acquired by learners in schools, colleges and universities, and what the world of industry demanded of them. He insisted that 'it was the right (and even the responsibility) of central government to see that this was delivered by those within the education system' (Lowe 2007: 3). Callaghan also made reference to aspects of pedagogy and what he described as the 'unease felt by parents and others about the informal new teaching methods' and what some perceived as a decline in standards in schools (Callaghan 1976). He called for the need for greater 'value for money' and 'as high efficiency as possible', arguing that 'we cannot be satisfied with maintaining existing standards . . . we must aim for something better' (ibid.).

In many ways, Callaghan's speech was a watershed moment for educational provision in England and was to pave the way for unprecedented governmental intervention in the curriculum and greater accountability for teachers. Successive governments were to ensure that the 'educational experience' (i.e. both the content of the school curriculum and how it should be taught) would no longer be left to the teaching profession, but would be determined by the State and a host of closely aligned external agencies. The most conspicuous of these agencies to emerge over the last three decades in England and one that has played a significant role in policing the curriculum as well as elevating the importance of classroom observation as a means of gathering data about classroom teaching is Ofsted, as discussed further on pp. 21–23.

Unwittingly perhaps, Callaghan's speech also prepared the ground for the radical right initiatives of the Thatcher era during the 1980s and a redefinition of educational objectives along with the introduction of a national curriculum. Many of these initiatives were underpinned by principles that had been taken from the world of private enterprise and were to become commonly known as the three 'E's (i.e. Economy, Efficiency and Effectiveness). There was also a direct appeal to market forces with increased emphasis on competitiveness, attempts to measure performance and the decision to make school inspection reports public, along with the publication of exam results in league tables in later years. These were all key elements of the introduction of performance management systems designed to control educational policy from the centre. Mahony and Hextall (2000) quote from Hoggett (1996) to illustrate the controlling and regulatory technologies designed to enhance the ability of government to steer policy from the centre:

> In virtually all sectors operational decentralization has been accompanied by the extended development of performance management systems. Such systems seem designed to monitor and shape organisational behaviour and encompass a range of techniques including performance review, staff appraisal systems, performance-related pay, scrutinies, so-called 'quality audits', customer feedback mechanisms, comparative tables of performance indicators including 'league tables', customer charters, quality standards and total quality management.
>
> (Hoggett 1996: 20, cited in Mahony and Hextall 2000: 31–32)

These 'regulatory technologies' were to become what Foucault (1980) refers to as the 'apparatuses of control' of successive governments in their attempts to improve education standards from the Thatcher regime to the current coalition government. We will return to discussing Foucault's 'apparatuses of control' on p. 24, but before then it is worth outlining some of the key reforms that have given rise to the increased reliance on classroom observation over the last three decades.

Government reform, performance management and the creation of the 'new professional' in schools and colleges

In the case of schools in England, the process of reform was encapsulated by several key legislative changes, which were to change the education landscape as well as the role of teachers immeasurably. The most notable among these were: the 1988 Education Reform Act (ERA), the introduction of a National Curriculum, the Local Management of Schools (LMS) in 1991, the introduction of a national teacher appraisal scheme in 1992 and the implementation of a new inspection regime. Each of these reforms was underpinned by an ideology of increased accountability and greater parental choice, ultimately rendering schools more answerable to central government.

In the mid-1980s the then Secretary of State for Education, Keith Joseph, declared that 'the only way to remove unsatisfactory teachers from a profession where they can do much harm' (cited in Wragg *et al* 1996: 9) was by introducing a system of teacher appraisal, which would be based on classroom observation. This policy became a legal requirement in 1986, yet it was not for another decade before it became common practice for teachers to be observed. As Wragg *et al* (1996: 141) describe:

> The introduction within appraisal of a formal system for observing teachers teaching was for many teachers the first time they had been officially observed since they were

trainee teachers or probationers ... until appraisal it was rare for teachers to be observed with the specific purpose that their teaching should be analysed and commented on.

Teacher appraisal for schools prescribed two classroom observations bi-annually, an appraisal interview with the member of staff's line manager and the subsequent drawing up of a list of targets to be achieved within an agreed time scale. Yet, as Middlewood (2001: 126–127) comments, formal evaluations of the teacher appraisal scheme 'presented pictures of limited effectiveness' and it was not long before 'other priorities quickly took over for school managers and leaders, notably school inspections in the 1990s'. Referring to Wragg *et al* (1996), Montgomery (2002: 2) highlights the low percentage of teachers that were observed and remarks that 'it was left largely up to the teachers to decide on the focus for the observation', as though this autonomy in decision-making were immediately presumed to have negative consequences, or, at the very least, were to be frowned upon. She also touches on the area of feedback by stating that 'only 60 per cent' (ibid.) of those teachers observed felt that it had improved their professional practice.

Ofsted identified a number of weaknesses to the appraisal system, amongst which they listed 'infrequent or ineffective classroom observation' (Montgomery 2002: 1). Ofsted's Chief Inspector of Schools at the time, Chris Woodhead, was critical of the appraisal scheme and insistent that it was not doing enough to improve the performance level of teachers. Furthermore, Middlewood (2001) makes the point that the grading of teachers' performance during Ofsted inspections became a practice in the late 1990s and this was 'a process to which teachers inevitably paid more attention' than the appraisal system. In some ways it could be argued that this coincided with the rise of a new generation of younger teachers eager to climb the career ladder and embrace this new 'performative' culture in order to progress professionally (see p. 17 for further discussion of the concept of 'performativity'). Maguire (2010: 63) argues that 'in the public sector there is an awareness that the new education professional is an entrepreneurial individual, someone who seeks performance-related rewards, who is compared with and compares him/herself against his/her "colleagues"'. In a small-scale study of newly qualified primary school teachers, Wilkins (2011: 403) talks about the emergence of a 'post-performative professional identity', where these new teachers have a 'generally positive view of the managerial culture of teaching' on account of the fact that they have never known anything else. By the time they started school, performance management systems were already firmly embedded in the working cultures of institutions. Thus along with their teachers, as learners they were nurtured and immersed in regimes of accountability and performativity.

In the case of FE, the 'incorporation' of FE colleges under the 1992 Further and Higher Education Act was the key turning point in the history of the sector. In some respects 'incorporation' was similar to the LMS policy implemented in the schools' sector, though it was to have much more far-reaching consequences. It triggered a fundamental restructuring of FE (Ainley and Bailey 1997), which meant that 'colleges became corporate institutions completely independent of local authority control with governing bodies dominated by representatives from business and industry' (Hyland and Merrill 2003: 14). FE colleges were given charitable status as all power and decision-making capabilities were removed from Local Education Authorities (LEAs). Though colleges continued to be funded by the State, a key change was that this would be controlled by a newly appointed national body, the Further Education Funding Council (FEFC).

The FEFC introduced a new and complex unit-based funding regime. Ideologically, the new regime was based upon an output related funding mechanism driven by a political desire to instil measures of accountability into public spending, consistent with a wider 'value for money' policy promoted by the Conservative government at that time. This financial regime was commonly referred to by FE teachers generally as the three 'Rs', i.e. Recruitment, Retention and Results (Achievement), and was considered by some to constitute the single most noticeable cause of disempowerment amongst FE academic staff (e.g. Randle and Brady 1997). Others (e.g. Gleeson 2001) suggested that its introduction accelerated the spread of 'new managerialism' (see p. 16) and the overt business values and discourses associated with that culture (efficiency, target setting etc.).

The creation of the FEFC was one of a collection of far-reaching changes to occur in FE during the post-incorporation period and reflected a wider political agenda for the public sector. The Conservative government of the time implemented an ideology that sought to erode the powers and influence of local councils in public services (Ainley and Bailey 1997). Its plan for FE, and indeed for the education sector as a whole, was thus to engender a shift from a locally controlled to a more centralized system of governance, but also one where market forces would play a key part in future development (Newman 2001). At the heart of both the 1992 Further and Higher Education Act and its earlier counterpart for schools, the 1988 ERA, was the belief that financial independence, coupled with the adoption of core business values from the private sector, represented the most effective way forward to raising standards and improving provision.

In short, the 1988 ERA and the post-incorporation period in FE signalled the emergence of a culture of 'new managerialism' (Avis 1996). Wallace and Hoyle (2005: 9) have argued that new managerialism 'is underpinned by an ideology which assumes that all aspects of organisational life can and should be controlled. In other words, that ambiguity can and should be radically reduced or eliminated.' From the early 1990s onwards, the culture of new managerialism was to redefine the working traditions of schools and colleges nationwide and impact significantly upon the professional identity of teachers (Ainley and Bailey 1997; Lowe 2007).

From the mid-1980s in schools and the start of the 1990s in colleges, teachers went through a period of 'de-professionalization'. The speed with which reforms were implemented led to a dramatic increase in the administrative bureaucracy of teachers and a rise in levels of dissatisfaction and stress amongst the profession as a whole. The Chief Inspector of the time, Chris Woodhead, was for many teachers seen as public enemy number one and epitomized the stance of the New Right. He was repeatedly critical of the calibre of teachers, their commitment and professionalism and argued that the low standards in English schools were solely attributable to the high numbers of what he perceived as poor or incompetent teachers.

Prior to these reforms, the term 'professional' had generally conferred an elevated social status to teachers, valuing their subject knowledge, pedagogic skills etc., as well as key qualities such as trust, respect and integrity, which in turn had traditionally afforded them a high degree of autonomy (Hoyle and Wallace 2005). As a result of the reforms, the notion of professionalism was to become reconfigured. The professional autonomy of teachers was to be substantially eroded and these key qualities were to be superseded by a set of technicist skills that formed part of a new culture of 'performativity' (see p. 17 for further discussion).

These technicist skills were to be acquired through standardized training and an opening-up of the profession to market values and systems, giving rise to the birth of the 'new professional' to deliver a set of 'outcomes' or customer service in accordance with managerially assured accountability procedures (Hoyle 1995). Maguire (2010: 61) refers to this as the reconstruction of the teacher as 'state technician, trained to deliver a national curriculum in the nation's schools'. She goes on to argue that (2010: 62):

> The reconstructed teacher is produced out of sets of recipes for action, systemic rules, technologies of performance and routine classroom actions that are designed (by others) to 'deliver' quality and 'assure' high standards. The teacher is reconstituted as a technical 'risk manager' who, in McWilliam's terms (2008: 36), makes 'learning outcomes more visible, more calculable and thus more accountable' in a context where, to some extent, any competing versions of the teacher have been erased.

In the case of FE in England, recent research claims that 'it arguably still is characterized and perhaps dominated by new managerialism' (James and Biesta 2007: 9). It is to this development that the next section turns its attention and in so doing seeks to examine the related contexts and cultures and how the emergence of observation fits into this changing landscape.

A culture of new managerialism, performativity and accountability

New managerialism can be seen as a by-product of a wider political and economic neo-liberal agenda, which 'extends the logic of the market to all corners of the earth and all spheres of social life, liberalizes trade, drives down the price of labor, and employs financialization as a principle strategy of capital accumulation' (Lipman 2010: 241). According to Randle and Brady (1997: 125), new managerialism was a 'style of management which emerged in the UK in the early 1980s and gradually spread throughout the Public Sector'. It essentially comprised a package of management techniques taken from the private sector that were considered *successful* and as such could subsequently 'be applied as a template for public sector institutions' (op. cit., p. 121) to improve levels of productivity and performance and to make the workforce more accountable. Underpinning such models of management were three notions commonly referred to as the three 'Es': Economy, Efficiency and Effectiveness.

The three 'Es' were captured by the Right during the Thatcher regime and employed as the guiding rationale for the neo-liberal agenda of privatization and marketization of public sector institutions. In the process they were removed from the realm of political discourse and subsequently re-packaged in an 'ideology of neutrality', which meant that such issues were conceptualized and discussed as being 'technical' rather than political or ideological ones. Writers such as Ball (2003), Clarke and Newman (1997), Ranson (1992) and Sachs (2001) all challenged the use of such discourse, contesting that these concepts were manipulated by the Right as both a means of justification and of deflecting criticism from their political agenda. Clarke and Newman (1997: 148) argued that this 'technicist discourse strips debate of its political underpinnings'. Ball (2003: 217) contested that this 'hyper-rational' and 'objective façade' was an attempt to explain complex social processes by converting them into 'simple figures or categories of judgement'. Besides, by adopting quantifiable performance indicators to assess accountability, they were, in the words of Ranson (1992: 72), endeavouring to hide behind the 'guise of neutrality'.

In the case of FE colleges, Robson (1998: 598) argued that the drive towards improving the quality of colleges' provision and widening participation 'was based on the belief that in the past the FE sector had been less efficient and effective than it could have been'. A central tenet of new managerialism was thus the view that workers could no longer be trusted to do their jobs efficiently and effectively. This led to the introduction of audit systems and mechanisms of accountability and 'performativity' to monitor output and performance (Ball 2003).

In discussing the importance of trust in the context of teacher professionalism, Avis (2003: 320) has argued that it is paramount for the development of a high-skills knowledge-based economy, as high-trust working environments are more likely to promote creativity and risk taking:

> Trust becomes a pre-requisite for the knowledge worker for, without it, risks will not be taken and therefore, new ideas will remain unexpressed and hinder the development of competitiveness as well as processes of continuous improvement. . . . Such argument would suggest the need to develop a re-formed teacher professionalism, one that would accord with the new conditions of risk and uncertainty within which the economy and education is set.

Avis believes that performative systems engender a low-trust working environment, as they are based on a 'blame culture' where 'accountability becomes a means by which the institution can call to account its members' (p. 325). There are certain parallels here to Foucault's concept of 'normalization' and the way in which graded models of classroom observation operate in schools and colleges (see p. 35 in the following chapter for further discussion of the concept of normalization).

Ball (2003: 215) has described performativity as a culture that 'requires individual practitioners to organize themselves as a response to targets, indicators and evaluations, to set aside personal beliefs and commitments and live an existence of calculation'. This culture of performativity promotes a new type of 'entrepreneurial' teacher who strives to be graded as 'outstanding' and 'successful' according to national testing schemes, not least when it comes to observing their classroom performance. Ball argues that this can lead to feelings of 'inauthenticity' as this new professional 'may offer what they believe to be a limited and diluted curriculum' (Maguire 2010: 62) in order to achieve the very targets by which their professional competence and performance are measured and assessed.

Ball maintains that performativity has become so engrained in education that it engenders a change not just in what teachers do, but, more importantly, in whom they are as people and how they interact with their learners and colleagues. Ball (2003: 223) summarizes this change very succinctly when he says that 'beliefs are no longer important – it is output that counts. Beliefs are part of an older, increasingly displaced discourse'. The suggestion is that this 'older discourse' has been superseded by a managerialist discourse, characterized by its prioritization of measurable outcomes. As Chapter 6 explores, this has been repeatedly played out in the agenda for national teacher standards and attempts to define what constitutes an effective teacher.

In more recent work Ball (2012) has developed his conceptualization of performativity further, accentuating his understanding of it as a form of moral, neo-liberal technology that seeks to control the psyche and conscience of teachers in everything they do in their working lives. His definition and analysis in the extract below clearly bears similarities to Foucault's (1977) 'disciplinary power' and, before him, Gramsci's (1971) concept of 'hegemony':

> Performativity is the quintessential form of neo-liberal governmentality, which encompasses subjectivity, institutional practices, economy and government. It is both individualizing and totalizing. It produces both an active docility and depthless productivity. Performativity invites and incites us to make ourselves more effective, to work on ourselves, to improve ourselves and to feel guilty or inadequate if we do not . . . . Performativity 'works' most powerfully when it is inside our heads and our souls. That is, when we do it ourselves, when we take responsibility for working hard, faster and better, thus 'improving' our 'output', as part of our personal worth and the worth of others.
>
> (Ball 2012: 31)

For Ball the culture of performativity is one in which the performances of teachers individually and schools and colleges institutionally are evaluated in terms of their productivity or output. The value or quality of the institutional or individual's performance lies within what he refers to as a 'field of judgement' and the key question is who controls this field of judgement? In the words of Ball (2003: 216): 'Who is it that determines what is to count as a valuable, effective or satisfactory performance and what measures or indicators are considered valid?' These are highly pertinent questions when discussing classroom observation, especially when it is used summatively in a performative context to assess teachers' professional practice. In such instances, observers control the field of judgement since they are empowered to categorize performance according to a predetermined scale. Whether they are Ofsted inspectors or school/college managers carrying out observation for teacher appraisal, they assume the role of custodians of effective practice. In turn, this raises further questions. For instance, how do teachers interpret this use of observation? What impact does it have on their professional development? What kind of professional is being produced through the use of such models of observation? These are matters that will be explored in more detail when discussing the findings of cognate studies into the use of observation in the educational arena in the chapters that follow.

It was in light of this culture of performativity that classroom observation came to the fore as an important means of gathering evidence for colleges and schools' QA systems and preparing for Ofsted inspections (see pp. 21–23). Although not the only context in and purpose for which observation is used, as subsequent chapters discuss, the dominant model adopted in the English education system to date has been driven by the performative goals of inspection and QA regimes that prioritize the practice of graded observation, i.e. where lessons are assessed and graded against Ofsted's 4-point scale as a key performance indicator (KPI) to gauge the quality of provision and determine funding. One of the defining characteristics of such models of improvement is the emphasis on competition.

The promotion of competition and market values as part of the 'Quality Agenda' for school improvement and effectiveness is a topic that has been explored by many educational researchers. Mahony and Hextall (2000: 85) have argued, for example, that:

> This drive for effectiveness and higher standards is directly tied into the National Curriculum, since the 'effectivity' is predominantly judged in accordance with critieria derived from it, mediated through examination results, assessment gradings and the performance indicators of Ofsted inspection reports. . . . The resulting league tables have subsequently been linked to the fostering of competition and a market orientation which is part of the drive for quality. . . . In the light of such pressures, schools and other educational institutions have been increasingly driven to market themselves and their qualities.

They go on to argue that one of their concerns about current definitions of school effectiveness is that they do not take into account 'where students come from, the nature of their life experiences, or their prospective destinations' (p. 86). This has repercussions for the model of the teacher and the nature of the teaching and learning process that is being presented through such an approach. In order to illustrate some of the implications of such an approach, they cite the work of Angus (1993: 337):

> [E]ducational practice is conceived of in a particularly mechanical way. . . . In keeping with economistic definitions of effectiveness, it is the bit that comes between 'input' and 'outputs'. It is seen largely as a set of techniques, the 'core technology', for managing 'throughput' rather than a complex and always unpredictable process of ongoing construction of educational practice. Practice is a set of techniques to be employed by teacher technicians on malleable pupils.
>
> (cited in Mahony and Hextall 2000: 86)

This is a discussion that will be explored further in Chapter 6 when examining the notion of teacher effectiveness, but for now it is worth acknowledging that the cultures and systems associated with managerialism and performativity have been instrumental in determining existing models of teacher effectiveness.

The prioritization of teacher improvement in the quest to raise standards: FE and the use of observation as a case in point

After almost 20 years of Conservative government, New Labour secured a landslide victory in 1997 with '*Education, Education, Education*' as its central slogan of the election campaign. Its decision to make education its number one priority was indicative of Tony Blair and Gordon Brown's firm commitment to investing in the 'knowledge economy'. The spread of globalization gave rise to the 'knowledge economy', which was underpinned by the philosophy that the economic prosperity of a country was significantly determined by the effectiveness of a country's educational provision. In other words, the more highly educated a country's population was, the more beneficial this would be to its economy, and 'central to this clearly lies the quality of teaching and learning in a nation's schools, colleges and universities' (Middlewood and Cardno 2001: 1).

While there were many similarities between New Labour's approach to education policy and that of the previous administration's – i.e. a continued emphasis on increased accountability, value for money, links to the needs of the market etc. – the intensity with which New Labour pursued its reform agenda was a clear statement of intent to prioritize the development of the education sector as a whole. As Mahony and Hextall (2000: 62) have commented: 'The Green Paper which was published in December 1998 (DfEE 1998) announced the Labour government's firm intention to introduce a thorough-going performance-management model to form the basis for the overall restructuring of the teaching profession within schools'. September 2000 saw the introduction of a performance management system in schools, whereby a direct link was made between pupils' attainments and teachers' performance. As was commented previously, the impetus for this change in policy was driven by the belief that the appraisal system that had been established at the start of the 1990s had either 'fallen into disuse in some schools and was perfunctory in others' (Montgomery 2002: 1).

New Labour pursued a similar reform agenda in the FE sector and although the discussion that follows focuses on the FE context, much of what is discussed is comparable with events that occurred in schools as part of the government's overarching reliance on a performance-management approach to improvement.

The sheer volume of policies and initiatives produced under New Labour was testament to its efforts to reform education, particularly in FE. One of the key drivers of this reform agenda was the prioritization of teaching and learning as the foundation on which to build improvement. This policy focus arose out of a wider political commitment on the part of New Labour to promote the role of FE in 'upskilling the nation' (DfEE 1999: 2), which in turn acknowledged that 'success depend[ed] on the skills of people working in the sector' (DfES 2004: 3). This resulted in the development of a package of initiatives and strategies designed to improve the professional skills and knowledge base of the sector's teaching staff, from which classroom observation surfaced as an important strategy.

During New Labour's tenure, FE was subjected to a continuous stream of policies and initiatives aimed at raising standards and improving the quality of teaching and learning, as evidenced by the raft of publications to emerge (e.g. DfEE 1999, 2001; DfES 2002, 2004, 2006). Key terms that have since become the mantra of education policy are *continuous improvement*, *quality* and *excellence*, and nowhere more so than in the domain of teaching and learning (James and Biesta 2007). The importance attached to improving the quality of teaching and learning coupled with an emphasis on reforming the professional development of teachers reflected a general shift in policy direction to prioritizing teaching and learning as the cornerstone on which improvement across the sector should be built (see Bathmaker and Avis 2005; Colley *et al* 2007; Finlay *et al* 2007).

Since the turn of the millennium two policy developments in particular can be linked to the increased use of classroom observation in FE and indeed in schools; the first of which was the introduction of a new set of professional standards and mandatory ITT qualifications for FE teachers by the Further Education National Training Organisation (FENTO), subsequently revised by Lifelong Learning UK (LLUK 2006) – new Teacher Standards for schools came into effect from September 2012 (see Chapter 6 for more discussion). The second development involved the formation of a new inspection framework, which saw Ofsted and the Adult Learning Inspectorate (ALI) working alongside each other from 2001 before merging into one inspectorate in 2007. These two policy developments were a concerted response by New Labour to address some of the concerns regarding the professional skills and knowledge base of FE teaching staff.

Before September 2001 there was no legal requirement for teachers in FE to undergo an ITT programme or possess a teaching qualification prior to employment. In 1999, FENTO published its *National Standards for Teaching and Supporting Learning in Further Education in England and Wales*. This document was followed by the introduction of national regulations for FE teachers that made it mandatory for all new entrants to the profession to obtain a qualification based on the FENTO standards and for existing staff to upgrade if their qualifications failed to meet the new requirements, which took effect from September 2001.

In 2004, a key government report (DfES 2004: 8) recommended more emphasis on the practical aspects of teaching and highlighted the importance of observation in particular: 'An essential element of teacher training is the observation of the trainee's teaching and constructive feedback'. It called for 'more effective observation of teaching practice' (p. 16). Another outcome of the report was that LLUK was commissioned by the government to develop a new set of professional teaching standards for FE. The catalyst for this was a set of recommendations made by Ofsted (2003), in which eight HEIs (HE Institutions) and 23 FE colleges were visited by both Ofsted and ALI inspectors 'as part of a national survey to evaluate the quality and standards of ITT in FE' (2003: 1). The overriding judgement of the report was that the FENTO standards '[did] not provide a satisfactory foundation of professional development for FE teachers at the start of their careers' (p. 2).

Observation was recognized as a particular weakness in existing programmes; 'few trainees receive effective mentoring in the workplace and their progress is inhibited by insufficient observation and feedback on their teaching' (ibid.). In short, the FENTO guidelines for observation were criticized for failing to regulate its use and not specifying precisely how often it should take place and the minimum number of assessed hours of observation required. This inevitably led to a lack of uniformity in practice across providers, an area which both Ofsted and LLUK were keen to rectify.

The *New Overarching Professional Standards* (LLUK 2006) were published towards the end of 2006. They were largely an attempt to respond to Ofsted's (2003) recommendations to revise the FENTO standards and to link them with existing standards for school teachers. The prominence given to observation as a key criterion in the assessment of trainee teachers in the LLUK standards was a noticeable modification to the previous FENTO ones, as those following the 'full teaching role' route were required to complete 'a minimum of 8 observations totalling a minimum of 8 hours' (LLUK 2007: 23). This was a clear attempt to address what Ofsted had originally identified as a lack of standardization of practice in the assessment of trainees' teaching as well as a sign of their growing sway over FE policy in the classroom. It is to Ofsted's role in influencing the increased use of classroom observation that much of the remaining discussion in this section now turns its attention.

Together with the introduction of the new professional standards and teaching qualifications (LLUK 2006), the decision to hand over responsibility for all FE inspections to Ofsted marked another significant act. On the one hand, it could be seen as an acknowledgement of how standards in teaching and learning were a high priority in the government's quality agenda throughout the sector. On the other hand, it might also have been indicative of an underlying aim to 'police' the sector (Gleeson *et al* 2005) to ensure that performance targets were met and *continuous improvement* remained at the top of the agenda.

Whilst it is important to acknowledge the role of the LSC (Learning and Skills Council) and other key players such as the Learning and Skills Improvement Service (LSIS) in this drive, the impact of these agencies on teaching and learning in FE has arguably been less tangible than that of Ofsted. Ofsted's involvement in and regulatory control over the FE sector grew considerably during New Labour. It was extended beyond its original remit of inspecting standards in colleges to one of defining them, as indeed it has been in schools. During the last decade it has taken a leading role in shaping the QA policy agenda, as evidenced by some of the key publications to emerge in recent years that have influenced senior management in FE (e.g. Ofsted 2003, 2004a, 2004b, 2008a).

As commented above, one of Ofsted's criticisms in its survey of ITT provision in the sector was that there was insufficient attention given to classroom observation under the FENTO validated programmes (Ofsted 2003), similar to the criticism levelled at the appraisal system in schools in the 1990s. The central role of observation in the self-assessment process in colleges was also underlined in two parallel reports that were later to become seminal documents for college senior managers: *Why Colleges Succeed* and *Why Colleges Fail* (Ofsted 2004a, 2004b), and more recently *How Colleges Improve* (Ofsted 2008a).

In the 2004 reports, 'underperforming colleges' were criticized for having observation schemes that were 'poorly conceived and implemented, concentrating too much on teacher performance as opposed to the achievement of learners' (2004a: 14). In colleges where there was evidence of 'a reluctance to grade observations which are viewed as developmental rather than quality control activities', Ofsted concluded that such schemes were 'insufficiently robust, partly because the observations are not graded' (ibid.). The diction of both reports (2004a, 2004b) implied that without the use of a grading scale such as Ofsted's, the observation data were deemed less valid and reliable. Similarly, in the 2008 report (Ofsted 2008a), graded observation was emphasized as an important tool in the performance management of standards in teaching and learning across colleges. There were references to observation on almost every page, thus highlighting the importance attached to it by Ofsted.

All three reports reveal an underlying value system that favours 'hard' (i.e. quantitative) over supposed 'soft' (i.e. qualitative) data on the basis that the former are measurable and thus considered more objective and credible. There is an implicit assumption that numerical grades (1–4) have an objective value comparable with that of calibrated measuring devices such as weighing scales or thermometers. By attaching a grade to the subjective judgement of the observer, people are seduced into believing that such judgements have greater objectivity and authority than they can, in reality, claim to have. No matter how spurious the precision of these measurements might be, these seemingly hard, numerical data acquire an 'aura of objectivity' (Gipps 1994: 5). Their captivating allure is illustrated in the following quotation from one of the interviewees of my own research (O'Leary 2011), Graham, the Director of Quality, who described how he was responsible for providing monthly statistical updates on his college's internal graded observation scheme:

> On a monthly basis I report to the executive team on the current formal graded observation profile so the stats that they are looking for is the percentage of lessons observed that were good or better and then the percentage of lessons that were observed as inadequate and what we're doing about it. So they don't routinely hear

about the other observation process in the college, which is the peer observation process.

Although this institution had an alternative to QA graded observation, i.e. a pre-existing, internal, peer observation scheme, Graham's comments indicated how this formative scheme was marginalized as attention became fixated on the 'measurements' generated by graded observations. His comments also highlighted the confidence invested in these data with the executive team routinely scrutinizing statistics showing how many lessons had been graded 1, 2, 3 or 4. These grades were accepted as valid and reliable measures of performance and trends within the college and had become a key tool in tracking progress as part of the continuous improvement agenda. They were relied upon to compare overall performance year on year, forming the basis for the college's self-assessment for inspection purposes. Graham, however, was sceptical about such practices: 'At the end of the year in our self-assessment report, we will report on the number of ones, twos, threes and fours and I think it's basically worthless'. He, nevertheless, conceded that, 'it's something that all colleges do at the moment because it's what Ofsted expects'. Thus, reliance on these quantitative performance indicators had become 'custom and practice' – an established feature of performance management systems.

As Mahony and Hextall (2000: 3–4) claim in relation to the term 'standards' and the importance of measuring performance:

> They do appear to hold out the promise of calculability. This is perceived as vital if it is considered important to construct some kind of basis on which the performance of the public sector can be judged or measured. . . . Standards provide a central part of the technology which is used both to deliver and legitimate the culture of performance which has become so ubiquitous within the whole public sector, not least in relation to schools and teachers.

In a related discussion about student evaluations of teaching, Brookfield (1995: 18) argues that such an epistemological stance 'serves individuals with a reductionist cast of mind who believe that the dynamics and contradictions of teaching can be reduced to a linear, quantifiable rating system'. Underpinning Brookfield's comments is a fundamental critique of new managerialist practices, embodied in systems of accountability and performativity, of which a graded approach to classroom observation can be seen as an example. As argued earlier in reference to Ball's critique of performative systems of managerialism, in an attempt to explain complex social processes by converting them into 'simple figures or categories of judgement', such systems endeavour to hide behind an 'objective façade' (2003: 217).

Labels of this kind (i.e. lessons graded according to a scale of 1–4) have a definitive quality to them that seems ill-suited to judgements that are essentially based on snapshots of performance. Satterly, in Harlen (1994), suggested that variations in performance from one occasion to another were one of the greatest threats to the reliability of assessment. This issue is very pertinent to classroom observation where there are potentially so many variables beyond the control of the teacher that can impact on the outcome of a lesson. This raises questions again about the reliability of observation as a means of assessing performance, a topic explored in further detail in Chapter 4 in particular. It also links to the question posed earlier by Ball (2003) as to who controls the 'field of judgement', which hits at the heart of the power–knowledge dynamic between observer and observee. Here the work of Michel Foucault is helpful in illuminating the relationship between power and knowledge.

For Foucault, power and knowledge are inextricably linked. This has particular resonance for classroom observation given that it is regarded as one of the most important means of collecting knowledge about what happens in classrooms and what it can reveal about teaching and learning. Thus, viewing observation through a Foucauldian lens inevitably connects its use to power, which means that if we are to construct a detailed understanding of observation then we must also understand the mechanisms of power that underpin it.

Foucault believed that knowledge is a social product created by a number of connected mechanisms, which 'determine how knowledge is accumulated by prescribing correct procedures for observing, researching, and recording data and for disseminating the results of investigations' (Brookfield 2005: 137). These mechanisms of knowledge production act as what Foucault refers to as 'apparatuses of control' to establish certain forms of knowledge as more legitimate than others. In reality what this means is those with the greatest command of such mechanisms are able to create 'regimes of truth' (Foucault 1980).

Regimes of truth are 'the types of discourse which it [society] accepts and makes function as true' (1980: 131). For Foucault *truth* is not to be understood in the conventional sense as an empirical fact proven and accepted to be true by society, but as a notion that is 'linked in a circular relation with systems of power that produce and sustain it' (2002: 132). These systems of power determine the *rules* or the 'ordered procedures for the production, regulation, distribution, circulation and operation of statements' (ibid.). Regimes of truth emerge from the connections formed between these dominant discourses. In paraphrasing Foucault, Brookfield (2005: 138) states that 'dominant discourses inevitably reflect and support existing power structures'. In the case of classroom observation, the production of such dominant discourses and regimes of truth is exemplified by external agencies such as Ofsted, who are the custodians of quality and standards for teachers. In her research into the effect of Ofsted inspections on an English secondary school, Perryman (2009: 616) has argued that:

> The discourse of OfSTED involves standards, quality, efficiency, value for money and performance. In order to be successful, schools need to accept that this discourse is the way forward, especially if they are in danger of failing. There is no room for schools to 'do their own thing' in terms of improvement.

The extent to which judgements made by Ofsted during inspections have helped to improve standards has been an issue of some contention ever since it was given the remit to inspect schools and colleges. According to a survey conducted by the National Association of Head Teachers (NAHT) in 1999, Ofsted inspections failed to improve standards, largely as a result of the negative approach adopted by focussing on failure. As Montgomery (2002: 100) suggests:

> It would be far more beneficial to have a system which focused upon strengths and motivated teachers to fulfil their professional duties rather than seeking to catch them out. . . . We learn from having our strengths identified and then we know how to

proceed. If our weaknesses are focused upon we only know what not to do and not how to put them right.

Recently Professor Dylan Wiliam, a renowned authority in the field of assessment, publicly questioned Ofsted's ability to make reliable judgements about the quality of teaching and learning during the course of inspections (Stewart 2012). Professor Wiliam's comments highlighted the limitations of the assessment framework used by Ofsted to judge the effectiveness of an institution's provision and in so doing touched a raw nerve with the inspectorate. At the same time, his comments seemed to echo the sentiments of many in the teaching profession. That is to say, the main criticism was based on the 'snapshot' nature of observations made during inspections and the extent to which accurate judgements can be made on the basis of such observations. Moreover, what is the impact of such judgements on improving quality?

In other developed countries like Australia or Germany, for example, there is no such thing as Ofsted, yet they continually outperform the UK in internationally recognized tests such as the Programme for International Student Assessment (PISA). In other words, they do not seem to have suffered from not having an inspection regime. Perhaps, then, it is worth exploring alternative approaches to the way in which standards of performance are judged? This is not a debate to explore in the context of this chapter but will be returned to in later chapters when discussing other ways in which observation might best be used to enhance the quality of teaching and learning. For now, the final section of this chapter will concentrate on outlining the continuing importance of observation as part of recent policy decisions made by the current coalition government.

The growing importance of observation under the coalition government

Since the coalition government took office in May 2010, the emphasis on teaching and learning as the main vehicle for driving up standards and extending the agenda for continuous improvement has entered a new phase of heightened scrutiny and performativity, the repercussions of which have resulted in even higher stakes assessment of teachers' practice in schools and colleges. In the light of this, classroom observation has become an even more prominent feature of professional life for teachers regardless of the sector within which they work. In the schools' sector, for example, the white paper, *The Importance of Teaching* (DfE 2010), promises greater use of observation and increased powers for head teachers in schools to 'sit in on as many lessons as necessary to root out under-performing teachers'. In fact, even before the white paper was published, the proposal drew criticism from the main teaching unions who saw it as a licence to 'endorse management bullying in schools' (Shepherd 2010: 6).

Both in schools and in colleges Ofsted has been responsible for raising the stakes higher still. In keeping with the agenda for continuous improvement and framework for excellence in teaching and learning, Ofsted proclaimed that 'satisfactory is not good enough' any more (Ofsted 2008b: 4). This stance has been reinforced as part of a revised inspection framework by Ofsted's Chief Inspector, where satisfactory is now deemed unsatisfactory (Sir Michael Wilshaw, BBC 2012). Ofsted's recent report *A Good Education for All* (2012c) recommended the replacement of the judgement of 'satisfactory' with 'requires improvement' and emphasized a position of zero tolerance to those institutions that fail to continue to improve.

In *The Importance of Teaching* (DfE 2010), classroom observation is identified as a key tool in the improvement of practice and is considered the principal means of re-instating what is regarded as 'core' in education. It notes disapprovingly that 'only 25 per cent of teachers report that they are regularly observed in classroom practice' (p. 19), denouncing restrictions in this area – 'we will make clear that there is no "three hour limit" on the amount of time a teacher can be observed' (p. 24). By coupling this measure with plans to ask Ofsted to focus 'its attention on . . . observing more lessons' (p. 69), the government declared its intention to promote 'an "open classroom" culture' that is a 'vital' ingredient in 'the most effective practice in teacher education and development' (p. 19). A 'much improved' primary school was used to exemplify this vision. It was a place where 'rigorous' formal observations and 'day-to-day drop-ins became part of accepted practice' (p. 26). Whilst the potential of formative assessment to improve the performance of individuals (thereby raising standards more widely), has been identified at different levels from early years through to higher education (Black and Wiliam 1998), the initiatives described above may also be viewed as stakes-raising measures in the context of teacher appraisal. Their efficacy rests on the viability of a dual-purpose assessment regime in which a formative function, through increased opportunities for informal observation and more regular feedback, can co-exist with a strengthened summative function involving more frequent scrutiny by senior managers and by Ofsted. This is a matter that is debated in the chapters that follow when considering the models, purposes and contexts in which observation is used.

Summary

This chapter has attempted to locate the emergence and use of classroom observation against the backdrop of recent education policy along with wider socio-political reforms designed to establish greater accountability and control over the teaching profession. The prominent position occupied by classroom observation as the main method of judging the quality of teaching and learning has been linked to the establishment of systems of performance management in schools and colleges and the increasing role of Ofsted, in particular, over the last decade and a half. Key education reforms such as the 1988 ERA, the 1992 Further and Higher Education Act, the introduction of teacher appraisal, a new inspection regime and the mandatory collection and publication of performance data have all been instrumental in central government exercising more control over what teachers do. These key reforms have also acted as the catalyst for the adoption of a predominantly performative approach to the use of observation in schools and colleges, which despite changes of government and the on-going policy churn, seems likely to continue in the future.

The next chapter will concentrate on discussing relevant literature and previous studies into classroom observation across the schools', FE and HE sectors in order to compare and contrast the role of observation. In doing so, it will examine some of the key themes and issues relating to its use in each sector and identify common and contrasting themes across the three sectors, with a view to establishing the significance of these themes and issues to all those involved in the process of classroom observation.

Discussion topics

1. *Origins of observation schemes in your workplace*
    Your task is to unearth the origins of the observation schemes in use in your workplace with a view to illuminating the connections between the past and the present. To help to frame your discussion, you might find the following questions useful:

    - Where did the current observation schemes in use come from?
    - Why did they emerge?
    - Who was responsible for their creation?
    - What were the key influences on their creation in terms of institutional and educational policy?

2. *Educational policy and the role of classroom observation in my workplace*
    Discuss with your peers the links between past and current educational policy and how observation is used in your workplace. You might want to think about this on a departmental as well as institutional level.

Chapter 3

A review of classroom observation in the English education system[1]

Understanding its role in schools, colleges and universities

Introduction

Classroom observation has a long-standing tradition in the assessment and development of new and experienced teachers in England. Over the last two decades it has progressively emerged as an important tool for measuring and improving teacher performance in schools and colleges. This chapter reviews relevant literature and studies across the three education sectors in England [i.e. schools, Further Education (FE) and Higher Education (HE)] in order to compare and contrast the role of observation. In doing so it discusses the key themes and issues surrounding its use in each sector and identifies common and contrasting patterns. It argues that in schools and in FE, observation has become increasingly associated with performance-management systems; a dominant yet contested model has emerged that relies on a simplified rating scale to grade professional competence and performance, although the recent introduction of 'lesson study' in schools appears to offer an alternative to such practice. In HE, however, there is limited evidence of observation being linked to the summative assessment of staff, with preferred models being peer-directed and less prescribed, allowing lecturers greater autonomy and control over its use and the opportunity to explore its potential as a means of stimulating critical reflection and professional dialogue about practice among peers. The chapter concludes with a synopsis of the recurring themes and issues to emerge across all three sectors with a view to establishing their significance to all those involved in the process of observation. These themes and issues will also serve as useful reference points for discussion in later chapters, where they will be re-examined in an applied context.

The schools' sector experience

Much of the existing literature on classroom observation is located in the schools' sector with a particular focus on the *practice* of observation, and takes the form of textbooks rather than research-based texts. Besides there being fewer studies in FE and HE, those that do exist have occurred mainly in the last decade. This in itself is significant as it highlights how observation has a longer history in the schools' sector (Grubb 2000; Wilcox and Gray 1996).

As discussed in the previous chapter, it was following the educational reforms of the 1980s and 1990s that observation materialized as well-established practice in schools. Although it had long been and continues to be a pivotal method of assessment in ITT courses, its rise to prominence for qualified teachers was closely linked to wider political reforms at the time, which demanded increased public accountability and an educational reform agenda determined to impose greater control over what teachers did in the classroom (Lowe 2007). Amid concerns about standards and the quality of teaching, observation emerged as a key method of collecting evidence on which to base subsequent systems of teacher appraisal. Marriott (2001: 3) argued that:

> The long term success of the school depends to a very great extent on the quality of teaching. . . . It is hard to see how the head teacher and other managers in schools can be fully aware of the quality of work unless they are gaining first-hand information by systematically observing in classes.

In a similar vein, back in the 1990s Wilcox and Gray (1996) referred to the 'dominance' of observation as the main method of collecting data about what went on in classrooms. This dominance was crystallized by the introduction of a cycle of inspection by Ofsted and formal appraisal for teachers as discussed previously.

Wragg's seminal work, *An Introduction to Classroom Observation* (1999), is one of the most widely cited textbooks on the subject to date. It is located in the context of English primary schools and covers a wide range of themes related to observation pedagogy and theory, although the emphasis is largely on the practical application of observation as a pedagogic tool. Given the breadth of coverage in Wragg's work it is helpful to use it as a starting point from which to explore some of the key issues and themes in the field and to relate these to other relevant studies.

At the beginning of his book Wragg raises the issue of the reliability of observation as a form of assessment. He remarks that 'we often "observe" what we want to see' (1999: vii). His comment draws attention to the subjectivity of observation and how events are 'inevitably filtered through the interpretive lens of the observer' (Foster 1996: 14). The subjectivity of observers' interpretations is a common theme in the literature, particularly when discussing notions of *good practice* (e.g. Fawcett 1996; Montgomery 2002; Tilstone 1998). Wragg maintains that 'mostly when we talk about a "good" teacher, an "effective" strategy or a "bad" lesson, we are referring to our own subjective perception (1999, p. 60). He exemplifies his argument by recalling a session in which thirty-five highly experienced teacher educators were shown a videotape of a student teacher's lesson and were asked to grade it on a scale of A–E (A at the top end of the scale and E at the bottom). Their grades varied from a D at the lowest end to a B+ at the top end of the scale. Such differing judgements illustrate the issue of observer subjectivity and reinforce the unreliability of observation as a sole method of assessment, especially when a grading scale is used to measure performance. Discussion of the issue of observer subjectivity will be explored in more detail in the following chapter and that of grading in Chapter 5, but for now it is simply noted that these are significant factors to consider when discussing observation, particularly in the context of teacher appraisal.

Wragg is critical of hierarchical grading systems as he claims that 'the nature of the levels can still be vague and diffuse, using words like "adequate" or "considerable" that are open to widely differing interpretations (1999: 103). It cannot be assumed that there is a shared understanding among observers or observees as to the meaning and interpretation of value-laden terms such as 'good' and 'outstanding', as used by Ofsted. Wragg (1999) argues that these terms, together with the assessment criteria that underpin them, need to be carefully defined when used and attempts made to establish a collective understanding.

But even when such attempts are made, for example standardization exercises for observers in observation systems and associated assessment criteria, the limitations of what they can achieve need to be acknowledged (Montgomery 2002). In other words, whilst they might be useful in raising collective awareness among observers, it is unrealistic to expect the assessment criteria to be uniformly and consistently applied. Besides, extant research suggests that experienced assessors are likely to judge intuitively, even ignoring published criteria. Though it has to be said that this is not a phenomenon specific to observation as a method of assessment, but reinforces more widely held beliefs among key researchers in the field that 'assessment is not an exact science and we must stop presenting it as such' (Gipps 1994: 167).

In their two-year monitoring study of teacher appraisal in English primary and secondary schools, Wragg *et al* (1996) highlighted what they described as a 'snapshot' approach to classroom observation (i.e. one-off observations) as one of the main obstacles to identifying incompetent teachers. The reason for this was because such teachers could deliver the 'rehearsed' lesson as a one-off performance, hence avoiding detection. Marriott (2001: 8) has also highlighted the limitations of a snapshot approach as 'the impact of teaching on learning, and therefore progress, is harder to evaluate in the context of one lesson'. As a means of mitigating such limitations, Wragg *et al* (1996) advocated the need for a series of observations to be carried out as part of a longitudinal approach to construct a more realistic picture of a teacher's classroom competence. However, in their research into teacher effectiveness, Campbell *et al* (2004: 133) maintain that 'even successive observations of a teacher will only ever supply a collection of snapshots rather than a full picture of teacher behaviour over the year'. While they acknowledge the importance of observation as a source of evidence for systems of teacher appraisal, they also remark that as a method of data collection 'it is often used with little regard for, or knowledge of, its characteristics' (p.133). What they mean by this comment is that despite its widespread use as a means of gathering data, there is a lack of rigour in its application and insufficient awareness on the part of those carrying out observation of its limitations as a method (further discussion of these methodological issues is taken up in the following chapter).

Wragg (1999: 3) succinctly summarizes some of the paradoxes involved with observation when comparing the ways in which teachers respond to the different contexts in which it occurs and its application as a multipurpose tool in the following comment:

> Skilfully handled, classroom observation can benefit both the observer and the person being observed, serving to inform and enhance the professional skills of both people. Badly handled, however, it becomes counter-productive, at its worst arousing hostility, resistance and suspicion.

The rules of observer–observee engagement are likely to differ according to who is observing whom, in what context and for what purpose. Underpinning Wragg's comment and the observer–observee relationship are the notions of power and authority. As Wragg comments, 'the actual or perceived power relationship between observer and observed is not just a sociological concept, but rather a reality that needs to be recognised' (1999: 62). For example, if a head of department is observing a newly qualified teacher (NQT), to what extent does the teacher feel able to challenge their assessment? Are efforts made to ensure that the observee's voice is heard? How many observation schemes actually choose to tackle this issue? What efforts are made, if any, to address the distribution of power?

These are questions that will be explored in later chapters but for now it is worth acknowledging that what links them is the degree of ownership and autonomy afforded to the observee.

Ownership and autonomy are identified as key features of successful observation schemes in schools, which are characterized by a move away from authoritarian models where observation is something that is 'done to teachers' to a more egalitarian approach in which ownership of the process is devolved to teachers (e.g. Metcalfe 1999; Tilstone 1998). Tilstone (1998: 59) advocates 'partnership observation', a term that she uses to express a more collaborative, democratic relationship between observer and observee. She argues that 'such partnerships will only work if the [observer] is not regarded as an authoritarian figure and is able to take on the role of facilitator with the teacher in control of direction of the observation and consequent actions' (p. 60).

Metcalfe (1999: 454) reflects on his experience of the use of observation from the perspective of both a researcher and an Ofsted inspector:

> What is becoming clear in schools is that classroom observation, as an aspect of monitoring and evaluation, is felt to be most acceptable when it is part of a broader approach . . . in which teachers work collaboratively as opposed to a 'bolted on' approach, which is felt to be connected with 'checking up', accountability and control.

These views can be seen to embody a wider, egalitarian philosophy of professional learning and development, sometimes referred to as 'democratic professionalism' (e.g. Sachs 2001; Whitty 2000), which is examined in Chapter 7. A similar approach to observation is supported by two of the main professional associations for school teachers, the National Union of Teachers (NUT) and the Association of Teachers and Lecturers (ATL) (ATL 2008; NUT 2006). It is their shared belief that observation constitutes an important element of a teacher's professional development and as such should be 'neither a burden for the teacher concerned nor an opportunity to "police" a teacher's performance' (NUT 2006: 5), but 'should be conducted in a manner that equates to a professional dialogue' (ATL 2008: 1).

The advantages of observation programmes that prioritize development over surveillance are well documented. As Wragg argues (1999: 17), 'good classroom observation can lie at the heart of both understanding professional practice and improving its quality'. When it is used insightfully observation can have a profound impact that 'can lead to a more open climate, greater trust between colleagues, and the development of strong professional relationships' (Marriott 2001: 3). One of the biggest obstacles to the creation of such a climate would appear to be the issue of grading.

Historically, graded observation has been a contentious issue in schools and provoked a resolute response on the part of the NUT and the National Association of Schoolmasters Union of Women Teachers (NASUWT) to campaign against its use (e.g. NUT 2007). Both unions believe that grading encourages school management to view observation as a surveillance mechanism with which to monitor the quality of teachers' work, instead of seeing it as a valuable means of stimulating professional dialogue. Marriott (2001) maintains that the grade can take on such importance that it threatens to undermine the value of the dialogue and feedback between the observer and the observee. Both parties can 'become hung up on what the grade means rather than how to improve the teaching' (2001: 46).

Such is the anxiety surrounding grading that the 'teacher may become over-concerned about whether he or she has "passed"' (ibid.).

One of the most recent developments in the field of classroom observation in schools has been the use of 'lesson study' as a model for improving teaching and learning. In drawing on Stigler and Hiebert (1999), Lieberman (2009: 83) traces the origins of lesson study to Japan, where it has a long and well-documented history and has been used as the most common 'form of teacher professional development in the improvement of mathematics and science education'. Unlike conventional models of observation that tend to be based on an atomistic approach, relying on evidence collected during a single, isolated observation on which to base judgements and formulate follow-up improvement action plans, lesson study 'challenges the status quo of teachers and their classrooms as islands – relatively unaware of events on other islands – with students floating in between' (Wang-Iverson 2002: 1). Far from being seen as a corrective mechanism to improve the practice of individual teachers, the planned impact of lesson study is meant to be collaborative and fully inclusive of all an institution's practitioners. The emphasis is placed on the observation of an entire curriculum unit rather than an isolated lesson, and how those who teach that unit can enhance greater student understanding and achievement. In short, lesson study is broadly based on an action-research approach to studying what goes on in classrooms where teachers work collaboratively as active researchers. Furthermore, one of its unique characteristics is how it seeks to involve the learners in the discussion and analysis of the observed lessons. According to Lieberman (2009), lesson study puts student and teacher learning at the centre of the observation process rather than teacher evaluation.

As part of a pilot project in England co-funded by the Teaching and Learning Research Programme (TLRP), the National College for School Leadership and the Centre for British Teachers (CfBT), teachers from twenty schools (both primary and secondary) across eight local authorities were involved in the trialling of lesson study with the aim of answering the project's key question: 'Would Lesson Study work in the UK and if so would it do so in a way which would add value to the range of professional development approaches already in use?' (Dudley 2007). The research was conducted in two phases: the first phase from 2003–06 and the second from 2007–10.

One of the findings to emerge from the first phase of the project was that lesson study was found to be a 'popular, powerful and replicable process for innovating, developing and transferring pedagogic practices' (ibid.). According to Dudley 'it was popular with both experienced and less experienced teachers alike' and had a 'demonstrable impact on the quality of teaching and on pupil progress and attainment' (ibid.).

The second phase of the research aimed to explore the 'critical features of teacher learning in lesson study' and what distinguished it as a form of classroom inquiry. Some of the key findings indicated that lesson study fostered joint risk taking among teachers, enabled teachers to develop evidence-based practice to inform their professional learning and empowered them to take control of their professional development through their own classrooms (Dudley 2008).

Dudley (2007, 2008) claims that the use of lesson study has subsequently become more widespread across schools in England in recent years, with particular emphasis on Mathematics and Literacy teaching, though this claim is not supported by any quantitative evidence. Notwithstanding the lack of data to support his claim, there is evidence of a growth in the use of lesson study as a form of intervention in teacher development in other countries. Lieberman (2009), for example, has reported on the popularity of lesson study increasing in the USA over the last decade. In her research, Lieberman (2009) found that lesson study encouraged greater openness among staff, which helped to expose vulnerability as an issue that affects both experienced and novice teachers. Reinforcing some of Dudley's (2007, 2008) findings, Lieberman argues that lesson study has helped to foster a collegial approach to teacher development through peer observation and thus prompted teachers to take more risks in their teaching. Chapter 8 explores the use of lesson study as an alternative approach to conventional models of classroom observation in more depth by discussing some of the key principles on which it is based as well as presenting an outline of its practical application.

The FE sector experience

There has been comparatively little research regarding the role of observation in FE. One of the first studies was Cockburn's (2005). His qualitative research consisted of interviews and focus groups with observers and observees as well as documentary analysis of the chosen institution's observation policy and feedback reports. The research was based in one college and, although the number of participants is not specified, one gets the impression that it was a relatively small cohort. The study's aim was to report on the perceptions and attitudes of staff to the use of observation.

Cockburn (2005: 376) provides what he refers to as a 'typology of resistance' of those who expressed negative views about observation. Some of the issues that he lists resonate with other studies (e.g. O'Leary 2006, 2011, 2012a; Wragg *et al* 1996). For example, he suggests that there is evidence of 'artificiality' in lessons as a result of being observed, which leads some tutors to adopt an 'orthodox style of delivering lessons' (p. 380) on the basis that there is a 'formula' for effective teaching. In a much larger and more recent research study (O'Leary 2011), my findings revealed that this 'artificiality' and 'orthodox' teaching style were largely due to the high stakes nature of the assessment and what I refer to as the 'normalization of practice', which resulted in many teachers 'playing the game' in order to ensure a successful outcome during graded observations (see below for further discussion).

In Cockburn's study the credibility of the observer also emerged as a contested issue amongst observees, specifically relating to their experience and suitability to perform the role. My research unearthed similar findings. Many of the participants' comments about credibility tended to converge around whether observers were still current practitioners. A popular complaint on the part of observees was that invariably observers were middle managers who had not taught for some time and thus had 'lost touch with the classroom'. Equally a significant percentage of observers stated that they thought it was essential to still be teaching for them to remain credible in the eyes of their colleagues (O'Leary 2011).

Related to the question of credibility in my research study was whether the observer had knowledge and experience of teaching the subject area of the observee. There were numerous instances of teachers having been observed by colleagues from curriculum areas that appeared to have little in common with their own. Gavin, for example, was an agricultural studies tutor who was observed teaching tractor driving to a group of teenagers by an IT specialist. Debbie, a special needs teacher, was observed teaching a dance and movement class to a group of young adults with severe learning difficulties by a manager from engineering whose students were mainly HE level.

Like Wragg (1999) above, Cockburn makes reference to the power relationship between observer and observee, arguing that 'the observer is commonly perceived as possessing greater power', which 'is legitimised by organisational arrangements' (2005: 384). This is a phenomenon that has been commented on by other writers in the field particularly regarding how it threatens to undermine the developmental potential of observation. This is accentuated when it is used to fulfil the dual purpose of performance-management requirements and the developmental needs/goals of teachers (e.g. Ewens and Orr 2002; O'Leary 2006).

In previous work I have argued that an assessment approach to classroom observation, like that employed by Ofsted and internal QA schemes, is ineffective in terms of its impact on improving the standards and quality of classroom teaching and learning. The primary purpose of such approaches 'is not to inform and improve current practice but simply to make a judgement about the quality of teaching and learning being observed' (O'Leary 2006: 192). One of the main problems with such approaches is that they 'place an inequitable proportion of control and decision-making at the behest of the observer, thus limiting the role of the person being observed (the *observee*) to that of a passive recipient rather than an active participant' (ibid.).

My recent research (O'Leary 2011) adopted a mixed-methods approach (i.e. it combined quantitative and qualitative data through the use of questionnaires and interviews) and was carried out in a sample of ten colleges situated across the West Midlands with a total of 500 participants, consisting of 50 from each college. The sample comprised teaching staff, middle and senior managers. One of the key findings to emerge from the research was how graded observation had become normalized as a performative tool of managerialist systems fixated with measuring teacher performance rather than actually improving it. The vast majority of colleges involved in the study adopted what I refer to as a 'restrictive approach' to the use of observation, typified by their reliance on the use of the Ofsted 4-point graded scale to measure performance, prioritizing the needs of performance management systems over those of their staff. Yet, in contrast, in those colleges where there was evidence of an 'expansive approach', grading was seen as less important, as the professional development needs of staff underpinned the way in which observation was used ('expansive' and 'restrictive' approaches to classroom observation are discussed in later chapters).

My research data also uncovered repeated examples of teachers being encouraged to demonstrate normalized models of 'effective practice' based on prescribed notions of 'excellent' or 'good' teaching, often cascaded from senior management, who were understandably keen to promote 'best practice' given the high-stakes nature of such observations particularly during inspections. One of the repercussions of this pressure on teachers to perform was how it encouraged what Ball (2003) refers to as 'inauthenticity' in teacher behaviour and classroom performance during graded observation. This was typically manifested in the delivery of the 'rehearsed' or 'showcase lesson', where the teacher concerned 'played the game' in order to succeed. For example, Terry, an Engineering teacher with over twenty-five years' experience, provided a candid and detailed account of how he followed a 'checklist' in the planning and delivery of a recent observation to achieve in order to ensure that he achieved a grade 1:

> So you know your lesson plan inside out. You make sure there's a plenary, a couple of plenaries in there at the start and the end of the lesson. Put a load of crap in with

regards to getting the students to do some sort of learning activity at the beginning to show that they have learnt from the previous week's work, put your core tasks in and don't forget that old chestnut about 'differentiating' in the tasks you include! Give them a little quiz, move on to the next one and then make sure you do a good summary and do a nice little feedback session with them. Fiddle your scheme of work so you're doing the lesson that you want to do, make sure that all the hand-outs have got the college logo on them and they're all nice and neat with no smudges, do a lot of questioning, do a lot of walking around, then bring some work in with you so you can show that you're giving them adequate feedback.

Terry was openly cynical of what was required to secure a high grade. His knowledge of 'which boxes to tick' was indicative of many astute teachers' pragmatic response to the use of graded observation and the need to 'play the game'. In other words, they were able to assimilate those features of pedagogy that had been identified as part of a *toolkit* for 'good' or 'outstanding' lessons and subsequently apply them to their own teaching when being observed. This resulted in such practice becoming normalized and adopted as the *default* model for all those striving to achieve a high grade, which itself raises questions concerning the validity and reliability of graded observation as a means of assessing classroom performance, two important factors that are discussed in the following chapter.

My research study (O'Leary 2011) drew on and was informed by the work of Foucault (1977, 1980, 2002) as its theoretical backbone, along with concepts discussed in the previous chapter relating to theories of new managerialism and performativity. Foucault's work, in particular, provided a suitable framework for analyzing the phenomenon of classroom observation as some of the key concepts he explored provided a useful lens through which to examine relationships of teacher agency and structure, as well as a language with which to describe and discuss the phenomenon of observation, for example, the concept of 'normalization'.

Normalization is a Foucauldian term that can be defined as the adjustment of behaviour to fall into line with prescribed standards. Perryman (2009: 614) states that:

> Normalization is a powerful mechanism of power which is achieved through the hegemonic internalization of discourses of control. In general, this means that those who are subjects of power internalize expected behaviours and learn these behaviours through acceptance of a discourse.

In the case of my previous work on the use and impact of models of graded observation, normalization can be seen as a means of conceptualizing the process by which teachers operate within the accepted norms of 'good practice', a concept largely determined by agencies such as Ofsted (O'Leary 2011, 2012a). In her research, Perryman (2006: 150) argued that it is the discourse of school effectiveness research that has been appropriated by Ofsted that forms the dominant discourse in the context of inspections, which 'uses performativity and normalization as its mechanisms'. Perryman identifies this as a classic example of the use of knowledge to convey power.

Foucault (1977: 184) asserted that 'the power of normalization imposes homogeneity; but it individualises by making it possible to measure gaps, to determine levels, to fix specialities and to render the differences useful by fitting them one to another'. The 'homogeneity' that Foucault refers to is imposed by the requirement for all teachers to demonstrate standardized notions of good practice during an appraisal observation. Those that are able to manifest such normalized behaviour become members of a homogenous community; those that fail to do so are identified through gaps in their assessed performance. The means by which such gaps are measured and levels determined is through a procedure that Foucault referred to as the *examination*, which 'combines the techniques of an observing hierarchy and those of a normalizing judgement' (ibid.). As discussed further below, graded observation epitomizes Foucault's *examination*, where a teacher's performance is categorized and differentiated by the observer according to Ofsted's 4-point scale.

Hardman's research (2007) adopted a case study approach in which the practice of observation was explored in three FE colleges and three HEIs. The three FE colleges in Hardman's study all had observation policies and procedures that sought to combine the purposes of QA requirements for Ofsted, together with internal staff development agendas. Observation schemes are undoubtedly time intensive and expensive for colleges. With limited budgets it is hardly surprising that colleges should attempt to dovetail two different purposes into one scheme. However, as Hardman suggests, the effectiveness of such a strategy is questionable. QA requirements appear to take precedence over the developmental needs of teachers. Furthermore, the use of observation for QA purposes is not without its controversies as has been discussed elsewhere.

My research revealed that the prioritization of the performance management agenda over the developmental led to the nullification of observation as a tool for CPD in many institutions (O'Leary 2011). As a result, teachers came to experience a growing sense of disempowerment, increased levels of anxiety and general discontent in relation to its use. A recurring theme from my data was the perceived lack of benefit of graded observation to teachers. Some said that the college management was the only beneficiary as it provided them with the necessary data to compare levels of performance with national benchmarks. Others referred to it as a 'tick-box' exercise that was more concerned with satisfying Ofsted than their development needs. Equally, senior managers were sceptical of the use of such data as they saw them simply as part of the 'evidence trail' required for Ofsted.

Postlethwaite (2007) states that 'observing classes as part of quality assurance procedures has become a contentious matter in many FE colleges' (cited in James and Biesta 2007: 168). This is a viewpoint shared by the main professional association for the sector, the University and College Union (UCU) who report that it has 'become an increasingly common flash point in colleges, triggering local negotiations, and in some places industrial disputes' (UCU 2009: 1). As a result, the union have 'call[ed] for a code of practice over how such work is carried out' (Lee 2007: 1) as, unlike the schools' sector, there is 'currently no national agreement on lesson observations with the Association of Colleges' (UCU 2009: 2). This is in response to complaints from members regarding the draconian, 'intimidatory and not supportive' way in which observation is being used by managers in some colleges (Lee 2007). At the centre of the debate is the issue of grading. My research data revealed that, in some cases, teachers are threatened with disciplinary action or denied annual pay increments if they continue to be rated satisfactory or inadequate on the Ofsted scale. In recent times the issue of unannounced observations has also become another hotly debated topic, as unions contest that it is a tactic that is being used by some unscrupulous employers to single out and harass specific individuals.

From 2006–09, researchers based at the University of Huddersfield published three separate reports (Burrows 2008; Ollin 2009; Peake 2006) into the use of observation in the context of ITT programmes as part of the 'Huddersfield Post-Compulsory Education and Training (PCET) Consortium'.

The first of these reports (Peake 2006) explored the perceptions of teacher educators and trainee teachers concerning the purposes of observation and sought to identify examples of good practice. The research methods consisted of two survey questionnaires, one for trainee tutors and the other for subject specialist mentors, as well as interviews with eleven teacher educators working at five different centres. In total there were 134 responses to the trainees' questionnaire and only four responses to the mentors' questionnaire, which had been sent to 12 mentors in total.

The key findings of the research revealed some interesting areas of discussion that resonated with issues covered in related studies. Below is an adapted summary of these:

- Importance of the observer being a subject specialist
- Conflicting purposes of ITT and QA observations
- Concerns regarding the lack of consistency and standardization of practice between observers across the consortium
- Trainees avoid taking risks in observed sessions
- Value of peer observation in professional development
- Observation is resource intensive – it is time-consuming and expensive.

The second report (Burrows 2008) focused on exploring trainees' perceptions of observation as part of the 'new curriculum', i.e. the increase in observation to a minimum of eight hours under the LLUK qualifications (2007), together with the undertaking of observation by mentors to support the development of subject specialist pedagogy. The project was underpinned by two aims: 'To identify the perceptions of trainees of observations within the new curriculum [and] to formulate an action plan to improve observations based upon the analysis of the research' (p. 5).

Although the research aimed to explore the main issues confronting both pre- and in-service trainees and their observers during observation, only the former were included as part of the sample. Eighty participants completed a questionnaire similar in focus and design to that used in Peake's (2006) study, followed by four focus groups in which sixty-five trainees participated. The key findings are summarized below:

- More structured training of observers needed, particularly subject mentors who are unfamiliar with the observation process.
- More than 50 per cent of respondents thought that ITE (initial teacher education) observation should not be graded compared with a third who thought that it should.
- Observation as 'formative' assessment is a key means of supporting professional development and more value should be attached to it than course assignments. Peer observation is highly valued.

The third report (Ollin 2009: 5) was carried out:

[I]n response to the introduction of Ofsted's new grading criteria for inspection of ITE in the [sector] (2009), which state that over fifty per cent of trainees need to be judged 'outstanding' for an ITE provider to achieve the highest inspection grade.

The research explored the implications of introducing the Ofsted scale for teacher educators across the consortium. Ollin remarked that the grading criteria on Huddersfield's programmes 'previously operated on a pass/fail basis' and that the transition to the Ofsted scale 'will influence the way that Certificate in Education/PGCE programmes are developed and delivered' (p. 7). This is a very significant point highlighting the challenges faced by providers as a result of having to adapt to changing policy, while also protecting the values and beliefs that underpin many ITE programmes; i.e. the emphasis being on encouraging teacher development through a combination of formative and summative assessment where the former is prioritized over the latter. However, Ollin fails to point out that providers are not obliged to adopt Ofsted's scale. It is the choice of an institution to decide to do so or not.

The underpinning aims of Ollin's (2009: 12) research were, 'To develop a working conceptualization of what constitutes "outstanding" teaching [and] to use this information to further develop staff and quality systems, taking into account issues of grading of trainees' practical teaching'. The research was 'qualitative and interpretive in nature' and used interviews and observations. These included a small sample size of nine case studies of 'outstanding' and 'weak' trainees during which the ITE tutors were observed carrying out observation and giving feedback, followed by a semi-structured interview 'focussing initially on understandings and judgements of "outstanding" related to the specific observation' (p. 15). Some of the key findings revealed:

- Mixed interpretations as to what constitutes 'outstanding'.
- The need to consider the effect of context on the notion of 'outstanding'.
- Tensions between the 'dual identities' of those in-service trainees observed on ITE programmes and as part of internal college QA schemes. In the first instance they are seen as 'students' with 'developmental needs' and in the second as employees with an obligation to prove their professional competence. Similar tensions were revealed by observers who were involved in observation as ITE tutors but also in college observation for QA purposes.
- Resistance on the part of observers to grading based on the premise that it undermined the developmental nature of ITE observation.

Ollin's research concluded that the Ofsted grading criteria are likely to have a significant impact on future ITE programmes across the Huddersfield Consortium and present a challenge in 'balancing the underpinning values related to the learning and development of trainees with increasing demands for standards of teaching to be monitored and assured' (p. 6). It is surprising though that there is no reference to previous studies carried out in this specific field (e.g. Cope *et al* 2003; Sharp 2006), which have argued that the graded assessment of observation for trainee teachers is unsustainable on the basis that:

> There is no published research which confirms that meaningful grading is possible. Attempts to implement grading schemes ignore the lack of support from research and imply that the assessment of teaching is based on measurement rather than professional judgement.

(Cope *et al* 2003: 683)

Finally, Lawson's recent research (2011) has explored the use of an 'observational partnership' between a university education department and three local colleges. Lawson carried out qualitative content analysis of the texts of 924 observation report forms collected between 2002 and 2009. The aims of the analysis were to 'establish an understanding of which practices may be successfully changed through observation of the classroom and which may be more resistant to transformation, as well as giving insights into the process of enacting change in the classroom' (p. 10).

Lawson's analysis identified two areas of teachers' classroom performance that appeared to lend themselves more easily to change ('planning for learning' and 'assessment for learning') and two that were more resistant ('questioning' and 'student involvement'). In relation to the former, the findings revealed no discernible patterns as to why these two aspects seemed more conducive to change than others. With regards to the latter though, Lawson argues that in the case of 'questioning', 'the practice is so complex and nuanced that it is difficult for teachers to develop their practice'. As for 'student involvement', Lawson puts this down to 'deeply ingrained habits and suppositions about teaching' (p. 17).

Lawson concludes by stating that 'sustained observation offers a robust way of changing some classroom practices and of making inroads in others'. He attributes the success of the partnership's observation scheme to its collaborative nature and its 'continuity', which has helped to establish a mutual understanding and trust amongst those involved as to what its purpose is i.e. to encourage an open, shared dialogue between observer and observee with a view to further improving teaching and learning. Notwithstanding this, he is mindful of how not all those observees involved were 'open to the possibilities of change' and this was manifested by them 'going through the motions' (p. 18).

The HE sector experience

It is only in recent years that observation has begun to emerge in HEIs. This has been partly fuelled by QA demands for greater accountability but more increasingly as a result of its potential for supporting the CPD of lecturers (Hammersley-Fletcher and Orsmond 2004, 2005; McMahon *et al* 2007; Shortland 2004). Unlike FE and the schools' sector, its use is much less commonplace or prescribed. There is less evidence of links to formal, centralized QA systems and it appears to operate mostly on an informal, voluntary and departmental basis. Hardman's research (2007) reveals that it also occurs as part of academic programmes of professional study for staff, such as the recently created postgraduate award in Learning and Teaching in HE; a compulsory qualification for new staff in many post-1992 universities.

The dominant model used in HE would appear to be 'peer observation' (Hammersley-Fletcher and Orsmond 2004, 2005; Peel 2005; Shortland 2004). Shortland (2004: 220) defines peer observation as 'peers observing each other's teaching to enhance teaching quality through reflective practice, thereby aiding professional development'. There are some researchers, however, who contest the generic application of peer observation in HE as an all-encompassing term for observation and instead prefer the label 'third-party observation' (Fullerton 2003; McMahon *et al* 2007). For them the term peer observation refers to a specific model of observation based on a collaborative partnership between peers, which is underpinned by 'equality between observer and observed'

(McMahon *et al* 2007: 500). This is a legitimate and helpful terminological distinction to make, especially if we are to avoid a blurring of the boundaries between the different models, contexts and purposes of observation as examined in the following chapters.

Extant research reveals a commonality in the key issues, most of which centre on the perceived opportunities and threats associated with the use of peer observation in HE. Peel (2005) is mindful of its potential danger as a surveillance tool on an institutional level. Research carried out among GP teachers revealed opposition to schemes that used peer observation to address the twin aims of teacher development and QA. Such schemes were considered 'unlikely to succeed if seen to be conveying quality assurance in the guise of tutor support' (Adshead *et al* 2006: 72). The transparency of the aims and objectives of any peer observation scheme in HE is regarded as fundamental to avoid it being viewed with suspicion by lecturers.

In a small-scale qualitative study involving eighteen interviews with lecturers from two academic schools of a post-1992 English university, Hammersley-Fletcher and Orsmond (2005) explored their experiences as participants in a peer observation scheme. Their findings revealed uncertainty regarding the expectations of their roles as both observer and observee. Some lecturers felt uncomfortable about providing critical feedback for their peers. The uncertainty and unease expressed by lecturers showed how a shared understanding of what was meant by the term 'critical feedback' was missing. It also exposed their lack of experience in providing constructive feedback.

In Hammersley-Fletcher and Orsmond's study the success of the peer relationship between observer and observee was seen to be dependent on the notions of trust and confidentiality. These were considered fundamental to facilitating honest reflection. It also emerged as an important issue in other studies (e.g. Gosling 2002; Shortland 2004). Gosling (2002: 2) talks about the need for staff to be seen as 'genuine peers in which there is real mutuality and respect for each of the participants as equal'. He suggests that the process can be undermined if the observer is senior in hierarchy to the observee, although his claim is unsubstantiated. His concerns seem to be based on the premise that such a relationship is likely to result in more senior members of staff taking charge, hence threatening the equality of the interaction.

In an autobiographical study, Peel (2005) reflects on her personal experiences as a new lecturer and examines the arguments for and against peer observation. She avers that it can be a useful means of facilitating reflection as long as it incorporates reflection on wider issues of the teaching and learning process and not just that of the observed lesson. She remarks that it was as a result of engaging in critical reflective thinking triggered by the feedback element that led to her successful CPD rather than discussion centring on the observation itself. Thus, peer observation is being used as a 'lens' to stimulate critical reflection (Brookfield 1995).

Following the Browne (2010) review into university funding, the president of the National Union of Students (NUS), Liam Burns, called for all university lecturers to be subjected to similar training programmes to those of their counterparts in schools and colleges (Boffey 2012). His rationale for the need for the introduction of such qualifications is set against the background of the significant rise in university tuition fees and the need to ensure QA mechanisms that students are being taught by appropriately qualified staff. If the government were to follow up this recommendation, it suggests that it may not be long before the use of classroom observation is introduced as a form of measuring quality/ standards in HE.

Synopsis of key themes and issues across the sectors

There are clearly recurring themes surrounding the use of observation in all three sectors. For example, its value as a means of stimulating reflection on practice by engaging in professional dialogue with colleagues, who act as 'critical mirrors' (Brookfield 1995) seems to be a shared interpretation among researchers and practitioners in all three sectors, albeit with the caveat that specific ground rules need to be established for this to work successfully; i.e. notions of mutual trust, respect, ownership etc. At the same time, there are divergences between the three that partly reflect their historical status and the history of policy in each sector. In FE and schools, observation appears to have operated principally to satisfy policy driven agendas of performance management systems. In HE, its role is less prescribed, thus allowing lecturers more autonomy and control over its use, though arguably this can be attributed to the fact that the observation of teaching is not included in Quality Assurance Agency (QAA) inspections of HEIs whereas it is one of the main sources of evidence in Ofsted inspections.

The use of graded observation has triggered debate regarding the reliability of observation as a form of assessment in schools (Wragg 1999) and more so recently in FE (O'Leary 2011). Although this discussion is continued in the following two chapters, it is important to note at this stage that graded observation is perhaps the single most contentious issue relating to the topic. Its performance focus is something that seems to have provoked strong reactions across both sectors. Brown (in Brown *et al* 1993: 51) compared such models of observation with the traditional examination in that both teacher and student are required to produce 'peak performance under stressful conditions with little opportunity for dialogue with the examiner and no real chance to gain meaningful feedback on how things are going'. There is a natural link here to Foucault's (1977) notion of the 'examination', where the performance of the teacher becomes subjected to a process of 'objectification' through the system of graded observation.

On pp. 16–18 the pervasion of systems of performativity and accountability in public life was discussed. For Foucault (1977: 184) these systems are embodied in the *examination*, which functions as 'a normalizing gaze, a surveillance that makes it possible to qualify, to classify and to punish. It establishes over individuals a visibility through which one differentiates and judges them'.

The examination is a pivotal mechanism of disciplinary power by which people are ranked. In relation to classroom observation, it can be seen as a metaphor for graded models of observation in schools and colleges, where a teacher's performance is categorized and differentiated by the observer according to Ofsted's 4-point scale. Foucault's notion of the examination is thus a useful theoretical tool for analyzing and discussing the application of observation, particularly the use of graded observation and to test whether it is applied 'at each moment to supervise the conduct of each individual, to assess it, to judge it, to calculate the qualities and merits' (1977: 143).

Some of the existing research in the field has highlighted how the performative nature of graded observation has resulted in a decline in the creativity and innovation of teachers' work in the classroom. There is a reluctance to want to 'take risks' for fear of being given a low grade. Teachers are aware of the need to 'play the game', which can result in them following a collective template of 'good practice' during observation. According to Simons and Elliott (1990: 83), this is an example of 'management exercising control over performance by preventing teachers from reflexively developing new understandings of the nature of teaching and learning tasks'. In FE, Peake (2006) has illustrated how even in the context of ITE trainees avoid taking risks during observation. Yet recent research into the use of lesson study among qualified teachers in schools seems to suggest a counterbalance to this.

With regard to the use of observation as a formative tool for CPD, there would appear to be a commonality across much of the literature in terms of some of the key concepts discussed: i.e. collaboration, equality, autonomy, ownership, trust etc. Much of this work has focused on the use of lesson study in schools and peer observation in HE, both of which are explored further in Chapters 7 and 8. Referring to Ramsden (1992), Jones (in Brown *et al* 1993: 31) comments that in order for observation to work it needs to be part of a teacher's professional development and not something that is 'done to them':

> Ownership of observation needs to be devolved down as much as possible to the participants in the teaching process. The closer the ownership of the process is located to the actual participants, the more likely it is that the aims will be achieved and the outcomes accepted by all concerned.
>
> (Brown *et al* 1993: 10)

To conclude, across all three sectors previous studies have revealed that observation is regarded as an important means of evaluating, reflecting on and improving the quality of teaching and learning as well as contributing to a greater understanding of these processes. Whether this occurs as part of QA systems or CPD programmes, the central role that observation has to play in the professional practice of teachers seems incontestable. Where the contestations start to emerge, however, is in relation to the stated aims behind its use, the extent to which the outcomes match these aims and the way in which the process of observation is operationalized.

Wragg (1999) argued that the *purpose* of observation should largely determine how it is used, but evidence in this chapter and those that follow suggests that the boundaries between different models, contexts and purposes have become blurred and contested. At the heart of these contestations lies a conflict between 'structure' and 'teacher agency', and related notions of power and control that manifest themselves in the sometimes paradoxical agendas of policymakers, the institution and its teaching staff. This conflict is epitomized by the way in which the developmental needs of staff and the requirements of performance management systems are forced to compete as they are often conflated into a 'one-size-fits-all' model of observation in schools and colleges, with the latter overshadowing the former.

Summary

This chapter has reviewed relevant literature and previous studies of classroom observation across the schools', FE and HE sectors. It has identified key themes and issues to emerge in each sector and provided a synopsis of areas of commonality and differences. Many previous studies and publications have focused largely on descriptive accounts of *practice* with limited discussion of the wider contexts and cultures in which it is situated. Where there have been links to context these have often occurred in relation to ITT. Nevertheless, more recent research in FE (e.g. O'Leary 2011, 2012a) has helped to develop a synthesis between the practice of observation and the contexts in which it occurs. The use of observation in the university sector is still relatively new, with much of the existing research focusing on models of peer observation and its application as a tool for reflection.

Finally, the key themes and issues explored in this chapter will serve as useful reference points for discussion throughout the rest of the book, where they will be re-examined and re-cycled in an applied context. This chapter brings Part 1 of the book to a close and moves on to Part 2 – 'Classroom observation as a means of assessing teaching and learning', where the first chapter will focus on the use of observation as a method for researching classrooms.

Discussion topics/tasks

1. *Learning from past studies*

   - What do previous studies into classroom observation tell us about its use in the education system?
   - What lessons can we learn from these studies?
   - How might the findings from past studies influence our current perspective and attitude towards observation?

2. *'Hot topics'*

   - What are some of the 'hot topics' surrounding the use of observation in your workplace?
   - To what extent do you consider these topics to be specific to your chosen sector? Are they specific to your subject area/department? Do they apply to all staff?
   - Which of these topics provoke the strongest feelings amongst staff?

3. *Evaluating union perspectives on observation policy in your institution*
   Appendix 1 is an example of a union position paper on the use of classroom observation in colleges. Drawing on this or similar papers from other unions representing college/schoolteachers, use this as the basis for assessing the current protocols and procedures for observation in your institution.

Note

1 This chapter is based on an article that first appeared in the journal *Professional Development in Education* (O'Leary 2012a). Included with permission.

Part II

Classroom observation as a means of assessing teaching and learning

Chapter 4

Classroom observation as a method for studying teaching and learning

Ways of recording what you see

Introduction

In recent years the use of classroom observation has increased as governmental agencies such as Ofsted and in turn schools and colleges have come to rely on it as a vital means of collecting evidence about what goes on in classrooms. Such evidence has been used to inform current conceptualizations of what makes for effective teaching and learning (see Chapter 6), along with providing the basis on which judgements about the competence and performance of teachers are made. Interestingly though, in spite of its elevated status as a key tool in the government's policy for teacher appraisal and development, observation remains an under-researched area with few texts having explored its strengths and limitations as a method of assessment or indeed its application.

The key aim of this chapter is to discuss observation as a method for studying and recording what goes on in classrooms, along with developing an awareness of its advantages and disadvantages as a method of assessment. At the core of this discussion is a comparison between quantitative and qualitative approaches to observation, which are situated in an applied context. Observation instruments are presented in order to illustrate the differences between these two approaches and what they are able to tell us about the process of teaching and learning. Validity and reliability, fundamental cornerstones of any research method, are discussed and considered in relation to the use of observation as a means of data collection, as well as the repercussions for subsequent judgements made about the quality of teaching and learning.

Quantitative and qualitative approaches to classroom observation: an introduction

What do we mean by the term 'classroom observation'? Interestingly, there are very few studies of observation that actually define what it is. Bailey (2001: 114) describes it as being 'the purposeful examination of teaching and/or learning events through the systematic processes of data collection and analysis'. Tilstone (1998: 6) offers a similar 'working definition' and describes it as 'the systematic, and as accurate as possible, collection of usually visual evidence, leading to informed judgements and to necessary changes to accepted practices'. The extent to which observation can be considered a 'systematic' or 'accurate' method of assessment is a matter of some debate. Much of this debate centres on the assessment tools or methodological approaches used to record and evaluate what happens in classrooms and this is something that will

Quantitative approach   Qualitative approach

Figure 4.1 The quantitative–qualitative continuum.

be discussed in detail throughout this chapter when examining different approaches to the use of observation.

Traditionally, the way in which classroom observation has been used as a method for recording the events of the classroom can be broadly categorized into quantitative and qualitative approaches. These two approaches can be seen as opposite ends of a continuum (see Figure 4.1), though this does not mean that they are necessarily mutually exclusive 'as they can often complement each other' (Wragg 1999: 20). As we shall see when discussing examples of current observation instruments in use below (see Figure 4.3 on p. 64), many often combine aspects of both. At one end of the continuum is the 'quantitative' approach, which attempts to record specific classroom incidents according to a structured, selective rating system with a view to gathering quantifiable data or data that can be converted into numbers so that they can be analysed statistically. It typically uses some type of scoring or tally system in order to record the data. At the other end is the 'qualitative' approach, which at its most basic form consists of an open-ended, chronological recording of what the observer sees, often in the form of hand-written text – i.e. non-numerical data. An understanding of the specific context in which the observation occurs is integral to the observer's accurate interpretation of events.

These contrasting approaches reflect a long-standing dichotomy between quantitative and qualitative research paradigms and the differing perceptions of reality of these two paradigms (see Table 4.1). In the case of quantitative researchers, they believe that reality is universal and can be studied and measured objectively. Thus most quantitative research aims to test out a hypothesis. In order to do so, it relies on counting and classifying data, as well as using statistical models of probability to make sense of and explain what is observed.

In contrast, qualitative researchers believe that there is not one external reality, but multiple realities. For the qualitative researcher, reality is socially constructed; it is a product of the human mind and as such each person's perception of reality is likely to vary according to their life experiences, social, cultural and educational background etc. Qualitative

Table 4.1 A synopsis of features of quantitative and qualitative research.

Quantitative	Qualitative
• Researcher as 'scientist'	• Researcher as 'explorer'
• 'Hard' data (i.e. numbers)	• 'Soft' data (i.e. words)
• Objective	• Subjective
• Explanatory	• Exploratory
• Hypothesis-testing	• Hypothesis-generating
• One notion of reality	• Reality is a construct of the human mind
• Generalizable results	• Idiosyncratic results
• One reality in a rational world	• Multiple realities open to interpretation
• Reality is 'measurable'	• Reality is complex and dynamic

research is concerned with collecting mainly textual and/or verbal data, which are subsequently analyzed in an interpretative manner where the researcher is often responsible for creating their own categories of analysis.

The common perception is that a quantitative approach to the collection of data through observation is deemed to be more 'scientific' and 'objective' than a qualitative approach, though this is a contested perception among those involved in the field of research. Table 4.1 presents a concise comparative summary of some of the key differences between these two approaches.

So, you may be asking yourself, what is the significance of these approaches to the way in which classroom observation is used as an instrument for observing and assessing classroom teaching and learning, and why is it important for those involved in the observation process to know about them? Firstly, we need to be clear about what can and cannot be discovered and subsequently claimed about teaching and learning through the use of observation. Like any other method of data collection, it has its strengths and limitations and it is important to be aware of these if we are to maximize its value. Secondly, if observation is to be used as the main source of data on which judgements about the quality of teaching and learning are to be formed, then it is in the best interests of all those involved that they should strive to ensure that the approaches and tools used to collect these data are not only fit for purpose, but also as accurate and reliable as possible. And thirdly, I would argue that developing awareness about what underpins these approaches and tools and how they operate is essential for helping both observer and observee to appreciate what data will be recorded, why and how they will be recorded during the course of the observation, thus leading to a clearer understanding for both parties.

The following two sub-sections of this chapter will concentrate on quantitative and qualitative approaches to observation, respectively. The key features of each approach will be discussed and relevant literature, as well as observation instruments, will be drawn upon to reinforce and illustrate this discussion.

Quantitative approaches to classroom observation

There are limited examples of the use of classroom observation as a quantitative research tool in England, unlike in the USA where it has a long history. Much of its use in the USA has concentrated on the collection of statistical data about classroom behaviour and teacher–student interactions rather than using it as a form of intervention to improve teacher skills and knowledge as Lawson (2011: 4) comments:

> The research purpose of classroom observation is mainly unconnected with changing the behaviour of teachers directly, but rather is a way of understanding and theorising about the behaviours that are observed. As such, classroom observation has mainly been used in an evaluative way and not as a transformative tool.

Thus early quantitative approaches to classroom observation tended to concentrate on keeping a tally of specific teacher behaviours according to categories specified in an observation instrument or schedule rather than keeping a descriptive record of what was going on in the classroom as a whole. For example, how often a teacher asked open-ended compared with closed questions during a lesson, how much time was allocated to particular practices or how often particular teacher–student interactions occurred etc. These early approaches came to be known collectively as 'systematic observation'. In referring to Croll's (1986) work, Foster (1996: 4) summarizes systematic observation as follows:

> The purposes of observation, the categories of behaviour to be observed, and the methods by which instances of behaviour are to be allocated to categories are carefully worked out before the data collection begins. This is why this approach is often referred to as systematic or structured observation. A variety of techniques are used to record observations, but all involve some sort of pre-set, standardized observation schedule on which a record, often in the form of ticks or numbers, of the type of behaviour of interest is made.

Systematic observation is also referred to as 'interaction analysis' in the literature, though this term is commonly associated with a particular model of systematic observation developed over forty years ago by Flanders (1970). Flanders Interaction Analysis Categories (FIAC) is a model of systematic observation that was influenced by the positivist tradition. How it works in practice is that observers are given a data recording sheet in the format of a grid containing empty squares and each line represents a minute of classroom time. Observers are required to record and code the events taking place according to ten pre-established categories every three seconds by noting down the appropriate category number 1–10 in their grids and then at the end to calculate the percentage of total codes for each of the ten categories.

As shown in Table 4.2, Flanders' framework of analysis divides classroom interaction into three broad domains: 1) teacher talk; 2) pupil talk and 3) silence. Whilst it seems that a lot of detailed data can be recorded in a short space of time, there are clear limitations to FIAC in that its categories are rather generic and do not fully encapsulate the complexity and diversity of classroom interaction, not to mention the differing purposes of classroom observation today. Still, it needs to be acknowledged that FIAC was devised more than forty years ago and as such is unlikely to reflect 21st century classrooms and teacher–learner roles. However, in theory, there is nothing to prevent it from being updated to make it more relevant to today's classrooms and the specific focus of the observation.

What systematic approaches like FIAC and others that have followed since have in common is that the observation instrument is structured to ensure that the observer records events according to a pre-determined set of categories. Thus, as Foster states above, the observers have already decided on what data they wish to observe and record before even entering the classroom. Of course, one of the limitations of this structured approach is that it is inflexible and does not allow the observer to change the focus or record aspects of classroom practice that do not correspond to the pre-determined categories. From a qualitative perspective, such approaches can be regarded as oversimplifying the complex nature of classroom interactions as they eschew the inclusion of contextual variables in their analysis.

On the other hand, one of the advantages of such quantitative approaches is that they allow the observer to limit their focus, thus making the process more manageable, whilst also minimizing the judgemental aspect, often associated with certain qualitative approaches. However, this might also be seen as a disadvantage as a lot of information can be missed or left out. Although it is rare to see instruments such as FIAC in use in classrooms nowadays, especially in England, quantitative approaches to observation are still popular elsewhere like the USA.

Table 4.2 Flanders' Interaction Analysis Categories.

Teacher Talk	**Response**	1. **Accepts feeling**. Accepts and clarifies an attitude or the feeling tone of a pupil in a non-threatening manner. Feelings may be positive or negative. Predicting and recalling feelings are included.
		2. **Praises or encourages**. Praises or encourages pupil action or behaviour. Jokes that release tension, but not at the expense of another individual: nodding head, or saying 'Um hm?' or 'Go on' are included.
		3. **Accepts or uses ideas of pupils**. Clarifying, building or developing ideas suggested by a pupil. Teacher extensions of pupil ideas are included but as the teacher brings more of his own ideas into play, shift to category five.
		4. **Asks questions**. Asking a question about content or procedure, based on teacher ideas, with the intent that a pupil will answer.
	Initiation	5. **Lecturing**. Giving facts or opinions about content or procedures: expressing *his own* ideas, giving *his own* explanation or citing an authority other than a pupil.
		6. **Giving directions**. Directions, commands or orders to which a pupil is expected to comply.
		7. **Criticising or justifying authority**. Statements intended to change pupil behaviour from non-acceptable to acceptable pattern; bawling someone out; stating why the teacher is doing what he is doing; extreme self-defence.
Pupil Talk	**Response**	8. **Pupil talk – response**. Talk by pupils in response to teacher. Teacher initiates the contact or solicits pupil statement or structures the situation. Freedom to express own ideas is limited.
	Initiation	9. **Pupil talk – initiation**. Talk by pupils which they initiate. Expressing own ideas; initiating a new topic; freedom to develop opinions and a line of thought, like asking thoughtful questions: going beyond the existing structure.
Silence		10. **Silence or confusion**. Pauses, short periods of silence and periods of confusion in which communication cannot be understood by the observer.

Source: Flanders (1970: 34).

More recently in the USA, large-scale programmes of classroom observation have become associated with improving learner achievement, and have used standardized instruments in an attempt to measure teacher performance (e.g. Pianta *et al* 2008; Pianta and Hamre 2009). Typically these instruments have included some type of statistical measurement of behavioural interactions in the classroom. As Lawson (2011: 5) observes,

> The main focus of these types of observation is the collection of data rather than to change teachers' practices directly, the creators of these scales are concerned primarily with issues such as content validity and inter-rater reliability (Van Tassel-Baska, Quek,

and Feng 2007) and not with impact. In most of these schedules the aim is not to change specific teachers' practices in the classroom but to generate principles of good practice that may or may not be taken up by the teaching community at large.

Lawson is critical of what he perceives as a disconnection between the data generated by the use of such instruments and how these data can be applied in a meaningful way to further enhance the professional development of teachers. One of the common claims of quantitative approaches to classroom observation is that the instruments they use are systematic and as such 'provide a standard way of measuring and noting teachers' strengths and weaknesses'(Pianta and Hamre 2009: 110).

An example of a current quantitative instrument of measuring teacher performance is the Classroom Assessment Scoring System or CLASS as devised by Pianta *et al* (2008). The CLASS is a standardized observation instrument that was largely developed for use in an early childhood setting in the USA and has since become a trademarked product. The CLASS attempts to provide a conceptual framework for categorizing classroom interactions and consists of three broad 'domains of quality': 1) emotional supports; 2) classroom organization and 3) instructional supports (Pianta and Hamre 2009: 111). Within each of these domains, classroom interactions are further organized into multiple *dimensions* and in turn a series of *indicators* that 'are presumed to be important to students' academic and/or social development' (p. 113), as illustrated in Figure 4.2.

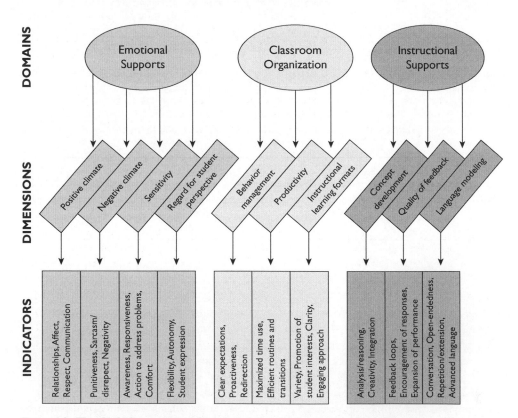

Figure 4.2 The CLASS conceptual framework for classroom interactions.

Pianta and Hamre (2009: 113) provide an overview of the conceptual framework of the CLASS and how they perceive it working in practice below:

> The CLASS framework starts with an understanding of the nature and regulators of developmental change at a given period (Hamre and Pianta, 2007; Pianta and Allen, 2008), then applies that understanding in an analysis of classroom settings and teacher–child interactions, maps that understanding back onto the rich and deep literature on classroom teaching and educational effectiveness, and then organizes this analysis within a framework that could inform measurement. . . . The latent structure in the CLASS model poses explicit, testable hypotheses regarding the organization of meaningful patterns of behavior (or behaviors) that are tied to underlying developmental processes. In this structure, meaningful units of teacher–child interaction are organized by patterns, which in turn are the basis for identifiable and scalable dimensions of interaction.

The design of quantitative observation instruments such as CLASS is often driven by a desire to make transparent and measure those aspects of teacher behaviour and teacher–student interactions that are considered effective in stimulating successful student learning and achievement. Put simply, what is it that an 'effective teacher' does in the classroom that impacts positively on the learning process and how can we replicate this? As Wragg argues in the following extract:

> Lying at the heart of the quantitative approach is a belief that the effectiveness of teachers can be improved if a body of knowledge is established which shows that they should do more of some things and less of others. Though this has an appeal, it has to be said that there are relatively few findings that can be said to be of wide general concern.
>
> (Wragg 1999: 9)

The 'belief' that Wragg refers to above is rooted in a positivist philosophy of knowledge production that seeks to quantify and measure what goes on in classrooms on the basis that the behaviour of teachers and learners is unambiguous and transparently observable. Although such approaches appear to offer the advantage of reducing the subjective interpretation of the observer as they tend to concentrate on the observation of low inference factors (see pp. 64–65 for further discussion of 'low' and 'high inference' factors), one of the key weaknesses of such an approach is that it does not provide a rationale as to *why* those events recorded have occurred in the first instance and thus fails to provide stakeholders with a more detailed understanding of classroom practice. Nevertheless, quantitative models of observation such as CLASS can be used to collect data on a wide range of specific aspects of the teaching and learning process at any given time. One of the advantages of such models is that they limit the focus of the observer, thus making it a more manageable process when it comes to collecting/recording data. In addition, as the observer is concentrating on their pre-determined focus, this means that they are freed from the constraints of having to make simultaneous evaluations, as is the norm with qualitative approaches in the context of teacher appraisal.

The scale of the sample involved in using CLASS is certainly impressive as it included roughly 2,500 classrooms, thus adding weight to the argument that such quantitative approaches to the observation of teacher behaviour generate data that are 'adequate in reliability and validity' (e.g. Hamre and Pianta 2005; Pianta *et al* 2005, cited in Pianta and Hamre 2009) and 'have shown promise in being usable at scale' (Pianta *et al* 2007, cited in Pianta and Hamre 2009: 111), which strengthens claims to the potential generalizability of the findings. Yet on closer examination of these observation instruments, they seem to share many of the features of combined quantitative–qualitative approaches to the assessment of teaching and learning associated with current instruments. Many of these instruments seek to combine both quantitative and qualitative aspects, as we shall see in the section that follows. Besides, the claims to standardization of quantitative tools such as CLASS are not as unproblematic as some of the researchers involved in these studies would have us believe. For example, one of the key variables noticeable in its absence from the discussion is that of human judgement in applying these instruments of measurement consistently. In some ways this is the proverbial 'elephant in the room' that seems to have been overlooked and it is an important issue that will be returned to in detail below.

An observation instrument such as CLASS may be useful in recording what type of behaviours and interactions occur in the classroom but not necessarily *why* they occur, which is the missing qualitative element. Unless the teacher and learners are active participants in the data collection and given the opportunity to explain classroom events, then we are forced to rely on the observers' explanations of these events, which can threaten to undermine the reliability and validity of the data. Besides, given the complexity of behaviours, interactions and compounding variables in any given classroom, it begs the question as to how useful or effective it can be to compile a list of events according to a series of pre-conceived categories.

Qualitative approaches to observation

Qualitative approaches to observation typically rely on observers keeping notes of what they witness in the classroom during the course of the observation, along with their evaluative interpretation of these events. Models can broadly be placed into three types: 1) the completely unstructured, 'stream of consciousness' type where the observer is given a blank canvas on which to record their notes as a 'running log' of events; 2) the semi-structured type where what the observer records is shaped by a set of pre-established categories, together with a list of assessment criteria and 3) the highly structured type, which shares many of the features of the previous type but divides the assessment of the lesson into individual performance indicators that are graded according to a pre-established rating scale such as the Ofsted 1–4 scale. In recent years there has been a tendency for many institutions to move towards the latter two types in an attempt to satisfy QA systems and the on-going demand for greater transparency and accountability, with the result that the 'blank canvas' model is rarely seen nowadays, other than in the context of peer observation or as part of a pre-agreed, unstructured approach between the observer and observee (see Chapter 7 for examples of this). Table 4.3 provides an example of a semi-structured model used by a university ITT department for assessing the performance of student teachers.

The report form shown in Table 4.3 is taken from the observation booklet of an ITT course, yet its overall structure and design is not unlike the type of forms used in some teacher appraisal schemes in schools and colleges. The observer is provided with a semi-structured framework in which to record their notes and assessment of the observed lesson.

Table 4.3 Semi-structured observation report form.

Teacher:	Observer:	Date:
Title:	Subject & Level:	Number in Group:

Preparation & Planning:

Learning & Teaching Activity:

Equal opportunities and safeguarding:

Resources:

Assessment:

Personal Qualities & Professionalism:

Areas to work on (discussed & negotiated between observer & teacher):

Teacher Self-Evaluation:

The overall assessment of this session = PASS/FAIL

Teacher's signature:	Observer's signature:

What makes this model 'semi-structured' is the fact that the form contains a set of pre-established categories to frame the observer's comments, which are also guided by an accompanying set of criteria for the observer to consult when recording their comments (see Appendix 2 – 'Criteria for semi-structured observation report form'). Although the specification of the categories might vary from one institution to another, there tends to be more similarities than differences between instruments as they are influenced by criteria and standards from validating bodies and/or external agencies such as Ofsted. Yet this does not mean that they are necessarily used in the same way as this can depend on factors such as context, purpose of the observation, observer training and so on. Some of these issues are discussed on pp. 60–67 and others in the following chapter.

Despite the structured framework of the report form in Table 4.3, it retains a predominantly qualitative approach to it insomuch as the assessment relies on the collation of interpretative comments on the part of the observer. These are then shared with the observee, who is given the opportunity to respond to them and offer their own interpretation of events, before a final decision on the assessment outcome is reached by the observer. Although the observer is able to consult a list of pre-determined assessment criteria to guide them in making their decision (see Appendix 2), the final decision rests largely with the judgement of the observer.

In contrast, the report form shown in Table 4.4 is an example of a quantitative–qualitative approach to recording data during the course of a classroom observation. It adopts a multi-graded framework that seeks to condense the assessment of teaching and learning into a set of 18 categories or 'performance indicators'. Each of these indicators is allocated a grade by the observer, based on an accompanying set of criteria (see Appendix 3 – 'Observation criteria for highly structured report form'), that are then added together to produce an overall aggregate grade at the end of the observation. At first glance, the form seems coherently structured and is clearly influenced by a positivist approach to assessment by the way in which it prioritizes the recording of numerical data (i.e. grades) over that of textual data (i.e. written comments). However, on closer inspection there are a number of aspects of design and implementation that are worth reflecting on in more detail.

Firstly, with regards to the assessment criteria on in Appendix 3, there are some issues concerning their validity and reliability (see 'Observation as a method of teacher assessment', p. 60 for further discussion of these terms). The observer is faced with a lot of information to read, digest and make evaluative decisions about simultaneously during the observation, which is likely to place them under a lot of pressure when forming their assessments.

Secondly, the descriptors for each of the four grades in the observation criteria fail to account for subject specific factors and are very generic. Following on from this, some of the language used to define the criteria for each grade and category are vague and ambiguous. For example, if we look at the grade 1 column, the term 'highly effective' is used repeatedly but no definition and/or illustration of what is meant by this is provided, leaving it open to interpretation. When comparing some of the criteria for a grade 1 and a grade 2, the main difference resides in the use of the terms 'highly effective' and 'good' respectively.

Thirdly, it is unclear what happens in the event of an observation where there is insufficient evidence of all 18 of the performance indicators having been met during the lesson. Do observers automatically award a grade 4 even if the circumstances are proven not to be conducive to satisfying those indicators? If so, how might this impact on the reliability of the aggregate grade?

Table 4.4 Highly structured observation report form.

Name of Teacher:	Centre: Course Code:	Number of students – on register: attending: late:
Payroll Number:	Course:	Length of Session: Length of Observation:
Date of Observation:	Lesson Type:	Teaching assistant/technician staff present:
Location/Room No:	Lesson Activity:	Name of above (if applicable):

OBSERVER JUDGEMENTS *(refer to Observation Criteria)*

Performance Indicator	Grade
1. Introduction, aims and learning outcomes*	
2. Pace and structure of learning*	
3. Assessment techniques*	
4. Learning methods*	
5. Identification and support of individual learning needs/ differentiation*	
6. Inclusive learning strategies*	
7. Teacher style and communication skills*	
8. Teacher knowledge*	
9. Review/recap/ summary of learning*	
10. Achievement*	
10. Management of learning	
12. Learning involvement and response*	
13. Attendance and punctuality	
14. Skills for Life – basic skills (key skill/functional skills) – identified and cross-referenced	
15. Learning environment	

16. Health and Safety	
17. Scheme of Work	
18. Lesson Plan	

* – Asterixed categories are fixed across all areas of the curriculum. These **must** be at least a Grade 2 to obtain overall Grade 1.

Comments by Learners (Minimum of 3):

Grade: Second observation necessary (if grade 4 awarded):

Overall Comments:

Comments from Observee:

Fourthly, in order to ensure that observers are able to evaluate these criteria accurately and reliably, they would need to receive regular, criteria specific training and guidance. This type of training is time consuming and costly and there are obvious financial implications involved. And finally, following on from a point made earlier, the form itself prioritizes the recording of numerical data over that of textual data, with the result that the qualitative feedback seems of less significance. Yet evidence from current research points to this type of feedback as being the most valuable aspect of the observation process.

It was remarked in the previous section that detailed observation instruments such as FIAC have largely fallen into disuse in England, yet the underlying philosophy behind them can still be seen in the documentation accompanying many current schemes. That is to say, contemporary 'structured' approaches to classroom observation are underpinned by an attempt to itemize classroom behaviour with a view to identifying, presenting and indeed prescribing specific practice as being more effective than others. This is evident in the approach encapsulated by the report form illustrated in Table 4.4. Such attempts to categorize and atomize the complex act of teaching and learning into a prescribed list of technicist skills are symptomatic of the pervasion of a culture of 'managerialist positivism' (see Smith and O'Leary 2013) that has hegemonized schools and colleges in recent years. The discourse of this culture demands the production of QA data that are 'measurable', 'transparent' and 'robust'. In other words, it prioritizes the production of quantitative data as proof of the efficiency and effectiveness of the provision and services offered by an institution.

Finally, qualitative approaches to observation are, at least in theory, considered to offer more freedom to the observer in what they record and how they record it, though this can depend on the specification of the instrument used as illustrated by the two examples above, along with the purpose and context of the observation (see Chapter 5). Regardless of the specific approach used, there are a number of variables, many of which converge around aspects of validity and reliability that need to be carefully considered and addressed when putting together an observation instrument. The next section moves on to discussing some of these variables and their significance in the application of observation as a method of assessment.

Observation as a method of teacher assessment: issues of validity and reliability

It was mentioned in Chapter 2 that Professor Dylan Wiliam, a recognized expert in the field of educational assessment, recently publicly questioned the ability of agencies such as Ofsted to accurately assess and judge the quality of teaching and learning (Stewart 2012). Wiliam's critique centred on the two key maxims of validity and reliability, widely regarded as 'the touchstone of all types of research' (Cohen et al 2011: 180).

Validity and reliability are fundamental issues to any discussion about the use of classroom observation as a method of assessment. But before discussing their importance, we need to establish what is meant by each of these two terms. Validity is a complex and multi-faceted concept that can be defined in various ways depending on the purpose of the assessment, although it is generally concerned with the extent to which an assessment samples the skills, knowledge, attitudes or other qualities it purports to measure. In other words, does the assessment measure what it claims to measure?

Validity is inextricably linked with reliability which is concerned with the consistency and accuracy of results: 'good quality assessment is inevitably the child of a union between reliability and validity' (Black 1998: 54). However, 'one can often be enhanced only at the expense of the other' (ibid.). Thus, this union is rarely an easy one. Evolving conceptions of validity have emphasized the on-going process of validation of an assessment for particular purposes as the following excerpt from Wiliam (1992: 16) highlights:

> One cannot validate an assessment; one can only validate a particular interpretation of assessment data. It follows that there can never be a set procedure for establishing the validity of a particular assessment process. Rather, validation is a never-ending process of marshalling the evidence to support the assertion that a particular assessment result has a particular meaning ... the onus is always on the users of the assessment information to establish that the inferences they make are warranted.

The validity of assessing teacher performance through the use of classroom observation has been a contentious issue for some time, as the following impassioned comments by Scriven (1981: 244) written over 30 years emphasize:

> Using classroom visits by colleagues (or administrators or 'experts') to evaluate teaching is not just incorrect, it's a disgrace. First, the visit itself alters the teaching, so that the visitor is not looking at a representative sample. This defect is exacerbated by preannouncing the visit. Second, the number of visits is too small to be an accurate sample from which to generalize, even if it were a random sample. Third, the visitors are typically not devoid of independent personal prejudices in favour of or against the teacher. . . . Fourth, nothing that could be observed in the classroom . . . can be used as a basis for an inference to any conclusion about the merit of the teaching.

Obviously Scriven was writing at a time prior to the introduction of performance management systems and a culture of audit and accountability in education, as such his views might even be regarded by some readers as belonging to a bygone era. Nevertheless, his comments still have currency as they highlight a number of interrelated factors that are the subject of debate when it comes to the use of observation as a method of assessment, and that converge around the notions of validity and reliability. Amongst these are: 1) the effect of the presence of an observer in the classroom, referred to as 'reactivity' or the 'Hawthorne effect'; 2) the extent to which individual observations can be considered a representative sample of a teacher's professional capabilities, knowledge and skills and 3) the subjectivity of observer judgement, or the issue of 'observer bias'. Let us now concentrate on discussing each of these factors in more detail.

The issue of reactivity in classroom observation

Reactivity, or what is also referred to as the Hawthorne effect, is a psychological term used to describe the extent to which the observed environment is influenced by the observer's presence. In other words, to what extent is a teacher's performance or behaviour in the classroom affected, consciously or not, by being observed? If we were to pose this question to a group of teachers, the response might well be a resounding, 'Well, of course it is!' And even more so if the observation forms part of a performance management exercise such as teacher appraisal or an external inspection, where the stakes are inevitably raised and the outcome becomes all the more important, thus encouraging the observed teacher to try even harder than might normally be expected.

It can therefore be argued that teachers' behaviour is affected by the mere act of being observed and this can have both positive and negative repercussions for some. For example, one of the teachers involved in my research into the use of observation in FE colleges remarked that, 'The observation process brings out the worst in me. I lose confidence in all the work I have done and become obsessive about the paperwork and end up making silly mistakes that I wouldn't normally'. Why observation should provoke such a reaction is perhaps indicative of how it has come to be viewed as a mechanism of surveillance in the workplace by some teachers. As Foucault (1977: 201) reminds us, 'surveillance is permanent in its effects, even if it is discontinuous in its action'. Yet, equally, some teachers embrace the opportunity to showcase their skills during an observed lesson.

In short, it cannot be denied that the act of observing is likely to have an effect on the classroom environment in some way, particularly the behaviour of the teacher but also that of the learners. The challenge facing all those involved in the observation process is therefore to minimize these effects as much as possible to ensure that the validity of the assessment is not compromised. Recent attempts to tackle this have included the use of remote video technology, where the observer is not present in the room (see case study three in Chapter 8 for more discussion), as well as the introduction of no-notice or unannounced observations (see Chapter 5).

The representativeness of the observed lesson

Another significant issue relating to the validity and reliability of observation concerns the representativeness of the observed lesson. For instance, in my research study (O'Leary 2011), reliance on one-off, annual observations as valid representations of 'true' performance was felt to be a particular bone of contention among college teachers. Teachers are aware that individual lessons can go much better or worse than anticipated – often for reasons beyond their control. As Debbie, an observee, reflected: 'on some days I could easily get a four and on other days I may feel it was great so why wasn't I observed that day?' Paula, a senior manager, noted: 'we all know when we've done a good session and then you may do a one-off that was outstanding and, if the observer was there for that, well aren't you lucky!'

Terry (observee), an Engineering teacher with over 25 years' teaching experience, described his own instrumental approach to securing a grade 1 when being observed as part of his college's annual graded lesson observation exercise:

> I knew I was going to get a grade one because I knew what boxes to tick . . . if I used PowerPoint, if I included a plenary, if I proved that I was checking learning, etc. I could rabbit them off and I just went straight through a list. I got a one and it proved nothing at the end of the day . . . if you know the rules . . . [and] you know the game then you've got the tick in the box.

Terry's cynical perspective (game playing, rule compliance, box ticking etc) is indicative of a system 'where assessment procedures and practices come completely to dominate the learning experience' and 'criteria compliance' comes to replace 'learning' (Torrance 2007: 282). Furthermore, recent research argues that observation systems that are based on a high-stakes approach to summative assessment can also be seen as ill-suited to tackling the problem posed by teachers capable of producing a competent performance but whose routine practice falls below acceptable standards (O'Leary and Brooks, forthcoming). For instance, Jackie recounted the example of a weak colleague whose observed performance seemed to bear little resemblance to his everyday practice:

> A member of staff was notoriously really bad and there were a lot of issues about his teaching and the curriculum manager picked him out that she was going to do it herself and he pulled out a perfect lesson. And I could hear the students saying, 'He doesn't normally do it like this'.

The 'enacted fantasy' of the 'spectacle' lesson (Ball 2003: 222) is actively promoted by many senior managers in schools and colleges. In the words of Jackie, an art teacher, 'They expect you to put on a good show and you have training and they say, "For your inspection, make sure you do this and this"'. Ryan, an observee in another college, agreed: 'You're told this by the management and you know that you are expected to put on a show and of course you do'. As was discussed in the previous chapter, it is unsurprising that such practice takes places given how high the stakes are for both individuals and institutions in a climate of performativity.

As was mentioned in 'The issue of reactivity', p. 61, recent developments in colleges and schools have seen a move towards no-notice or unannounced observations, though, as discussion in the following chapter reveals, this is a contentious matter in itself. In reality, such moves do not fully address the root of the issue, which is that discrete observations can only provide a partial snapshot of teachers' and learners' classroom performance and behaviour. In order to build a more comprehensive and accurate picture, information from other sources needs to be gathered e.g. appraisal interviews, students' work, course evaluations, student achievement rates etc.

Observer subjectivity and bias

One of the most contentious issues associated with classroom observation as a method of assessment concerns observer subjectivity and bias. According to Fawcett (1996: 3), 'we have a tendency to see what we are looking for and to look for only what we know about'. This inevitably raises the question of whether it is possible for observers to make an objective assessment of what they observe. This is an area that is fraught with a gamut of complex variables. For example, even before entering the classroom, is the observer aware of the teacher's theories and ideas about teaching? If the observer is unaware of, does not understand or even does not accept the particular pedagogic orientation of a teacher, then surely this is likely to impact on the way in which they interpret the teacher's classroom behaviour and performance? Some might suggest that this adds weight to the argument that being observed by someone who knows you is often more advantageous as their tacit knowledge about the observed teacher's pedagogic orientation is likely to be far greater than that of an outsider, which can help in making sense of classroom events and teacher decision-making. Yet, at the same time, it is important to acknowledge that such a model of observation is also open to critique in terms of increased opportunities for bias.

For all those involved in the observation process, it is important to remember that the observer's interpretation of events represents only one viewpoint and not the profession as

Low inference   High inference

Figure 4.3 The low–high inference continuum.

a whole. There are competing perspectives operating across all classrooms and this is something for all to be mindful of. In their description of a group of teacher educators who were asked to observe and comment on a video-taped lesson of a student teacher, Sullivan *et al* (2000: 259–260) drew attention to the subjective interpretation of those observers and how their feedback failed to take into account these competing perspectives:

> Their critique was presented as criticism of her personal action, rather than as a recognition of the existence of differing perspectives on teaching and learning. The majority of suggestions were presented as definitive statements rather than as comments with the potential to open up discussions about tensions in pedagogy.

In some ways it is inevitable that observer subjectivity is likely to feature as a significant variable when classroom observation is used as a method of assessment. After all, few would deny that human judgement plays a key role in the observation process and as such it is impossible to be certain that the way in which one observer interprets a sequence of classroom events is likely to be the same as another observer. The range of variance in observer interpretation is largely dependent on the instrument used and the extent to which the observer is concerned with recording 'low inference' or 'high inference' factors, as well as the purpose of the observation. These terms are best seen as part of a continuum rather than as polar opposites (see Figure 4.3). Typically, a high inference observation requires a significant degree of subjective judgement by the observer. In contrast, a low inference observation concerns factors that are considered more transparent and as such interpretations are less likely to vary widely from one observer to another.

In the context of a low inference observation, Roberson (1998: 5) maintains that the role of the observer is mainly that of a 'collector of descriptive data'. These data are meant to provide supporting evidence, or not as the case may be, of particular aspects of the teaching and learning process according to a predetermined and prescribed set of observation criteria. Thus as part of a low inference approach, at no point is the observer required to make a qualitative judgement about what they see as there is an assumption that the criteria are transparent and explicit and can be applied reliably regardless of who is carrying out the observation. This claim is not unproblematic as it is based on the premise that each observer views reality through the same lens. Yet, as Roberson (1998: 6) aptly illustrates with the following comment:

> Where one observer views a student's behaviour during an observation as a display of independent thinking, another may view the same behaviour as a classroom disruption. A third observer may find the behaviour irrelevant and not identify the behaviour at all.

It is typical for many ITT observation schemes to concentrate on low inference factors as they invariably include important skills for a trainee and/or newly qualified teacher to acquire at the start of their career as part of their classroom survival kit e.g. voice projection, clarity of instructions, pace of the lesson etc. Since such factors appear to lend themselves more readily to being 'measured', it is not surprising then that some also feature as part of assessment criteria upon which to base observations of experienced teachers as part of the appraisal process. However, I would argue that it is the more complex high inference skills that really determine the effectiveness of a teacher's performance in the classroom. That is to say, the types of judgements and decisions that are based on complex inductive reasoning, such as knowing when and when not to deviate from a lesson plan or when and how to change the group dynamics of a class in order to maximize the learning experience. Yet by their very nature such skills are more abstract, less easily identifiable and consequently less measurable, and as such are rarely acknowledged in observation instruments. As Richards (1998: 141) aptly comments, 'While teaching would appear to be an observable phenomenon, only aspects of it are in fact observable'. Similarly, Wragg (1999) acknowledges that not everything in a lesson is observable and as such quantifiable. For example, how does one go about observing and measuring the extent to which a teacher 'inspires' learners? In the context of graded observations, this 'inspirational' element is often seen as a key characteristic of grade 1 or 'outstanding' teachers, yet it is not defined by Ofsted and there is an absence of a collective understanding on the part of observers as to what it is or how to define it.

The ability to inspire is a good example of a high inference skill that is essentially qualitative, which means that a quantitative approach is therefore of limited use in assessing such skills. How then do we go about trying to assess these high inference skills given their qualitative nature? It would seem sensible to suggest that both observer and observee should explore such aspects in the post-lesson feedback session in order to aid the former's understanding of the events that have taken place in the classroom. The topic of feedback is examined in the following chapter but for now let us continue our discussion of issue of observer subjectivity and bias.

A study into teacher appraisal conducted by Suffolk Education Department back in the 1980s conceded that subjectivity was a major concern. As Graham (1987: 15) states, 'Objectivity about teaching seems to elude us. Frequently, teaching is described in general terms which are open to a range of interpretations depending on perspectives and experiences'. One of the aims of the project was to attempt to define effective teaching in the hope that systematic and objective approaches to assessing teaching could be achieved. In spite of their attempts to inject a greater degree of objectivity to the way in which observation was used, Graham was mindful of the impact of grading scales on the observer's judgement:

> Once any scale system is in use the 'halo effect' may come into operation, ratings being consonant with previous assessments. Errors can be made by observers always using the centre of the line, or by being consistently too tough or too lenient.
>
> (1987: 16)

The halo effect is also recognized by Marriott (2001) who, in relation to the role of the observer, remarks that 'one of the hardest parts is leaving your professional "baggage" at the classroom door' (p. 34). She acknowledges that observers are likely to have their own preferred teaching methods but stresses the importance of open-mindedness and acceptance of different approaches. Others have taken this argument on one step further by claiming that an observer's 'personal views on what constitutes effective teaching ultimately influence their judgements whilst observing' (O'Leary 2006: 193). As a means of guarding against the 'halo effect' and minimizing threats to the objectivity and reliability of judgements made during observations, some institutions turn to external observers. The rationale for such practice is that the external observer is likely to be less prone to bias in the judgements they make and as such more objective. Yet, at the same time, they are unlikely to possess the rich, context-specific knowledge of internal observers as argued above.

Regardless of whether an institution uses internal or external observers, it is important to acknowledge that 'observations are inevitably filtered through the interpretive lens of the observer', which can mean that 'observers' existing knowledge, theories and values will inevitably influence the data they produce and the accounts and evaluations they produce' (Foster 1996: 14). But should observer subjectivity necessarily be seen as a negative aspect of classroom observations?

The idea that it is only 'factual evidence' that is valued and to project one's subjective interpretation on to this evidence runs the risk of contaminating it is a well-known debate in the wider realm of educational research and encapsulates the traditional schism between the paradigms of positivism and relativism. Thus in order to achieve high levels of reliability and validity in data collection, researchers are encouraged to 'see the world as it is' rather than to allow their personal lens to influence their interpretations. This is what was discussed towards the beginning of this chapter as the 'scientific' approach to research and is based on the premise that the 'truth is out there'. Foucault would argue that this 'truth' is not a universally accepted scientific fact, but a product of the apparatuses of control that create 'regimes of truth' through the production of their dominant discourses.

In recent years, two noticeable strategies that have been employed in schools and colleges in an attempt to reduce observer subjectivity and bias are: 1) the use of ever-increasing lists of detailed assessment criteria and 2) the emphasis on observing the learners and the learning process rather than the teacher and teaching. Let us now consider each of these strategies in more depth.

With regards to the interpretation and application of assessment criteria, there is compelling evidence confirming the very considerable difficulties in eliminating bias from judgements (Wolf 1995), in ensuring that assessors adhere to published assessment criteria (Ecclestone 2001) and interpret them in a consistent manner and in reaching conclusions about the worth of a performance that are consistent and accurate (Brooks 2012). One of the ways in which many institutions try to mitigate these variables is through the training and standardization of observers.

Levels of training across observation schemes can understandably vary from one institution to another depending on size, provision etc. Yet if classroom observation is being used as a method of assessment, then one of the most important ways in which to ensure greater consistency and reliability across observers is by providing standardized and on-going training for those involved. Some have suggested that one of the main contributory factors in observer bias is what is perceived as inadequate or a lack of systematic observer training or preparation (e.g. Sheal 1989), with the result that observers have a tendency to rely on their own interpretations of effective teaching as a gauge and thus make the mistake of observing very impressionistically. Notwithstanding this, even if observers undergo rigorous training, it still seems difficult to deny the claim that their personal views on what constitutes effective teaching are likely to influence their judgements whilst observing as evidenced by the comments of participants from recent research (e.g. O'Leary 2011).

Debbie, a Health and Social Care and Special Needs teacher, described her experience of reporting to two programme managers. Although both had received training to standardize their practice, only one regarded the use of grade one as acceptable; the other 'thought no one could get grade ones because that would be perfection and no one's perfect'. Thus, 'Whoever was going to have the one person could be graded at grade one . . . the other one wasn't going to tick any of those boxes before she went in to observe'. Similarly, Karen, a Psychology and Sociology teacher stated:

> It does depend on who observes . . . everyone has their own idea about what a good lesson involves. I mean you have very didactic teachers and you have very activity-based teachers and teachers that prefer using IT and others that don't. Even when you use the same criteria you can interpret them in different ways. It's like marking exams . . . the mark scheme can be interpreted in different ways.

The perception of observees that observation was often deeply subjective was also reinforced by some observers. For instance, Gill confessed:

> I know this sounds awful, but . . . if you've been in education as long as I have I think you develop a feel for somebody who can be a presence in the classroom and who can relate to the students . . . I think you can tell that . . . within the first few minutes.

Gill's account of passing judgement quickly based on 'a feel for somebody' is consistent with existing research suggesting that experienced assessors are inclined to ignore published criteria, relying instead on their own intuitive judgement.

As for the switch in observation focus to the learners and learning, this is equally problematic. Ofsted inspectors talk about being able to observe learning taking place in the classroom. But can such a claim be reliably substantiated? Simply because a learner answers a question correctly in class or performs a task successfully does not necessarily mean that learning has taken place. Most recent observation schemes have tended to emphasize the importance of evidence of 'learning taking place' as the overriding factor in formulating judgements. Yet, if, as discussed above, aspects of teaching are intangible and by definition unobservable, then it would follow that not all aspects of learning can be recorded as 'seen' by the observer.

Learning is an extremely complex psychological process that largely operates on an internal level, which makes it very difficult to assess if it has taken place. But as observers can only report on what they see, inaccurate assumptions and conclusions may be drawn from the classroom experience. Even if we assume that we are able to assess learning taking place, it is questionable how much or how little we are able to observe. Whilst it cannot be denied that experienced observers are able to make an informed judgement, such judgements cannot nor indeed should not be regarded as absolute. In order to strengthen the validity and reliability of such judgements, they need to be supported by additional data to provide a more credible and accurate reflection of a teacher's competence and performance.

Summary

This chapter has sought to provide a panoramic perspective on the use of observation as a method for studying teaching and learning by comparing quantitative and qualitative approaches and discussing their application. Despite some of the shortcomings associated with quantitative and qualitative observation instruments, one cannot deny that each has a role to play in researching classroom behaviour and/or teacher–learner interactions. There are undoubtedly certain aspects that lend themselves well to quantitative study and others that are more suited to a qualitative approach. As has been discussed in this chapter, the current norm is for many institutions to adopt a mixed-methods approach to the use of observation by combining qualitative and quantitative aspects. Yet it has also been argued throughout this chapter that by itself observation may only provide a partial view of teaching and learning, thus highlighting the importance of gathering information from other sources in order to be able to form a well-rounded judgement. The next chapter moves on to exploring differing models of observation in use, the contexts in which these models are used and their underlying purposes. Much of this discussion centres on performance management approaches to observation, the protocols and procedures typically connected to observation in this context and the respective roles of observer and observee.

Discussion topics/tasks

1. *Comparing observation approaches across institutions*
   Your task is to compare the observation approaches of two different institutions (your own and another). In order to do this, you will need to gather the documentation/paperwork of each institution (see Appendices 4 and 5 for examples). Take time to evaluate the documentation, identifying those features that seem to reflect qualitative or quantitative approaches to observation. Discuss with a colleague your evaluation of the documentation.
2. *Analysis of observation instruments in your workplace*
   Analyze the pros and cons of the observation instrument(s) used in your workplace. Think about how your analysis might lead to an improvement in the instrument itself. Now produce a 'mark II' version of the instrument.
3. *Experimenting with different instruments*
   Choose an observation instrument that is unfamiliar to you e.g. Flanders FIAC or CLASS discussed above. Together with a peer or work colleague, arrange to observe each other using this instrument. Your follow-up discussion should concentrate on your experiences of using the instrument itself rather than the actual content of the lesson. What did you like/dislike about it? What were its strengths/limitations?

Chapter 5

Typologies of classroom observation

Contexts, models and purposes

Introduction

Classroom observation is an omnipresent mechanism that permeates the working lives of teachers throughout their careers. For many, their first experience often comes as student teachers undertaking teaching practice during an ITT programme. Upon qualification and entry to the profession, teachers' future involvement with observation typically occurs in the context of teacher appraisal and CPD schemes. It is hardly surprising then that teachers inevitably tend to associate it with an assessment of their professional capabilities from the beginning to the end of their careers.

This chapter explores differing typologies of observation in relation to its use as a means of assessing teaching and learning. It begins by discussing and comparing models of observation, the contexts in which these models are used and their underlying aims. The 'Ofsted model' is included as part of a wider discussion centring on performance management approaches to observation, along with the issue of grading and its effects on teacher identity. An outline of the typical protocols and procedures surrounding assessed observations is provided in which the recent development of unannounced or 'no-notice' observations is discussed. Finally, the chapter shifts its focus to the topic of feedback with a view to developing the understanding of observer and observee as to their respective roles, whilst also providing pointers as to how best to make use of the feedback discussion for both parties.

Exploring contexts, models and purposes of classroom observation

Broadly speaking, models of observation can be placed on a continuum according to their purpose and emphasis as illustrated in Figure 5.1. At one end of the continuum lies the 'performance management' model/context and at the other 'professional development'. Although some institutions seek to combine these, the aims underpinning these models/contexts are different and arguably incongruous.

Models of observation underpinned by professional development goals tend to be based on a discursive approach whereby collaboration between observer and observee is – or at least should be – less hierarchically delineated and driven by a desire to nurture pedagogic knowledge and skills rather than simply passing judgement on the professional competence of the observee on the basis of an isolated observation. In contrast, most performance management models adopt a top-down approach, where the observer retains the sole power

Performance management   Professional development

Figure 5.1 Continuum of observation models/contexts.

to pass judgement on what constitutes effective teaching and learning and to offer advice on which areas of practice need to be improved, though feedback to the observee has not traditionally been a feature of Ofsted inspections and is more commonly associated with internal observation schemes. In evaluative models of observation, the role of the observee is largely passive with limited opportunity for input. The observee's perspective is perhaps best encapsulated in the words of a teacher who said that 'observation is something that is *done* to you' in her workplace (O'Leary 2011). In reality, such models of observation are shaped and influenced by the Common Inspection Framework (CIF), as much of the QA activity in colleges and schools is invariably geared towards gathering data for bodies such as Ofsted in order to ensure that they are 'Ofsted ready'.

Studies exploring observation contexts, models and purposes are somewhat limited. As a reference point this chapter focuses on Gosling (2002) and Wragg's (1999) typologies because they provide contrasting means of categorizing observation. Gosling's framework of analysis categorizes observation into three *models*, whereas Wragg's is grouped into *contexts*.

Gosling (2002) categorizes observation into three distinct models, all of which he labels as 'peer observation'. A description of each model is shown in Table 5.1. As noted in Chapter 3, the term peer observation is generally agreed to have very specific connotations and thus it is terminologically inaccurate to use it in the generic way that he does. It is only his third model, which he refers to as the 'peer review model' that can be described as a genuine example of peer observation. Nevertheless, his 'models' still have value as a way of examining the different contexts and purposes for which observation is used.

Gosling's 'evaluation model' typically reflects the approach taken in formal QA processes such as teacher appraisal whereby senior staff observe teachers. The observer carries out an assessment of their professional competence, culminating in a summative judgement. QA systems such as external inspections, internal audits and probationary periods for NQTs typically fall into this category, though admittedly the latter can have a development focus.

The purpose of Gosling's second 'development model' is for observees to 'demonstrate competency' and for the observer to 'improve teaching competencies'. The observer adopts a formative and summative approach, as it is envisaged that the observation will be graded on a pass/fail basis and the findings will lead to recommendations for improvement and inform a future action plan. This model reflects some aspects of practice commonly found in ITT and CPD programmes. McMahon *et al* (2007: 502) argue that 'Gosling suggests that this model can be clearly differentiated from the first but, in practice, the boundaries are anything but clear'. Thus the distinctions between these two models are rather blurred and the summative element of Gosling's model often overshadows the formative as discussed previously in Chapter 3 and in recent research (e.g. O'Leary and Brooks, forthcoming).

Table 5.1 Gosling's Models of Peer Observation of Teaching (2002: 4–5).

Characteristic	Evaluation model	Development model	Peer review model
Who does it and to whom?	Senior staff observe other staff	Educational developers observe practitioners; or expert teachers observe in department	Teachers observe each other
Purpose	Identify under-performance, confirm probation, appraisal, promotion, quality assurance, assessment	Demonstrate competency/improve teaching competencies; assessment	Engagement in discussion about teaching; self and mutual reflection
Outcome	Report/judgement	Report/action plan; pass/fail PGCert	Analysis, discussion, wider experience of teaching methods
Status of evidence	Authority	Expert diagnosis	Peer shared perception
Relationship of observer to observed	Power	Expertise	Equality/mutuality
Confidentiality	Between manager, observer and staff observed	Between observer and the observed, examiner	Between observer and the observed – shared within learning set
Inclusion	Selected staff	Selected/sample	All
Judgement	Pass/fail, score, quality assessment, worthy/unworthy	How to improve; pass/fail	Non-judgemental, constructive feedback
What is observed?	Teaching performance	Teaching performance, class, learning materials	Teaching performance, class, learning materials
Who benefits?	Institution	The observed	Mutual between peers
Conditions for success	Embedded management processes	Effective central unit	Teaching is valued, discussed
Risks	Alienation, lack of co-operation, opposition	No shared ownership, lack of impact	Complacency, conservatism, unfocused

Gosling's third model is what he refers to as a 'peer review model', where tutors observe each other as part of a formative process. This is what was referred to earlier as 'peer observation'. Bennett and Barp (2008: 563) remark that this model 'specifically assumes an underlying dynamic of equality and mutuality of learning where feedback from the observer is non-judgemental and constructive, in a spirit of co-participation'. Thus, the value of observation is mutual and serves the dual purpose of promoting the development of observer and observee. There are parallels to lesson study as an alternative model, discussed further in Chapter 8.

In contrast to Gosling, Wragg (1999) chose not to categorize observation into *models*, but rather into the *contexts* in which it occurred (Table 5.2).

Wragg also chose to explore these contexts through descriptive prose in a separate chapter entitled 'Classroom observation in context' rather than in tabular format like Gosling. However, to facilitate comparative analysis between the two and to condense Wragg's original chapter, I have chosen to present a summarized version of the 'major contexts' he discusses in a table (Table 5.2) with a description of the key features of each context.

Wragg's first two contexts, 'ITT' and 'INSET and CPD' share many similarities. For example, in both instances there is an emphasis on the value of peer observation and its

Table 5.2 Wragg's major contexts of observation (adapted from Wragg 1999: 82–101).

Major contexts of observation	Summary description
ITT	• Value of observing others for trainee teachers' development • Peer observation discussed in the context of reciprocal pair work i.e. observer acts as 'another pair of eyes' • Supervision and mentoring – role of mentor carried out by teacher in the school where the trainee teacher is placed and/or a tutor from the ITT institution • Importance of the mentor–trainee relationship, underpinned by 'trust' and 'respect'
INSET and CPD	• Very similar focus to ITT • The focus tends to concentrate on developing skills of self-reflection amongst practitioners • Teachers are observed by more senior staff, or by their peers and vice versa • Peer observation identified as the principal use • Can occur across institutions
Studying pupils	• Learner-centred focus i.e. tracking pupil behaviour, ability to work in pairs/groups etc.
Curriculum development and evaluation	• Focus on how aspects of the curriculum are being implemented by the teacher • Principal use is 'to match intent against action' i.e. 'Is there a mismatch between intention and strategies?' • Observer usually senior member of staff e.g. deputy head
Job analysis	• Audit of what teachers typically spend their time doing in the classroom e.g. how much time is spent on assessment? • Holistic view of teacher's role i.e. observation forms part of a collection of data for job analysis
Teacher appraisal	• Observation forms an integral part of the formal appraisal process but part of a collection of different data • Appraisal of teaching competence must be both retrospective and prospective, looking back at what has been achieved and forward to what might be done in the future in order to make an impact • Most common form is a 'supervisor–subordinate model' i.e. more senior person observes junior colleague • Links with disciplinary action against 'incompetent teachers' • Problem of 'snapshot' observation highlighted

reciprocal benefits for observee and observer in their professional development. Though Wragg does not define his use of the term peer observation, it is generally used in a way that is consistent with previous definitions i.e. collaborative, constructive and non-judgemental. For Wragg, distinctions between the use of observation in ITT and INSET are governed by its underpinning purpose. In ITT there is a tendency for trainee teachers to observe experienced others' teaching (live or recorded lessons) as an important means of seeing particular skills and methods in action, which they will be expected to master and demonstrate in their own teaching when observed by a school-based mentor and/or an ITT course tutor in a formative and summative capacity. In an INSET context, Wragg argues that the emphasis is on developing the skills of self-reflection among teachers, implying a movement towards greater self-sufficiency and empowerment for the experienced teacher in shaping their own professional development.

Wragg's contextualization of observation can be regarded as more extensive than Gosling's. A good example of this is how he includes contexts that extend beyond the standard conceptualization of observation as centring on the observed teacher. For example, contexts three and four, 'studying pupils' and 'curriculum development and evaluation' illustrate how the focus of observation does not always have to be on the teacher's performance and/or development as is the case with Gosling's models. It is difficult to find any evidence of these two contexts of observation in FE or HE, which suggests they may be specific to schools and even primary schools. In fact, there are many similarities between these two contexts referred to by Wragg and the recent development of lesson study in schools (see Chapter 8 for more discussion).

Wragg's sixth context of observation, 'teacher appraisal', is similar to Gosling's 'evaluation model' insomuch as a teacher's professional competence is what is judged. Both also highlight the significance of the hierarchical nature of the power relationship between observer and observee as the former is usually a senior member of staff. Wragg's conceptualization of observation in the context of appraisal differs to Gosling's in two respects. Firstly, it situates the use of observation as part of a 'collection of data', thus recognizing that it is one of several sources of evidence in the formal appraisal process. Secondly, it highlights the shortcomings of adopting a 'snapshot' approach to appraisal through observation previously discussed by encouraging both a 'retrospective' and 'prospective' approach. Wragg's decision to categorize observation with reference to contexts rather than models also suggests that this is a more meaningful way of configuring it as it avoids the blurred boundaries between Gosling's models.

Gosling's 'evaluation' and 'developmental' models share two noticeable characteristics. The first is that they are observer-led and the second is that they are indicative of Freire's (1972) 'banking concept of education'; i.e. that the observed teacher is an account waiting to be filled with deposits of wisdom from the observer, thus suggesting an imbalance of power and expertise in the observer–observee relationship and the degree of autonomy afforded the latter. Tilstone (1998) refers to this as a 'non-collaborative' approach that was very much rooted in early practices within ITT and the assessment of NQTs whereby the observer would sit at the back of the room and make a list of prescriptive judgements or 'sitting next to Nellie'. Yet in his conceptualization of the role of observation in ITT, Wragg (1999) infers a more equitable mentor–trainee relationship underpinned by the importance of mutual 'trust' and 'respect' in order for it to be successful.

It is only Gosling's third 'peer review' model that reflects a more equitable relationship, which offers teachers the opportunity to take ownership of their own professional development. As McMahon *et al* (2007: 502–503) remark, 'it is the only model in which the reflection does not take an inevitable second place to concerns about managerial/inspectorial judgements'. Such a remark reinforces earlier discussion surrounding the power-dynamic between observer and observee and how performance management models of observation have come to be used as a surveillance mechanism, whilst simultaneously leading to a sense of disempowerment amongst teachers.

In the FE context in England, Coffield (2012a) has identified what he sees as four different models of observation:

1) *Managerial*: where lessons are typically observed by the observee's line manager, Advanced Practitioner or similar and graded according to the Ofsted 4-point scale. Their purpose is to act as a mechanism for policing teacher competence and performance.
2) *Developmental*: where 'expert' observers are tasked with identifying areas of the observee's classroom practice that need to be improved.
3) *Peer review*: where teaching staff observe each other's lessons in a supportive and non-judgemental exercise of mutual collaboration.
4) *Peer development*: where staff chose a specific area of their practice that they wish to improve in collaboration with a colleague(s).

Coffield's four categories are similar in focus and nomenclature to Gosling's. The only noticeable distinction between the two is that Coffield uses the term 'managerial' to refer to his first category. I would argue that the use of this term is no coincidence but a deliberate recognition of how observation has become normalized as a performative tool of managerialist systems designed to assure and improve standards, performance and accountability in teaching and learning, as discussed below and elsewhere (e.g. O'Leary 2012b).

Classroom observation in a Quality Assurance context: the use of the 'Ofsted model' as a performative tool

In recent years it has become custom and practice for colleges and schools to design their observation schemes to replicate the Ofsted model as closely as possible. Examples include the grading of observed lessons according to the Ofsted 4-point scale (see pp. 81–3 for a discussion on grading), along with the standardization of associated systems and audit trails, typically reflected in the normalized production of the 'course/class file', which includes documentation such as an up-to-date scheme of work, past lesson plans, pen portraits of the learners, samples of learners' assessed work, a plan for the observed lesson and so on. Since the publication of the white paper, *The Importance of Teaching* (DfE 2010) and the subsequent move by Ofsted to unannounced or 'no-notice' inspections (see p. 81), the need to be 'Ofsted ready' has become an even more pressing concern.

As part of the data collection for my empirical research (O'Leary 2011), I was keen to develop a panoramic view of the contexts and purposes for which observation was being used across ten colleges in the West Midlands. As such, questionnaire respondents were asked to indicate the context that best described their most recent experience of observation in the last year. Table 5.3 summarizes their responses.

The most common response selected by two-thirds was the internal quality review option, sometimes referred to in the sector as the QA model. This model reflects the

Table 5.3 Observation contexts.

Context	Frequency	Per cent	Valid per cent	Cumulative per cent
Inspection	26	9.9	9.9	9.9
External Consultation	12	4.6	4.6	14.5
Internal Quality Review	172	65.6	65.6	80.2
Professional Development	32	12.2	12.2	92.4
Other	20	7.6	7.6	100.0
Total	262	100.0	100.0	

approach adopted by Ofsted when carrying out observations during inspections i.e. lessons are evaluated using their 4-point grading scale (1 = outstanding, 2 = good, 3 = requires improvement and 4 = inadequate) although, unlike Ofsted inspectors, observers are expected to provide formative feedback. 'External consultation' also follows the Ofsted model and is mostly used as 'mock inspection', conducted by external consultants, in preparation for inspection. Thus the first three contexts listed all adopted a similar graded approach to observation that, when combined, yielded over three-quarters of responses. These statistical data suggested that observation had predominantly come to be regarded, and indeed implemented, as a mechanism for 'measuring' teacher performance – a practice that gave the underlying purpose a summative rather than a formative orientation.

The statistical data from questionnaires supported claims made in other studies (e.g. Armitage *et al* 2003) that observation is predominantly associated with QA and performance management systems in FE, although previous work has not been underpinned by the same type of statistical data presented here. These findings from the quantitative data were reinforced qualitatively in the comments of interviewees from SMT (senior management team), middle managers and teaching staff. Table 5.4 reveals a small random sample of responses to the question: 'What do you see as the main function(s) of classroom observation in your college?'

There was a commonality expressed in the diction of the extracts in Table 5.4 that seemed to permeate all levels of college hierarchy. The words 'quality' and 'standards' were particularly conspicuous as either one or both appeared in each comment, which was indicative of responses to the question given by the vast majority of interviewees. Such language is commensurate with the 'dominant discourses' (Foucault 1980) of QA divisions in colleges, large schools and academies. The notion of *improvement* of the 'learner experience' or of the overall 'quality of teaching and learning' was also prominent in the above responses and this reflected a consistent pattern across all colleges, though the extent to which there was agreement among senior, middle managers and teachers regarding how successful QA observation was in achieving the aims of CPD was a contested matter.

The fact that there was such uniformity to the language used by participants to describe the main function(s) of observation was neither a coincidence nor an idiosyncrasy of observation as a form of assessment, but a reflection of a wider discourse associated with the education reform agenda. Given that institutional policy is largely determined by government policy and that of key external agencies such as Ofsted, all of whom are linked by a shared agenda of continuous improvement, it follows that the dominant discourses produced by them are likely to be assimilated and applied by SMTs in the creation of internal policies. The repeated reference to quality and standards in Table 5.4 is a

Table 5.4 Sample of interview responses to main function(s) of observation.

Participant	Comment
Graham, SMT	It's to improve standards, to help improve learner experience, success rates, etc.
Paula, SMT	Improving the quality of learning for learners, definitely.
Polly, observer	I think their primary purpose is to maintain standards.
Cyril, observer	I think observations first and foremost are for ensuring that quality is maintained and to ensure our learners are getting the best possible deal.
Debbie, observee	I think the idea of it is to make sure everyone is teaching to the same standards but I also think the college [management] genuinely wants to improve the quality of teaching and learning.
Ryan, observee	Well, one of the reasons is because we've got to have them. It's part of all these quality claims, you know, ensuring standards and improving quality.

case in point, as well as the emphasis not simply on maintaining but on continuously improving them.

The decision of institutions to adopt the standard practice of graded observations for performance management purposes is indicative of how Ofsted casts its 'normalizing gaze' (Foucault 1977: 184) over the education sector and thus effects a form of panoptic control as the 'all-seeing' eye. It seems that Ofsted has hegemonized institutions to view the main function of observation as a performance indicator for categorizing teachers according to its 4-point scale.

Phil, an observer working in the field of Business and Professional Studies, neatly summarized Ofsted's panoptic presence when he said that 'the whole quality system for teaching and learning is based around collecting evidence for Ofsted'. Ofsted expects such data to be gathered by institutions on an on-going basis as part of their self-assessment. The culture of collecting numerical/written evidence of continuous improvement is, as the term suggests, continuous. In the words of Foucault: 'Surveillance is permanent in its effects, even if it is discontinuous in its action' (1977: 201). It would appear that this is precisely the type of mind set that the agenda for continuous improvement seeks to induce among teachers. In a related discussion, Graham, the director of the quality department at a large college, talked about his college's plans to move towards a system of 'no-notice' observation. Graham's prophetic comments encapsulated this desired mind set:

> We firmly believe that within two to three years Ofsted will, they already now have the right to do no notice . . . so if a group of students ring up Ofsted and say this college is 'crap' and it's not performing then they can turn up the next day, but we do firmly believe we'll be in the same place as schools within a few years and feel we need to get our staff into that mode of thinking that you're going to turn up on a Monday morning and the [Ofsted] team will be here and they will be out and about in those classrooms so you *have* to be prepared at all times.

Graham's comments about teachers needing to be prepared to be observed at all times are a persistent reminder of the panoptic presence of Ofsted in this case, but they also exemplify Foucault's (1977) concept of 'disciplinary power' and the desire to create a culture of perpetual self-regulation where teachers and their work are under constant (self) surveillance. In the following exchange between Donna and Anne, two Basic Skills teachers, Anne alludes to performance management observations as a form of panoptic control of teachers' professional practice:

Researcher: How would both of you describe the main function of observation in your institution?

Donna: Twofold: quality assurance and pay mechanisms I would say.

Anne: And thirdly, scaremongering amongst staff! It's like trying to say to some staff, 'we're keeping an eye on you so pull your socks up!'

Donna: I wouldn't have said supportive.

Anne: No. I would have said an attempt to try and keep you on your toes or make you believe that you need to be at a certain level to be teaching here.

Anne's interpretation of this type of observation as a form of panoptic control was a recurring theme to emerge from observees' data in my research (O'Leary 2011), although the way in which teachers responded to this varied. Some displayed strong feelings of resentment that they were 'being checked up on', reinforcing the notion of their work being 'policed', while others accepted it as an inevitable part of the job. Debbie summed up the feeling of many of her colleagues:

> The truth is though that most of us actually just find it a pain because it's extra work. We're busy anyway and there is that nugget of resentment there that I would really rather put my thought and effort into planning this lesson and creating resources instead of having to spend all this time putting this paperwork together for this observation . . . I suppose you could say it's sort of a necessary evil though.

Debbie's reference to observation as a 'necessary evil' is symptomatic of the paradoxes associated with its use but it also offers a balanced and realistic reflection of the thoughts of many teachers. That is to say, they are committed to providing the best learner experience they can and acknowledge the role that observation potentially has to play in this. Yet, at the same time, they resent the additional bureaucracy involved in having to compile the necessary 'evidence' associated with performance management observations and are mindful of its limitations as a means of measuring performance.

One of the biggest challenges for SMTs when deciding which model(s) of observation to use is how much choice or ownership of the observation process can be devolved to teachers whilst still ensuring that the performance management requirements of the institution and/or external agencies are met. This is a real conundrum and one with which so many institutions struggle to find a happy medium. Some insist on keeping observation models separate. So, for example, some may decide that the 'formal' observations (i.e. those that form part of a performance management cycle that includes appraisal) are carried out on a regular basis by a specific team, usually middle or senior managers, depending on the size of the institution, or even a group of external consultants. Whereas other observation models, such as 'developmental' models referred to above, might be the responsibility of teaching and learning coaches, subject specialist mentors and the like.

An essential ingredient of the success of any observation scheme is that the method/ approach employed should suit its purpose(s). Wragg (1999: 4) argues that in theory 'the

Table 5.5 Diagnostic review of your institution's observation policy.

Questions to consider

- Is the current policy working effectively?
- How do current models of observation connect with the CPD of the institution's teaching staff?
- What observation instrument is in use?
- Are the criteria used for assessing observations effective?
- Are the criteria up-to-date?
- Do the criteria allow observers to identify teachers who are at different stages of their professional development?
- Does the observation instrument capture everything it needs to?

purpose, timing and context of an observation should largely determine its methods'. For example, if the focus of the observation is meant to be collaborative and developmental, as discussed above with peer observation, then it would seem inappropriate for the observer to undertake a summative assessment of their peer. It would appear, however, that the theoretical delineations between different models, contexts and purposes of observation have become blurred in practice.

As a starting point, it is useful for all institutions to carry out a diagnostic review of the fitness for purpose of their observation policy. Table 5.5 above provides some useful questions to help guide such a review.

Let us now move on to discussing some of the typical protocols and procedures surrounding the use of observation when it is employed as an assessment tool.

Protocols and procedures of observation as an assessment tool

Institutional policy: purpose and rationale

Most institutions have a written policy in place regarding the use of observation, which is often ratified by its governors and, in some cases, the relevant professional bodies representing staff. These policies usually seek to combine several purposes and/or outcomes, though most tend to include the following type of aims:

- To improve the quality of teaching and learning
- To evaluate the overall quality of the learners' experience
- To benchmark performance against the Common Inspection Framework (CIF)
- To inform and provide an evidence base for the institution's self-assessment/self-evaluation systems
- To promote a culture of continuous improvement amongst staff
- To identify staff development needs.

Depending on the size of the institution, this policy document may reside in the quality unit, personnel or another administrative department. If you are not familiar with the documentation in use in your workplace it is certainly worth asking to see a copy. Among the most common strengths of institutions identified as having an effective observation policy during inspections is a transparency to its underpinning rationale as well as a focus on improving the experience of the learners.

The following sub-sections will now discuss some of the procedural features of an institution's observation policy, though naturally the scope of this chapter only allows for a broad outline rather than a detailed analysis.

Who is observed and how often?

Most institutions aim to observe all full-time, fractional and part-time teaching staff at least once in an academic year. In smaller institutions the frequency of these observations may increase depending on the resources available and the profile of the staff. For example, NQTs can expect to be observed on a more regular basis during their probationary year. Similarly, staff whose previous observation was assessed as 'inadequate' (grade 4) are normally prioritized for re-observation within a two to three month period. This can also apply to those assessed as a grade 3 ('requires improvement') in some institutions. In contrast, those who have been assessed as 'outstanding' (grade 1) in two consecutive years may be granted an 'observation holiday', exempting them from observations for that year, though this can vary from one institution to another and individual contexts. It is not unusual for some institutions to insist that those teachers whose lessons have been adjudged as outstanding are required to cascade their practice to others as part of their 'observation holiday', which some teachers might regard as more onerous than being observed again. Finally, the typical duration of an observation ranges from forty-five minutes to an hour.

Who are the observers?

Who observes often depends on the size of the institution and whether it has a recognized observation policy in which this is stipulated. Observers can typically include head/deputy head teachers, line managers or others in a managerial role, Advanced Practitioners, teacher educators, external consultants and Ofsted inspectors. In a small school, observations are likely to be carried out by the head/deputy head teacher. In larger schools/colleges, this is often unfeasible and so the responsibility is delegated to heads of department/faculty. In some institutions there is a dedicated team of observers who observe across all subject areas, though this is not without its problems/critics.

One of the findings to emerge from my own research was how teachers emphasized the importance of the observer having experience in the subject area(s) they observe, a recommendation that has been repeatedly supported by Ofsted in recent reports. There is also the expectation that the observer will still be a practising teacher themself. Some institutions even have it written into their observation policy that to be able to continue working as an observer that person must themselves have been graded as a 1 or 2 in their most recent observation. Added to this, it is usually a requirement for observers to undergo initial and on-going training and standardization whilst practising.

There are some institutions that choose to use external observers to carry out their performance management observations. The assumption is that the experience and expertise of the outside observer (i.e. someone who does not work closely with the observed teacher) means they are better equipped to judge the teaching and learning events than internal observers. There is also an added argument that by using outside observers, this enhances the objectivity and reliability of the assessment, though equally it could be argued that they are unaware of some of the complex, contextualized factors that might impact on the teaching and learning process.

How are observations recorded and what is done with the data?

If a college/school has a formal observation policy in place, then it is common for this to include approved documentation relating to the observation process. This documentation normally comprises a set of standardized forms such as an observation report together with a list of the categories of assessment criteria against which the observed lesson is assessed and a follow-up development/action plan. Although there can be differences in the criteria across institutions depending on context and other variables such as shifting national priorities (e.g. promoting equality and diversity, embedding functional skills in lessons and an explicit focus on assessing learning are amongst some of the priority areas in the 2012 CIF), the questions that underpin observers' judgements about the quality of teaching and learning in classrooms should remain the same; i.e.:

*   Is there sufficient evidence to suggest learners are learning?
*   What are they learning?
*   Why are they learning it?
*   How do we know they are learning it?
*   Are they learning it in the 'right' way?
*   Are learners interested in and motivated by their work?

These key questions serve as a common reference point for all those involved in the lesson observation process. SMTs, for example, might like to use these as the basis of a mapping exercise to compare the extent to which their own institution's current observation criteria address each of these questions. Equally it can be helpful as a standardization exercise for observers and/or a pre/post-observation meeting between observer and observee to share and discuss their perspectives on these questions. Appendix 6 provides a useful checklist of more specific questions relating to the focus of the CIF but readers are advised to consult current Ofsted inspection handbooks for more detailed and up-to-date coverage as priorities can and often do change.

Practices inevitably vary across institutions when it comes to the recording of evidence from an observation and what is done with that evidence, but there are some common features that are worth highlighting. In the first instance, it is recommended that observers establish some ground rules with the observee (preferably in a pre-observation meeting) in which they should check understanding of the aims of the observation, the assessment criteria, duration of the observation etc. It is also important to emphasize the confidentiality of the discussion and the oral/written feedback.

It is common practice for the observer to provide both oral and written feedback in which the strengths and areas of improvement are clearly highlighted. This is also accompanied by a follow-up action plan outlining the development points that need to be addressed. In addition to the observee receiving a copy of this documentation, a copy is also usually sent to their line manager and/or Head of School/Faculty along with the Quality/ HR department of the institution. It is normally then the responsibility of the observee's line manager or whoever is charged with supervising their performance and progress to meet to discuss the subsequent action plan, perhaps as part of the appraisal process, and authorize any additional support/resources required accordingly.

No-notice or unannounced observations

Up until recently in schools, teachers could be observed for a maximum of three hours in any academic year for performance management purposes. Following the publication of the white paper *The Importance of Teaching* (DfE 2010), this restriction was removed, though it has never existed in the FE sector. Notwithstanding this, head teachers have always had the authority to enter classrooms and observe their staff whenever they want, though any observations carried out in addition to the three-hour performance management limit could not be used for these purposes. There is no restriction on other types of observation such as informal visits but if any teacher feels that they are being unfairly singled out for repeated observations then this could be challenged as a form of harassment.

Unannounced 'drop-in' observations are a relatively new development for teachers. In the past, teachers were usually given at least a week's notice as to when they were to be observed. This change in approach has emerged largely as a response to Ofsted's move to 'almost no notice of an inspection with inspectors calling head teachers the afternoon before an inspection takes place' (Ofsted 2012a). According to Ofsted the rationale for this change in policy is that it is likely to lead to a more accurate sampling of provision, thus increasing the reliability of inspectors' judgements as institutions are unable to prepare in advance. However, it is a change that has not been welcomed by the teaching profession, as it is seen as a further extension of the surveillance culture in which teachers are forced to operate. Some teaching unions have vociferously opposed such practice and argued that it is disruptive, erodes trust and could be used as a means of bullying some staff (e.g. UCU 2012).

There seem to be two key arguments against the introduction of unannounced observations. The first is that as a matter of professional courtesy all teachers should be notified in advance if anyone intends to visit their classes. The second is that teachers need to be given the opportunity to showcase their knowledge and skills in the classroom, even though the 'showcase lesson' might not be deemed an accurate representation of their everyday practice. This argument relates back to some of the early research into classroom observation carried out by Samph (1968).

Grading: its effects on teacher performance, identity and self

There are differing schools of thought when it comes to the use of graded observations. Some argue that grading has counterproductive, deleterious consequences for the teacher and the improvement of teaching and learning as a whole. Others maintain that it is a crucial aspect of teacher accountability and plays an important role in measuring professional competence.

One of the common arguments put forward by those in favour of grading is that it helps to reward 'effective' or 'outstanding' teachers by acknowledging their classroom performance, which in turn can act as a strong incentive for those same teachers to continue to improve their practice as well as something for their peers to aspire to. In FE, for example, my research revealed that some colleges operate what can best be described as a form of performance related pay where teachers' appraisal and salary increments are linked to the outcome of their annual graded observations. In addition, one college involved in the study offered a one-off 'bonus payment' of £1000 as a financial incentive to staff who managed to achieve two grade 1s in consecutive years (O'Leary 2011). Yet there is a flip side to this too.

My findings also revealed compelling evidence of implicit and explicit labelling of teachers' performance across institutions, in spite of the hackneyed stance that it was the 'learning' that was being judged rather than the teacher. In some instances college-wide congratulatory emails were sent by SMTs, clearly flouting the confidentiality clause contained in many observation policies, as teachers who had achieved a grade 1 were often named explicitly. In other instances, staff were sent 'letters of concern' if they had failed to achieve 'good' or 'outstanding'.

Terms such as 'outstanding' and 'inadequate' are value laden terms, which carry with them potentially far reaching consequences for the observee. They have a longevity to them that belies the snapshot judgement on which they are invariably based. In discussing the effects of assessment on learners, Rowntree (1987) argued that grades act like 'averages', smoothing out and '[concealing] irregularities and variability', commenting that skills and qualities differentiating one individual from another are 'obliterated by the baldness of grades' (p. 69). The interpretation and subsequent conversion into a grade is, according to Rowntree, 'an act of reification, erecting a pseudo-objective facade on what is a very delicate personal judgement' (p. 70).

Wragg (1999: 24) argued over a decade ago that the use of grading has become a means of controlling teachers:

> One of the major problems with rating scales is that they appear objective, but are in practice heavily laden with the values of those who conceived them. They can be misused, becoming a crude device for overriding teachers' individual professional judgement and making them strive to achieve the goals of their superiors, especially if the observation takes place in the context of assigning merit awards or carrying out appraisal.

The depth of feeling expressed in the two comments below taken from a questionnaire respondent and interviewee in my study (O'Leary 2011) neatly encapsulate some of the tangible effects of grading teachers' performance:

> The grading of observations is divisive – we are given tables of how many people got which grade – it has almost become unhealthy competition – it's unnatural too. Personally I hate the process though I get good grades. I live in fear of failing next time.
> (Unnamed)

> When you mention the word observation in our college it provokes feelings of both panic and defensiveness that people are going to be judged. They cause a lot of stress and nervousness amongst staff. . . . We feel like we're being checked up on.
> (Rosie)

A recurring theme from observees' responses was how the use of graded observations often led to increased levels of anxiety, stress and staff questioning their self-efficacy. In short, the use of grading in some colleges seemed to have had a restrictive and often negative impact on teachers' professional identities and their notions of self.

Observation feedback: practice and priorities

The term 'feedback' is used in its broadest sense in this section and throughout the book as a whole 'to refer to any information that is provided to the performer of any action about that performance' (Black and Wiliam 1998: 24). Feedback can be considered the most important stage of the observation process as it is the feedback that is meant to have the most tangible impact on future development. The extent to which this stage is dealt with effectively by both observer and observee can largely determine whether or not the observation can be considered a worthwhile exercise. As a result of the discussion during feedback, teachers become more aware of their classroom practice (or not in some cases!) and are able to explore ways in which they can develop their existing knowledge and skills. Yet it is surprising how little attention is given to managing the feedback stage or even acknowledging its importance in terms of timetabling and the training of observers and observees in this important process.

My research into observation feedback in college observation schemes revealed that it is often overshadowed or its importance is compromised, as emphasis is placed on having to compile the necessary audit trails of documentation for performance management activities such as self-assessment and Ofsted inspections. While many observers expressed a commitment to maintaining the importance of building in sufficient time for a detailed feedback discussion with observees, their ability to uphold such a commitment was compromised by the prioritization of the QA agenda coupled with the challenges of managing a heavy workload (O'Leary 2011).

For example, Phil, an observer, describes below how the CPD aspect of the observer's role was further squeezed when his workplace was approaching an inspection due to the pressure on observers to 'get more in':

> We're trying hard to have this as a normal part of the developmental cycle but the problem is because of the nature of Ofsted, everyone has to collect data and evidence and that tends to go against a smooth developmental process. . . . As an Ofsted looms, there's more frenetic activity to ensure that the maximum number of observations are undertaken. It's suddenly, 'Get more in, get more in', and as it's part of a line manager process, I do wonder if it puts a lot of pressure on some of the line managers that perhaps the observations they do are not as developmental as they should be. They get through them, fill the paperwork in, get a score and I think it's a case of 'job done'.

Preparation for Ofsted is thus all-consuming for observers. As Phil insinuates, one of the consequences is that observation becomes a perfunctory exercise for some observers as they struggle to get through a large volume of teachers. This results in QA requirements taking precedence over development needs.

Statistical data from questionnaires regarding the duration of feedback also seemed to support this theory, as illustrated in Table 5.6.

More than a quarter of responses revealed that feedback had lasted less than 10 minutes and almost half of them between 10 and 20 minutes. It is difficult to imagine a professional dialogue of any substantive consequence for a teacher's developmental needs occurring in

Table 5.6 Duration of feedback.

		Frequency	Per cent	Valid per cent	Cumulative per cent
Valid	1–9 min	66	25.2	25.5	25.5
	10–20 min	123	46.9	47.5	73.0
	21–30 min	58	22.1	22.4	95.4
	31–40 min	10	3.8	3.9	99.2
	41+ min	2	.8	.8	100.0
	Total	259	98.9	100.0	
Missing	99	3	1.1		
Total		262	100.0		

such a short space of time, reinforcing Tilstone's (1998) critique of 'non-collaborative' models of observation where the feedback dialogue is predominantly one-way. I would argue that for feedback to be useful, it should last at least 30 minutes.

Tilstone (1998) puts forward a persuasive argument for institutions to formally acknowledge the importance of timetabling the feedback stage to allow sufficient time for reflection and discussion, and recommends that this be factored in on a strategic level in terms of its inclusion in the institution's development plan. I would extend this argument further and say that those institutions that attach as much significance to the feedback and feed forward process as they do to the observation itself often prove themselves to be the most successful in improving the quality of teaching and learning.

When it comes to models of observation feedback, there tends to be little variation regardless of the context and/or purpose of the observation, though there are some notable exceptions as will be discussed in Chapters 7 and 8. Conventional models adopted in most evaluative observations seek to combine a summative and formative approach to feedback where the observer relays the perceived strengths and areas of improvement to the observee following the observation. This usually takes place after the observation or at the next available break but preferably within a day of the observation. The typical format of this feedback model tends to be as follows:

Lead-in: The observer starts the discussion by inviting the observee to provide a self-evaluation of the lesson. Some exemplar opening questions might include:

'So, how do you think the lesson went?'
'How would you rate your performance in that lesson?'
'What are your initial thoughts on the lesson?'
'Do you feel the lesson went according to plan?'
'Are you happy with the lesson?'

Observer evaluation: The observer provides an oral summary of their written comments. This often takes the form of what is commonly referred to as the 'feedback sandwich' in which the observer sandwiches constructive criticism between layers of praise. For example, 'I liked the way in which you asked a range of open-ended questions to test the learners' understanding of the text as this was an effective strategy, but remember that if you want to ensure that certain learners don't dominate then you need to think about targeting questions and nominating particular learners to respond'.

Some observers choose to provide a synopsis of the key strengths and weaknesses/areas to improve of the lesson as a whole before embarking on a discussion of each activity or stage of the lesson. One of the dangers of this approach is that if there is a long list of weaknesses/areas to improve then this can overwhelm or even dishearten the observee. As was discussed in the context of grading above, they may only notice the negative and thus the formative element of the feedback can be lost. This is a problem that can be exacerbated in schemes that operate according to a long list of prescribed criteria and where the observer is required or expected to comment on each area. One of the ways to guard against this is to limit the criteria and for the observer and observee to agree beforehand to focus on a specific set of criteria. Other observers will recount their notes from start to finish in chronological order and elicit the thoughts of the observee intermittently.

Round-up/closing: The observer and observee discuss the follow-up action plan in which the key areas for development are listed. Depending on factors such as the nature of the relationship between observer and observee, the experience of the observee and the context and purpose of the observation, future areas for development may be negotiated jointly, although it is common for the observer to stipulate these. Observers and observees are also often encouraged to ensure that the follow-up action plan contains a list of 'SMART' (Specific, Measurable, Achievable, Realistic and Timed) targets that can be reviewed at an agreed future meeting.

Some have argued for delayed feedback on the premise that by allowing time to reflect on the observed lesson before conducting the feedback the observee is more likely to be able to distance themself from the emotions of the observation and to reflect more critically (and perhaps objectively) before discussing their thoughts with the observer (see Williams and Watson 2004). Added to this, there is an argument that in order for the feedback discussion to recognize the value of the observee's perspective, they should be allowed to reflect and write up their self-assessment before the oral discussion so that the observer has a record of their viewpoint which they can use to inform their final assessment. This is undoubtedly a very time-consuming model of feedback but has certain advantages in that subsequent action points are then more meaningfully negotiated between the observer and observee.

Given the undoubted importance of feedback in the observation process, it would seem essential that observer and observee develop a clear understanding of the skills and qualities required to ensure that the feedback discussion maximizes opportunities for professional learning and growth. Let us now move on to considering some guidelines for observers and observees to giving and receiving feedback.

Giving feedback: guidelines for observers

Underpinning the success of the observer–observee relationship are the principles of trust and respect, though these principles are not enough by themselves to ensure a productive dialogue occurs. Below are ten practical pointers that will help observers manage the feedback discussion effectively:

1. Try not to make purely evaluative or judgemental comments – focus on what you see rather than an impressionistic interpretation of what you think was happening. If in

doubt, it's always a good idea to pose searching questions rather than making absolute statements.

2. Be sensitive. Overtly critical comments can be off-putting and dent the person's confidence considerably. Try to avoid 'offering solutions'; i.e. 'Well, this is what I think you should have done . . .', unless specifically invited to do so.

3. Avoid making generalized statements such as 'You need to work on your classroom management skills'. Instead, make sure you provide practical suggestions for future classes, based on concrete examples of classroom practice that the observee can relate to.

4. Vary the types of questions you ask and try to use questions that are more geared to encouraging reflection or eliciting a detailed response from the teacher e.g. 'You chose to do "x" at that point in the lesson, why was that?' 'Can you explain to me what you were hoping to achieve with this task?'

5. Provide 'constructive criticism' or 'balanced feedback' i.e. feedback that is honest but helpful in developing the observee's practice and that accentuates the positives as well as the areas for improvement. Think about what they did well and why it was successful. Remember that highlighting strengths is as helpful as recognizing and describing what seem to be the challenges faced by the person teaching.

6. Feedback should be a two-way process. With this in mind, try to encourage the observee to take an active role in the feedback discussion, thus taking ownership of their learning and development.

7. Allow the observee the opportunity to explain their decision-making, to provide a rationale for why they did what they did in the classroom.

8. Encourage a shared discussion and agreement as to the key areas for future improvement/development and what support, if any, needs to be provided. With your guidance the observee should be encouraged to self-evaluate and identify their professional development needs.

9. Prioritize areas for development. With NQTs and trainee teachers there are likely to be a lot of areas for development. It would be both demotivating and unfair to present the observee with an exhaustive list of areas to develop so as part of your role as an experienced practitioner you will need to use your professional judgement when deciding what the main priorities are for the observee to focus on in the short term.

10. Make sure feedback is timely i.e. ideally it should take place within a day of the observation, but certainly no longer than a week after.

Receiving feedback: guidelines for observees

Whenever you are observed, you are encouraged to reflect on and self-evaluate your lessons. Table 5.7 contains a list of prompts that can provide you with a framework to follow after each lesson. Your responses should also provide you with a concrete set of notes to inform your feedback discussion with your observer. Common practice for most observers in the feedback discussion after the lesson is to start off by asking you how you felt about the lesson before sharing their feedback with you. In addition to the prompts in Table 5.7, which should help you to pre-empt many of the observer's questions and respond to their comments, here are some suggestions on how you can prepare for and make best use of the feedback discussion in general:

• **Remain calm and detached:** Try to remain as objective about your lesson as possible and avoid reacting defensively if your observer makes a comment that you disagree

Table 5.7 Self-evaluation prompts for observees.

1. What do I think I achieved during the lesson?
2. What am I most proud of?
3. Did my learners learn what I intended?
4. Were my learners productively engaged in the activities?
5. Was I satisfied with my planning, selection of resources, teaching and assessment strategies?
6. What have I learnt about the learners and my chosen teaching and assessment strategies?
7. To what extent did the lesson satisfy the observation assessment criteria?
8. What worked/didn't work? Why? Why not?
9. What have I discovered about myself as a teacher?
10. What happened that I didn't expect to happen?
11. If I could teach this lesson again, what would I do differently? Why?
12. What is the key thing that I want to improve for next time?
13. What do I need to do to bring about this improvement?

with or see as a criticism. See the feedback session as an opportunity to enhance your knowledge and skills and treat all comments as 'constructive criticism'.

- **Learner lens:** When you are reflecting on your teaching and that of others, it can be helpful to try to see things from the eyes of the learners. By doing so means that you are less likely to analyze the events from a very personal viewpoint and focus exclusively on the teacher's perspective. To help you do this, it can often be a good idea to invite one of your peers to observe you teaching with a view to following the progress of one or perhaps two learners for the duration of the lesson and then share their notes with you at the end of the lesson.

- **Take an active role in the discussion:** The greater the ownership you take of the feedback, the more tangible future improvement is likely to be. This means that it is important for you to engage in a two-way dialogue with your observer where you ask questions and put forward your perspective.

- **Don't be afraid to ask:** Ask for clarification if you're not sure about any of the oral or written feedback. Remember that your observers are often highly experienced teachers themselves and sometimes they might unconsciously use a term that is unfamiliar to you or make a comment that requires further explanation. Don't be afraid to say you don't understand something or ask them to give you an example of what they mean.

- **Keep a record of the discussion:** Take lots of notes so that you have a record of the key points that were discussed. Alternatively, you might even want to think about using a digital voice recorder so that you can listen to the discussion again at a later point. However, if you do decide to use a voice recorder, make sure you check with those involved in the discussion beforehand that they are happy for you to record it.

- **Future action points:** Your observer usually makes a list of key areas for future development to emerge from the lesson. Spend some time thinking about these and how you plan to tackle them. Don't be afraid to ask others for their thoughts and ideas.

Summary

This chapter has explored the models and contexts in which observation occurs as a tool for assessing teachers' classroom performance and competence. Much of the discussion has centred on how in recent years this has been driven by a performance management agenda in which the adoption of the 'Ofsted model' of graded observation has become normalized practice in schools and colleges. The typical protocols and procedures surrounding the use of observation for appraisal purposes have been outlined. The final section of the chapter has concentrated on the feedback and feed forward phases of the observation process with a view to enhancing the awareness of observer and observee about their respective roles and to ensure a productive focus to the discussion. Chapter 6 shifts its focus to the topic of teacher effectiveness and what it means to be an 'effective teacher' in the 21st century. It seeks to understand the policy–practice relationship, what the repercussions are for new and existing practitioners and how best to make sense of them.

Discussion topics/tasks

1. *Evaluating models of observation in your workplace*

   - What are the current models and contexts in which classroom observation is used in your workplace?
   - What are the stated aims for its use?
   - How well do the outcomes match the aims?
   - How could these models be improved?
   - To what extent do teachers in your workplace feel they are involved in evaluating the observation process?

2. *Observation through images/mind mapping*
   On a blank piece of paper, create a picture/set of visuals that best encapsulates the views, experiences and feelings of staff in your workplace towards the use of observation. Once you are satisfied with your picture/set of visuals, present it to colleagues and talk them through the significance of the imagery.

3. *Comparing links between the quality of teaching and student outcomes*
   It is common for each college/school to produce a yearly self-evaluation document (SED) or annual monitoring report (AMR). These documents typically include data relating to the quality of teaching and learning and student outcomes/achievement. Based on your institution's most recent SED/AMR, analyze the links between the data that reflect teacher performance and student achievement. Is there a correlation between these two data sets? How do you explain any differences between the two? Are there any contextual variables and/ or mitigating circumstances to take into account as part of your analysis? Produce a short report that reflects your analysis.

4. *Feedback*
   Think about a recent observation in which you were involved either as an observee or observer. Focus on the feedback discuss and consider the following questions:

   - Was the discussion useful? Why/why not?
   - How did you feel when delivering/receiving the feedback?
   - What did you find most challenging about the discussion?
   - Was there anything that you would change about this experience if you could do it again?

Chapter 6

Being an effective teacher

Models of teacher effectiveness

Introduction

In addition to the performance and accountability agenda discussed in previous chapters, classroom observation has also figured as a key data collection tool in the pursuit to capture/define 'teacher effectiveness' or the skills and qualities typically associated with the 'effective' or 'outstanding' teacher. This in itself raises several questions. For instance, can such skills and qualities be observed and subsequently taught? Are some more observable and teachable than others? And, if so, what are the implications for the training and education of the current and next generation of teachers?

It is interesting to note that at the time of writing, current government policy seems to be that teacher qualifications and ITE programmes are of limited value and even unnecessary, though it has to be said that this appears to be based on the unsubstantiated theory embraced by some members of the Cabinet that good teachers are 'born not made' and as such it is only 'learning on the job' that matters. This debate concerning the value of teacher education and professional qualifications makes it all the more timely and important to discuss notions of teacher effectiveness and explore some of the key developments in the field to date, which is the focus of this chapter.

One of the underlying arguments running through this chapter is that when it comes to assessing the quality and effectiveness of teaching and learning through observation, most models continue to rely on competency-based approaches, the criteria for which are ultimately defined and determined by politicians, policymakers and aligned agencies rather than by representatives of the teaching profession itself. This chapter presents a critical analysis of the principles and constituents of such models as well as discussing what the implications are for teachers in the workplace and how best to make sense of and engage with them. Mindful of the practical needs and interests of teachers, it provides a broad set of key principles for 'good' or 'effective' teaching that should be applicable to all subject areas and contexts and compares these against state-defined standards.

Contextualizing the pursuit of teacher effectiveness

A common theme overlapping the different contexts and purposes of classroom observation is the notion of teacher effectiveness. Campbell *et al* (2004: 3) broadly define teacher effectiveness as 'the impact that classroom factors, such as teaching methods, teacher expectations, classroom organisation, and use of classroom resources, have on students' performance'. They are critical, however, of what they see as its narrow conceptualization by some involved in the field, where a 'goal-oriented model for measuring teacher effectiveness' (p. 61) has been the preferred approach. For them, too much importance has been attached to the notion of student achievement when attempting to measure teacher effectiveness. They argue that although learning outcomes are the most common form of measurement, there is no clear evidence to suggest that there is a cause and effect relationship between the two. In their view such simplistic models fail to consider many variables often beyond the control of the teacher that can affect students' performance in any given lesson. Yet government policy over the last two decades appears to have disregarded such research perspectives as it continues to emphasize student achievement as one if not the most important variable on which to base judgements about the quality of teaching and learning. But here lies a clash of interests and agendas as to what constitutes teacher effectiveness and how it is best measured.

On the one hand we have the 'academic' community, comprising researchers and practitioners in education who by and large are interested in increasing understanding of the factors deemed integral to effective teaching and how these might feed into future improvements in the teaching and learning experience. On the other hand there is the 'political' community, principally comprising politicians and policymakers who are driven by a results-led agenda that wants/needs to be able to arrive at an unequivocal set of criteria to be able to measure performance and success rates as well as the effectiveness of individual teachers.

As Middlewood and Cardno (2001: 1–2) commented over a decade ago when emphasizing the significance placed on *outcomes* and the *measurability* of performance by governments:

> The significance for teaching and learning and consequently for any assessment of teacher performance is that comparisons and competitiveness inevitably have meant that governments have placed the emphasis upon education *outcomes*, such as proficiency in literacy and numeracy, examination results, test scores, and numbers of students continuing beyond statutory schooling. The significance of these is that outcomes have to be seen to be measurable, because only in measurable outcomes can comparisons be visibly made.

They go on to quote from Preedy (2000: 95), who provides a concise critique and identifies some of the risks associated with models of assessing teacher effectiveness that rely heavily on measurable outcomes:

> Many of the most valuable outcomes of education are multi-dimensional, complex and long-term. . . . By focusing on measurable outcomes against pre-specified objectives, the product evaluation model ignores unplanned outcomes, and fails to explore the value and worth of the prescribed objectives and purposes. There is also a tendency to de-emphasise contextual factors.

Middlewood and Cardno (2001: 2) went on to argue that if the success or failure of a school or college is judged against these outcomes then it is a logical next step for the notion of teacher effectiveness to be seen as embodying that which achieves those outcomes:

> The temptation therefore is for national bodies to promulgate a model of teaching which lends itself to this and to appraise teachers accordingly. In the UK, the model of

effective teaching as presented by Ofsted, and against which teachers' lessons were formally graded during one-off inspections, was widely criticized, not because it was an invalid model but because it was the only model. It was above all an outcomes model because the inspection model of the UK in the 1990s was itself essentially one concerned with inspecting schools' attainments.

Although Middlewood and Cardno were referring to models of inspection in place during the 1990s in schools, their comments still have currency twenty years later as the emphasis on learner attainment remains a key form of measurement during inspections and one that continues to play a key role in the overall judgements made both on individual teachers observed during the course of an inspection and on the quality of teaching and learning across the institution as a whole as recent national priorities identified by Ofsted have emphasized (e.g. Ofsted 2013: 5).

According to Montgomery (2002) it was not until the 1980s that discussion surrounding notions of teacher effectiveness in schools in England came to the fore. Much of the ensuing discussion was characterized by what she describes as the 'lack of a coherent and shared theory and practice of teaching' (p. 18). She emphasizes the importance of defining the characteristics of teacher effectiveness if the assessment of teachers via observation is to become a legitimate and meaningful activity. Yet, at the same time, she is critical of competency-based models used for teacher appraisal that adopt a 'checklist' approach to observation, as they reduce the teacher's role to that of a technicist. Kincheloe (2004) is equally critical as he argues that 'teachers in the technicist paradigm are conceived as a unit of production of an assembly line' or 'operatives' who perform a set function (p. 60). For Montgomery (2002), competency-based systems exist only to serve 'auditing and accounting purposes' (p. 19). They do little to respond to teacher behaviour that is deemed unsatisfactory or ineffective, as the '*how* to do it' is very often left unanswered (p. 39). This is an issue to which I will return when discussing how teacher effectiveness is assessed on p. 102 as well as identifying and supporting 'ineffective' teachers on p. 104, but first let me draw together the contextualization of teacher effectiveness as a whole.

One of the key drivers of the 'teacher effectiveness' pursuit from the outset has been the desire to establish a clear definition of effective teaching that can be applied to all contexts of classroom observation. In principle this seems like a noble and reasonable pursuit and one that would appear difficult to contest as worthwhile for all those committed to improving the quality of education. Yet in practice, as highlighted on p. 94, it is a highly contested area that continues to divide policymakers and practitioners alike.

Lowe (2007: 61) put forward the theory that the failure of the teaching profession to 'reach any agreed consensus on what constituted best practice meant that [it] was at the mercy of whichever political wind was blowing'. Whether or not one agrees with Lowe's hypothesis, it immediately raises the question as to why it has proved so difficult for teachers as a professional body to agree on a set of core principles against which standards of professional competence can be judged. Could it be that 'best practice' is just far too complex a notion to define? Or could it be due to the fact that there is no singular professional body representing practitioners that regulates the profession?

In comparing education with the field of medicine, for example, the General Medical Council (GMC) has a long-standing history in regulating standards in its profession. Yet one might argue that the professional capital of a body such as the GMC far outweighs that of the teaching profession as its powers are enshrined in law (e.g. the Medical Act 1983). Following the Teaching and Higher Education Act (1998) passed under New Labour, the

General Teaching Council (GTC), a professional body for schoolteachers in England, was established. Shortly after the coalition government was elected in 2010, however, the Secretary of State for Education, Michael Gove, announced the decision to abolish the GTC, illustrating the fact that its existence was always subject to the mercy of political change. Many would argue that part of the problem lies with the fact that such bodies like the GTC were created and sponsored by the State rather than formed and financed independently from the ground up. At the time of writing, little has changed to address this problem among school teachers, as in April 2012 the 'Teaching Agency' (TA) was created as an executive agency of the Department for Education, thus reinforcing State control of the profession. In FE, however, the situation is different and more complex as the once State-financed Institute for Learning (IfL), a professional body for teachers in the sector, appears not to have suffered unduly as a result of the removal of State funding and its subsequent transition to an independent body financed by members' fees.

To conclude this opening section, the pursuit to pinpoint teacher effectiveness has involved the academic community and the State over the last few decades. Whilst the motivations of each of these groups for wanting to reify teacher effectiveness might differ, one of the fundamental issues uniting them has been the attempt to arrive at a definition of what is meant by the term teacher effectiveness. This question is examined in detail in on pp. 94–99, but first we shall look at some of the findings from recent research into teacher effectiveness.

Researching teacher effectiveness

Over the last two decades the notion of teacher effectiveness has been the subject of extensive research on an international scale. It is not within the scope of this chapter to provide a review of this field of research but I do wish to touch on some examples of the kind of research that has taken place as it has informed the on-going debate. Large-scale studies have been conducted in England and internationally, each of which has attempted to arrive at a definition or formula of what makes an effective teacher or at least identify the optimum conditions for good teaching to occur (e.g. Campbell *et al* 2004; James and Biesta 2007; Muijs and Reynolds 2005). Although the findings from each of these studies have differed, one common theme to emerge has been the importance of 'context' in making judgements about effective teaching.

In 1999 the DfEE in England commissioned a private firm of consultants, Hay McBer, to carry out a large-scale project whose primary purpose was to provide a framework for describing effective teaching. In the following excerpt Ingvarson (2001: 167) is not only critical of Hay McBer's findings but the research methodology adopted:

> The approach used by Hay McBer is *circa* 1970s process-product research on teacher effectiveness, which seeks to find correlates between generic teacher behaviours and student outcomes. It does not reflect the major paradigm shift that has taken place over the last fifteen years in research on teaching, based on extensive evidence that what expert teachers know and do is fundamentally subject and level specific. Consequently, the Hay McBer research does not reflect well what highly accomplished teachers know about how to help students learn what they are teaching. . . . Generic characteristics of effective teaching lend themselves to the development of observational

checklists that managers who do not know much about the field of teaching they are assessing can use.

The findings from the Hay McBer report stressed the need for effective teachers to 'create trust', 'challenge and support', build 'confidence' in learners and 'respect for others'. Ironically, as Ingvarson (2001: 176) has noted, 'these standards do not appear to have been applied by the government to the way it works with the teaching profession in England'.

Muijs and Reynolds' (2005) research concentrated on exploring the impact of teaching and teaching factors on student outcomes and achievement. Their findings revealed that some of the key features of effective teaching included things such as clearly planned and well-structured lessons, appropriate pacing, effective modelling by the teacher and a variety of group interaction i.e. individual, paired and group activities. No surprise there then some might think. They also found that up to 25 per cent of variance in student outcomes could be attributed to classroom level variables (i.e. socio-economic background of pupils, literacy levels etc.), but a striking 75 per cent of that was attributable to teacher behaviours (i.e. classroom climate, teaching approach etc.). Sammons (2008) also found that teaching matters more to progress than pupil background. Similarly, Hattie (2003) has argued that teachers account for approximately 30 per cent of the variance of achievement, and that the learners themselves and 'what they bring to the table' account for 50 per cent of the variance. In other words, what all these studies emphasize is the key role that the teacher has to play in educational achievement.

Muijs and Reynolds (2003) also found that the impact a teacher has on learners' achievement is differential. Their findings revealed that teacher impact was greater on minority ethnic learners, low achievers and those with a low socio-economic status (SES) and that correlations between teacher behaviours and student gains were three times higher in low SES schools than high SES schools. These findings for differential effectiveness have been echoed in other studies (e.g. Hattie 2005; Sammons 2006).

Muijs (2008) has argued that classroom practice needs to be measured in more diverse but also in more discrete ways. There needs to be a greater use of mixed methods studies, what Campbell *et al* (2004) have referred to as a 'multi-dimensional' approach. According to Muijs (2008), there is a need for a 'rigorous study of the impact of teaching and pedagogical interventions in a field often dominated by snake-oil salesmen'.

In 2007 McKinsey and Company carried out a large-scale research study that sought to examine why it is that some school systems consistently perform and improve faster than others. As part of their research sample, they studied twenty-five of the world's school systems, including ten of the 'top performers'. Their findings identified three key contributory factors:

1. Getting the right people to become teachers ('the quality of an education system cannot exceed the quality of its teachers');
2. Developing them into effective instructors ('the only way to improve outcomes is to improve instruction'); and
3. Ensuring the system is available to deliver the best possible instruction for every learner.
    (taken from McKinsey and Company 2007: 7)

The McKinsey report has since had a tangible influence on policymakers internationally, not least the current coalition government in England, who made several references to it in the 2010 white paper. At the same time, it has also been the subject of a lot of criticism from educational researchers who have argued that it is methodologically flawed, simplistic and selective in its data analysis and reporting (e.g. Coffield 2012b). An example of this can be seen in the weight attached to the first of the three key factors listed above. Whilst it is certainly a welcome finding for the teaching profession as a whole to have the importance of the teacher's role in educational success formally recognized, it does not take into account other important variables such as the 'student' and 'what they bring to the table' (Hattie 2003) amongst others. One of the dangerous repercussions of reports such as this is that their findings can appear to offer a 'quick fix' to governments and policymakers. A case in point can be found in England concerning the issue of 'getting the right people'.

There has been some debate in recent years in England around the academic entry qualifications for schools' ITT programmes with government directives stipulating that entrants must have a 2:1 or First class honours degree as a minimum entry requirement. The theory is that only the best graduates make the best teachers, though there is limited (if any) evidence to corroborate such a standpoint. Nevertheless, the consequences of such a policy mean that some of the best potential teachers are barred from entering the profession based on an arbitrary judgement about their academic performance in their first degree. This is a discussion that could be extended but as I mentioned towards the start of this section, its scope is limited. Let us now shift the focus to examining attempts to define teacher effectiveness.

Defining teacher effectiveness

Moore (2004: 9) argues that the concept of 'good teaching' is a contested area and as such cannot be easily defined. His theoretical positioning is clearly rooted in a social constructionist view of knowledge as the extract below reveals:

> The words 'good' and 'teaching' are conceptually contestable, and perhaps demand rather more contestation than they often receive, particularly when they are bracketed in this way. . . . This notion of the ideal professional self that we carry with us will have been *constructed* from a wide variety of (re)sources over time and through social experience rather than having 'appeared' somehow as the internalisation of some universal truth.

Moore (2004: 25) maintains that 'any search for a simple model of good teaching is ultimately doomed to failure'. He believes that it is every teacher's responsibility to 'discover their own "best way(s)" of doing things'. For him the notion of a good teacher is linked to that of a good school, both of which can vary from one context to another and as such this makes the search for a universal model of 'good teaching' ultimately futile.

Moore (2004) is certainly not alone in highlighting what a difficult task it is to identify the skills and qualities of the 'good teacher'. Not only are the terms themselves contested areas, but they are also moving targets. In the following extract, Mahony and Hextall (2000: 84) summarize some of the complexities involved in the role of a teacher:

> Commentators have long endeavoured to explain and account for the changing form and character of teachers' working lives. The work which teachers do occupies an

intersection of many, often paradoxical, influences. . . . Teachers have always had to negotiate, reconcile and struggle with competing priorities – it goes with the territory. Of course the territory is different in different schools and different contexts. Working with seven-year olds is not the same as working with teenagers, the rural is not the urban, culturally diverse contexts are different from the 'white highlands'.

The key point to take from Mahony and Hextall's quote is the importance of the role of 'context' and how any definition of good teaching and learning needs to be situated accordingly. Brown *et al* (1989) argued back in the 1980s that 'knowledge is situated, being in part a product of the activity, context and culture in which it is developed and used' (p. 32). This viewpoint was reinforced in the findings of the Transforming Learning Cultures (TLC; Hodkinson *et al* 2005) project, the largest ever research project of its kind carried out into teaching and learning in FE:

> Rather than looking for universal solutions that will work always, everywhere and for everyone, the improvement of learning cultures always asks for contextualised judgement rather than for general recipes.
>
> (James and Biesta 2007: 37)

The TLC in FE project was part of the Economic and Social Research Council's (ESRC) Teaching and Learning Research Programme (TLRP). It was a large-scale, longitudinal project into the practices of teaching and learning in FE and was carried out over a four-year period (2001–2005). Its findings challenged several 'common-sense and officially sanctioned assumptions' (2007: 103) about teaching and learning in FE, particularly the idea that 'good practice' is essentially the same regardless of context and is 'infinitely transferable' once identified. What it means to be an effective teacher is likely to vary according to context. What works in one context and for one group of learners may not if it is applied to a different group of learners in different contexts as Mahony and Hextall remark in the quote above.

The work of Coffield and Edward (2009) has also drawn attention to the contested nature of 'good practice' and the complexities involved in defining it. For them it is an exercise that is fraught with compounding variables and any claim to have arrived at a definition of 'good practice' needs to be met with the following list of questions: 'Who says so? On what evidence? Using what criteria? "Best" for whom? Under what conditions? With what type of students?' (2009: 376). Not only are these questions indicative of Foucault's (1980) 'apparatuses of control' discussed in Chapter 2, but they also highlight the importance of context in defining and assessing teacher effectiveness (see p. 102). Policymakers and government agencies tend to avoid the 'context specificness' of effective teaching, as it is an area fraught with complexities and does not lend itself to the creation of positivist, outcome-driven models of accountability that crave 'transparent' methods of measurement.

Following on from this, trying to transmit 'good practice' to practitioners is equally as complex and this brings with it additional challenges, which Coffield and Edward (2009: 380) suggest are often overlooked or oversimplified by policymakers:

> The intensely complex processes of learning and transfer are thought of as a simple matter of delivering packets of 'good practice' to professionals, who apparently digest

them without difficulty and then pass them on to colleagues who absorb them with similar ease.

Notwithstanding the inherent complexities involved in attempting to define 'good practice' discussed above, Moore's work (2004) identifies and explores three dominant discourses of 'good teaching' that provide us with a useful point of reference to explore notions of teacher effectiveness:

1. The competent craftsperson
2. The reflective practitioner
3. The charismatic subject.

Moore associates the first model, the 'competent craftsperson', with competency-based models of good teaching and argues that this is the preferred model of central government and aligned agencies. One of his criticisms of this model is that notions of good teaching inevitably end up being historically situated. What this means in practice is that the sands are constantly shifting and that judgements on what constitutes effective teaching may become quickly outdated and/or invalidated. As I have commented previously in relation to the teaching of English as a second and/or foreign language:

> Different teaching methodologies and techniques seem to drift in and out and back into fashion with an alarming sense of regularity. Thus, to espouse the virtues of the current methodological flavour of the month is a precarious position to adopt and one that is inevitably bound to have a limited shelf life.
>
> (O'Leary 2006: 195)

Moore's second model, the 'reflective practitioner', is widely supported and embraced among teacher trainers and educators as it encapsulates the values and beliefs underpinning many teacher education programmes in England. That is to say, running centrally through ITE programmes is the notion of the reflective practitioner; i.e. someone who continually reflects and self-evaluates their classroom practice as this is considered integral to what it means to be a conscientious teacher and someone who is committed to their learners' improvement and their own CPD (see Chapter 7 for further discussion). Thus the reflective teacher is typically someone who is analytical and has the ability to assess their teaching objectively with a view to identifying areas of practice that need to be developed or improved to meet their learners' needs.

Moore's third model, the 'charismatic subject', is one whose popular appeal is portrayed in filmic and media representations from 'Goodbye, Mr Chips' to 'Dead Poets Society'. It is this model that arguably resonates most with the general public when asked to recall an 'inspiring' teacher or someone who made a positive impression on them during their education. When asked to list the reasons as to why these teachers made such a positive impression on them, people typically tend to identify 'human factors' rather than specific pedagogic 'skills' of the charismatic teacher. Frequently occurring terms used to describe such teachers include: 'passionate', 'enthusiastic', 'exciting', 'accessible', 'kind', 'funny' etc. Interestingly all these terms focus on the 'human' aspect of the teacher or even teacher personality rather than pedagogic and/or subject specific knowledge.

To what extent then do current conceptualizations and/or definitions of 'good teaching' reflect some and/or all of the features identified in Moore's three models? Let us begin by looking at the Ofsted 2011/12 annual report for schools, which identified the following characteristics of outstanding teaching and its impact on learning:

- Excellent leadership of behaviour and attitudes
- Lessons that challenge every pupil
- Good opportunities for pupils to learn independently
- Excellent use of questioning
- Outstanding subject knowledge
- Highly effective feedback to pupils.

(Ofsted 2012b: 21–22)

The model that these characteristics seem to correspond most closely to is the competent craftsperson. The dominant discourse also appears to be one that accentuates the teacher as 'leader' rather than facilitator. When examining these more closely there is also a noticeable emphasis on the individual responsibility of the teacher, giving the impression that they have the ability to control the many variables that impact on the teaching and learning process. When comparing these characteristics from the schools' sector with those from FE, there are indeed a number of overlapping areas as one might expect, but equally there are context specific factors that not only reflect the diversity of the sector and its learners, but also draw on a wider range of aspects from across Moore's three models. For example, the IfL (2010) report, *Brilliant Teaching and Training in FE and Skills*, notes that good teachers in FE:

- Make time for reflective practice and critically analyse their own objectives
- Learn from others and are willing to share practice and engage in peer support, mentoring and collaborative action research
- Continually listen and respond to learners, bringing enthusiasm and creativity to learning
- Are passionate about their subject and do not feel it is a chore to teach it.

(taken from IfL 2010: 6)

The IfL model moves beyond the predominantly competency-based list described in Ofsted's model of the outstanding school teacher and attempts to embody a richer description of the practitioner who values belonging to a community of practice. One might speculate that this reflects some of the inherent differences between the two sectors in terms of the teacher's role, the learners and the curriculum. Equally, however, it could be argued that Ofsted's conceptualization of teacher effectiveness is narrower than the more all-encompassing IfL model and this reflects their differing starting points and agendas. As the inspectorate for schools and colleges, Ofsted's remit is largely about *measurement* and *surveillance* rather than any direct engagement with improvement, as has been argued previously. In contrast professional bodies such as the IfL work *with* teachers rather than *on* them.

Despite the difficulties previously discussed in defining good teaching, this does not mean to say that it is impossible or pointless, as Moore suggested above, to devise a set of 'guiding principles'. It is one thing to produce a prescriptive list of 'dos' and 'don'ts' as to

Table 6.1 Ten principles of 'good teaching'.

Principle	Description
1. Subject knowledge & pedagogy	The good teacher has a sound knowledge of the subject area and the necessary pedagogic skills to impart their knowledge effectively to learners.
2. Contextualized learning	The subject matter is contextualized in a meaningful and memorable way that enables learners to assimilate it to their existing knowledge and skills and to relate it to the wider world.
3. Learner engagement	Good teaching stimulates active, cognitive engagement among learners, regardless of the pedagogic approach adopted by the teacher and often involves an element of fun or excitement.
4. Learner ownership, experimentation & hypothesis building	Good teaching encourages learners to take ownership of their learning in terms of the content and process. The good teacher provides learners with the opportunity to hypothesize and to test out their understanding of the subject matter.
5. Learner differentiation & inclusivity	A good teacher is someone who has the ability to manage the differentiated needs of individual learners, whilst simultaneously maintaining an inclusive classroom culture.
6. Managing & monitoring the learning experience	A good teacher embraces their responsibility for managing and monitoring the learning experience of their learners on an on-going basis.
7. Maximizing learner potential	A good teacher is committed to all learners and their learning, and strives to ensure that every learner maximizes their full potential.
8. Learning as a social act	Good teaching promotes learning as a socially interactive and collaborative process.
9. Teacher as reflective practitioner	A good teacher actively reflects on their classroom practice and experiences, and is committed to improving their professional skills and knowledge throughout their careers.
10. Teacher resilience	Teaching can often be emotionally demanding. Developing resilience to cope with the demands of the job is vital for the good teacher to protect their wellbeing and maintain their professional commitment and enthusiasm for the job in the long term.

what constitutes good teaching but another to theorize about some of its underpinning principles. With this in mind, what might such a set of principles or assumptions comprise? Table 6.1 is my attempt to produce a broad set of principles of 'good teaching', though not necessarily in a particular order.

Table 6.1 is not meant to be an exhaustive list, but should provide a broad framework for discussing the topic within and across institutions. It might also be used as a set of prompts on which to base the development of a more tailored instrument for assessing practice across the institution through the medium of classroom observation and other relevant mechanisms.

State-defined notions of teacher effectiveness

Mahony and Hextall (2000: 91) are critical of what they see as narrow definitions of the 'effective teacher' as prescribed by the state:

> A major concern is that, apart from the 'thin democracy' of consultations, definitions of 'good' teaching, 'relevant' professional development and career enhancement have all been placed beyond debate. For example, we have already seen that criteria for 'effectiveness' have increasingly been tied to central prescription and what can be measured.

Commentators such as Ingvarson (2001) have argued that many of the reforms and initiatives designed to transform and 'modernize' the teaching profession in England have been carried out *on* teachers rather than in collaboration *with* them. Although Ingvarson's research focused on the educational policies of New Labour from the end of the 1990s to the start of the millennium, many of his comments still resonate with the position of current government policy:

> Policymakers in the UK have not brought the profession along with it in these reforms, nor capitalised on the many opportunities they provide to enhance the responsibility the profession undertakes for the development of standards and assessment of teacher performance. Professional involvement has been minimal. Managers manage teacher performance and teachers teach. The threshold reform treats assessment *as an event not a process for learning.*
>
> (2001: 176, emphasis in original)

Successive governments have missed out on an opportunity to empower teachers to take responsibility for defining standards in the profession and to create a workable framework for assessing teacher performance. However, some might argue that this is no accident but reflects the continuing stranglehold of central government in what teachers do and how their work is measured.

In discussing teacher education, Maguire (2010) is critical of the de-politicization of courses on an international scale, where according to her government intervention has become normalized:

> One way of ensuring teacher quality is to reform teaching at source by regulating and controlling pre-service teacher education. Many nations, including the US, UK, New Zealand, Australia, Canada and countries in Europe and in the Asia-Pacific region, now seek to manage recruitment and pre-service training through the generation of lists of competencies that have to be met before the teacher can be licensed to practice. . . . And many of these competencies include prescriptions about what constitutes 'best practice' that intending teachers are expected to adopt and perform in the practicum element of their course. Thus, the emphasis, more and more, is on successful in-school experience, technical skills such as teaching literacy through centrally prescribed methods, behaviour management, familiarity with testing regimes etc. Other matters, for example, those of commitment, values and judgement are frequently sidelined, made optional or simply omitted. Put simply, the teacher is reconstructed as

a state technician, trained to deliver a national curriculum. The emphasis is on compliance with competencies rather than thinking critically about practice; focusing on teaching rather than learning; doing rather than thinking; skills rather than values. This regime is maintained (and justified) by the regular production of local, national and international league tables that exert pressure to raise the stakes and raise the game at every opportunity.

(Maguire 2010: 60–61)

Researchers like Sachs (2001) and Shain and Gleeson (1999) were some of the first to write about the 'compliance' associated with the 'new professional', where effective teachers are only deemed to be effective if they are able to embrace and engage with managerialist systems of efficiency and performativity. This conceptualization of the 'new professional' is one in which the teacher is seen as a functionary of the State (Gale and Densmore 2003). In addition to the national curriculum, another regulatory mechanism that has sought to consolidate the teacher as a 'state technician' in England in recent years has been the introduction of professional standards for teachers.

Teacher standards

In 2012 Michael Gove, the Secretary of State for Education in England, commissioned a panel to draw up a new, more simplified set of standards for teachers (DfE 2012). The 2012 Teachers' Standards were the fifth version to be created since their introduction in 1992. The previous standards for Qualified Teacher Status (QTS) and the core Professional Standards (2007), devised by the TDA (Training and Development Agency for Schools) and GTC respectively, contained thirty three standards in total, each of which was broken down into further sub-sections and were deemed by some to be too cumbersome and time consuming to work with. The findings of the panel concluded that there should be a reduced set of eight key 'Teaching standards' (Part one) along with a separate statement on 'Personal and Professional Conduct' (Part two), which could be applied to assess all teachers, regardless of where they are in their careers and their working contexts. As the document states, 'the new standards define the minimum level of practice expected of trainees and teachers from the point of being awarded QTS' (DfE 2012: 2). The 'preamble' to the standards reads as follows:

> Teachers make the education of their pupils their first concern, and are accountable for achieving the highest possible standards in work and conduct. Teachers act with honesty and integrity; have strong subject knowledge, keep their knowledge and skills as teachers up-to-date and are self-critical; forge positive professional relationships; and work with parents in the best interests of their pupils.
>
> (DfE 2012: 7)

This preamble is meant to serve as an overarching mission statement for all teachers and 'summarises the values and behaviour that all teachers must demonstrate throughout their careers' (p. 3). It is interesting to compare it against the ten principles listed in Table 6.1, as indeed are the standards themselves. Whilst there are certainly some similarities, there is a noticeable emphasis on the civic responsibilities of the teacher in the references to 'work with parents' and the commitment to 'uphold public trust in the profession and maintain high standards of ethics and behaviour, within and outside school' (p. 10) in Part two. Though it has to be said that the ten principles listed in Table 6.1 are targeted specifically at classroom practice and as such are not meant to reflect the wider roles and responsibilities that one would expect to see in a set of professional standards. The eight key standards listed in Part one deal directly with teaching and are worded as follows:

1. Set high expectations which inspire, motivate and challenge pupils
2. Promote good progress and outcomes by pupils
3. Demonstrate good subject and curriculum knowledge
4. Plan and teach well-structured lessons
5. Adapt teaching to respond to the strengths and needs of all pupils
6. Make accurate and productive use of assessment
7. Manage behaviour effectively to ensure a good and safe learning environment
8. Fulfil wider professional responsibilities.

(DfE 2012: 7–9)

These eight standards are broken down into related sub-standards, each of which specifies more precisely what is expected. Whilst they are certainly more concise than the previous standards, it is perhaps too early to judge whether they are more workable and transparent in their application given that they only came into force on 1 September 2012. Notwithstanding this, they certainly allow for greater professional judgement on the part of senior management as to how they might be interpreted and what evidence, or lack thereof, might be drawn on when making judgements. In fact, it is stated in the document itself that 'the professional judgement of head teachers and appraisers will therefore be central to appraisal against these standards' (p. 3), as it is at their discretion how to apply them to NQTs, mid-career teachers and more experienced practitioners. Some would argue that this makes the assessment process more subjective and as such leaves it open to bias.

The purpose of any set of teacher standards is ultimately to define the roles and responsibilities of teachers and how best these can be assessed to monitor the effectiveness of their performance. As with any other form of assessment, the more valid and reliable the assessment is, the more credible it is seen to be. As Ingvarson (2001: 165–166) has argued, this involves two specific aspects of validity:

> The first concerns the process by which the standards are defined and who is involved, or *procedural* validity. The second refers to whether teachers who meet the standards are more likely to provide higher quality learning opportunities to learn than those who do not. In measurement terms, standards aim to define the domain of what is to be assessed. In other words they should also have *content* validity. Content validity also relates to the match between the assessment tasks and the construct of the interest.

In addition to the issue of validity in assessing teacher effectiveness is that of reliability i.e. the extent to which the methods used to assess teacher performance can be reliably and consistently applied from one assessor or observer to another and from one context to another. As Ingvarson (2001: 169) has commented, 'it is one thing to write a list of standards, and quite another to establish clear guidelines as to what counts as meeting that standard'. Defining the 'what counts' is often left to the judgement of the individual appraiser or observer, thus increasing the threats to the reliability of the assessment itself.

In discussing the development of National Professional Standards (NPS) for teachers in England carried out by the Teacher Training Agency (TTA) during the 1990s, Mahony and Hextall (2000: 32) were critical of the regulatory nature of these standards:

> In these wider settings of education policy and public policy there has occurred a drift from developmental to regulatory orientations towards standards. In the latter sense the development of NPS can be seen both as providing a centralised specification of 'effective teaching' and as the codification of relations between managers and managed. This takes place in the context of a centralisation/decentralisation nexus where 'policy steering' is achieved through much tighter regulation by the centre and managers become locally responsible for staff compliance.

They go on to draw attention to the limitations of the assessment framework used to monitor such standards:

> In this ideology, 'standards' often obscure the ways in which evaluation processes are inescapably mediated through human subjectivity. They emphasise what can be 'measured' at the expense of the immeasurable (Broadfoot 1999), which leads to an over-concentration on the 'operational' (Devereux 1997) and patrols the boundaries of what is allowed to count as 'quality'.

Mahony and Hextall (2000: 32) summarize their critique neatly when they say that '"Standards" do not guarantee standards'. They illustrate this poignantly with the following comment:

> Standards are fundamentally grounded on achieving the subject knowledge and craft skills necessary to teach and assess the school National Curriculum. Thus some people have questioned whether today's new teacher might even be able to adequately achieve the Standards while at the same time being indifferent or ill-disposed to the young people they teach.

(p. 51)

This reinforces previous discussion in Chapter 2 regarding the impact of systemic changes, as a result of the proliferation of mangerialism, on what it means to be a teacher in the 21st century and the point made by Ball (2003) about beliefs and values no longer being regarded as important in the eyes of policymakers.

Assessing teacher effectiveness

Few in the teaching profession would argue against the need to retain some form of assessment of what teachers do in the classroom, not least because their actions have an important impact on student learning but also because every conscientious teacher should be committed to their CPD. What is more disputed is the 'How'; i.e. what form of assessment is used to judge teacher effectiveness and who is tasked with making such judgements. Ingvarson (2001: 163) sees this as a tension between 'political and professional responsibility' at the heart of which lie the following questions:

> Where does legitimate authority rest for teacher evaluation and accountability? On what conceptual foundation should teaching standards be based? Who has the authority, or the expertise, to develop standards for what teachers should know and be able to do? How should procedures for assessing teacher performance be developed and validated? Who should apply those procedures and how should they be trained?

Ingvarson (2001: 164) is critical of managerial models of teacher evaluation or appraisal on the basis that they fail to capture the complexities of what it means to be a teacher and can often 'descend into mere annual routines and rituals':

> Many teacher evaluation schemes also fail because they are conceptually flawed. At the heart of many performance management schemes lies a mismatch between teachers' work and the means used to evaluate it. The criteria often underestimate what teachers are trying to achieve. Indicators of performance may belittle the sophistication of what good teachers know and do. Teachers are held accountable for student test scores instead of the quality of learning opportunities they provide. Standards for practice are not owned and valued by the profession.

Findings from my own research into the use of observation reinforce and add to some of Ingvarson's claims. My data revealed examples of variables outside the teacher's control, often not included as part of the published assessment criteria, were being factored into the grading. For example, some observees cited the 'temperature' of the room as a common reason for which they were 'marked down' if it was judged to be too hot or cold. Anne described her experience of such an incident:

> I teach virtually in a shed that's been condemned for ages, and the first thing that the observer said to me was that it was freezing in there. Well I'd got three heaters on, it's like a colander you know, we've got gaffer tape over the holes what do you want me to do? It's the only classroom I can use but I got marked down a grade for that and she told me that in the first three minutes of the lesson!

Some observers spoke of occasions when they were given explicit instructions by their college SMT to 'drop a grade' if certain 'criteria' were adjudged not to have been met. Examples of such 'criteria' included the failure to exhibit students' work on the walls of the classroom, punctuality, attendance of students and even the cleanliness of the room.

Middlewood and Cardno (2001: 4) argue that some of the key qualities of the 'good teacher' are often not observable or very difficult to assess as part of an observation but this does not lessen their importance. Some of the qualities they refer to include: 'intelligence, commitment, compassion, sense of humour, determination etc'. They go on to argue that:

> These lists of qualities draw attention to the vitally important point that a measurable outcomes only assessment model ignores i.e. that teachers are not automatons. Teachers are persons with emotions, aspirations, and need for self-esteem; and their success in their jobs will depend upon the extent to which these are successfully channelled.

Yet these 'human' qualities and characteristics are rarely considered in any assessment of teacher effectiveness whether through the medium of classroom observation or other means. By definition they do not lend themselves to transparent models of measurability, but as was discussed when examining Moore's three models earlier, they certainly play a significant role in the conceptualization of the good teacher. Just because they are difficult to measure, does this make them any less worthwhile trying to identify? This is undoubtedly a sensitive and complex issue as what is being discussed here ultimately amounts to the teacher's personality or at the very least their classroom persona. How, for example, do we make judgements and recommendations about a teacher's sense of passion and enthusiasm in the classroom without it being interpreted personally and it being seen as a potential threat to their professionalism and that of the profession as a whole? Should we even attempt to do so? In the current climate of intense teacher accountability and performativity, this is indeed dangerous territory. Yet to ignore the role that these human factors play in the teacher's overall effectiveness would seem naïve and even remiss if we are to develop a deeper understanding of the profile of the effective teacher. I would argue that this would require a significant cultural shift on the part of the profession to open itself up to exploratory inquiry into these factors, but also the State to allow the academic community to take ownership of any such inquiry and decide what to do, if anything, with the findings. Given the heightened levels of evaluative scrutiny and surveillance that the profession finds itself subjected to at present, it is unlikely that such a shift is likely to occur any time soon and so teachers find themselves having to make sense of the current set of standards that have been created for them by others.

Identifying and supporting 'ineffective' teachers

One of the issues to emerge from my research into the use of classroom observation in colleges was how yearly graded observations were proven not to be a particularly effective means of identifying ineffective teachers (O'Leary 2011). This was in part due to the advanced notice given to teachers to prepare for these observations, but also as a result of their snapshot nature discussed previously.

In discussing the use of classroom observation for supporting under-performing teachers, Jones *et al* (2006: 35) acknowledge that assessment through observation can be and often is 'prescriptive' and 'judgemental'. As a means of counterbalancing the subjective judgement of the observer they suggest adopting an 'open-ended approach' in which the observer keeps a descriptive log of the events in the classroom rather than using a 'prescriptive observation sheet'. Their rationale for such an approach is that it 'can present the teacher being observed with a non-judgemental account which may be a better starting point for initial self-reflection and follow-up discussion'. As a means of attempting to increase the validity and reliability of the evidence collected during the observed lesson(s), they suggest that the chosen observation(s) should:

> [T]ake place with the teacher's 'worst' class and without the teacher making special preparation for the observation [as] this is likely to 'capture' more of the reality of the learning experience in the classroom and lead to the production of an action plan for real improvement.
>
> (ibid.)

Such an approach resonates with findings from my own research (O'Leary 2011), where in those institutions considered to embody what I refer to as an 'expansive' approach to professional learning and development through observation, teachers asked for their 'worst' classes to be observed. Why did this happen in some colleges and not in others? And what can we read into such practice? As explored in more detail in the following chapter, such practice was indicative of those colleges in which a culture of trust and collaboration was seen to be at the heart of working relationships among colleagues.

Jones *et al* (2006: 17) emphasize the importance of the language used to describe and categorize 'under-performing' or 'ineffective' teachers according to a set of differentiated terms, which ranges from 'ineffective', 'struggling', 'under-performing', 'sinking' to 'stuck' teachers. In illustrating the major influences on teachers' under-performance, their conceptualization embodies three concentric circles, each of which is seen to intersect with each other. In the inner circle lies the individual teacher whose under-performance can be attributed to 'negative personality traits', 'limited training', a 'limited repertoire of skills' and 'inappropriate relationships' (p. 25). The two outer circles reflect the immediate working and wider school contexts, both of which make reference to the importance of supportive line management and leadership. Interestingly, in some colleges involved in my research, those teachers who were assessed as a grade 3 or 4 in their appraisal observations were treated as individual problems. They were subsequently assigned to mentors whose role was akin to that of 'repair technicians' entrusted with the task of repairing the 'faulty goods' and re-circulating them into the system once they had passed the approved 'safety standards'. As Abdul, an observer and teacher educator pointed out, unless the observee was able to improve their grade in the follow-up observation six weeks later, they were likely to be faced with disciplinary procedures. In many ways, such restrictive approaches to observation are indicative of a technicist view of teaching and learning and encapsulate Freire's (2005) theory of the punitive use of teacher evaluation that 'we evaluate to punish and almost never to improve teachers' practice. In other words, we evaluate to punish and not to educate' (p. 13). It is to the matter of educating through the use of observation that the final part of this book now turns its attention.

Summary

The pursuit to define what it means to be an effective teacher has been the subject of on-going inquiry in recent years, which has given rise to competing conceptions among the political and academic communities. The 'state defined' conception is one where teachers are regarded as functionaries of the State and as such are considered to have a prescribed role to fulfil as laid down in regulatory mechanisms such as the Teachers' Standards. This is a conception that individualizes the teacher in seeking to attach sole responsibility to the individual for the achievement of their learners. In contrast, the conception of the academic community is one that whilst recognizing the importance of the teacher in learners' achievement rates, accentuates the role played by other significant variables such as the learners themselves and context. Teacher effectiveness is thus seen as a more complex and contested notion that is likely to vary to differing degrees from one context to another as a result of particular variables. What this means is that it makes the process of measurement more problematic across institutions when using the same instrument. Is it possible therefore to establish common ground between these two conceptions?

I would argue that there is a need for a more consultative and collaborative approach when it comes to identifying what makes for teacher effectiveness or ineffectiveness. Such consultation should seek to involve all the relevant policy stakeholders rather than a top-down approach driven by political agendas or government policy. In the final section of this book (Part 3), the focus of the discussion shifts to exploring examples of collaborative and more democratically oriented approaches to using classroom observation to promote professional learning. The first chapter, Chapter 7, begins by looking at contextualized examples of what I refer to as 'expansive' approaches to professionalism and professional learning through the use of observation.

Discussion topics/tasks

1. *'Fields of judgement'*
   Who is it that controls the 'field of judgement' in your school/college? How are such judgements made?

2. *Professional/teacher standards and observation*
   What role do the professional/teacher standards play in observations in your workplace? Are they incorporated into the assessment criteria for observations? If so, can you explain how and where?

3. *Effective teachers*
   Carry out a survey (oral or written) of your colleagues and/or learners of what makes an effective teacher. Once you have collected the responses, compare and map them against the relevant standards for your sector i.e. schools (Teachers' Standards 2012; DfE 2012), colleges (LLUK 2006). Here are some useful prompts to guide your analysis and discussion:

   • Are there any patterns to your responses?
   • Are there significant similarities/differences to your responses and the standards used in your sector?
   • Do any skills/qualities in particular stand out as the most important?
   • Do your responses identity any skills/qualities that are not listed in the 'official' standards?
   • What are the implications of these responses for you and your colleagues?

4. *Models of 'good teaching'*
   Using Moore's (2004) three models as a framework, assess your own practice as a teacher and/or that of peers against these three models:

   • The competent craftsperson
   • The reflective practitioner
   • The charismatic subject

   ▪ Do you/your colleagues fit one model more so than another? If so, which?
   ▪ How is this manifested in the classroom?
   ▪ Do you/your colleagues wish to develop and/or experiment with incorporating aspects of other models into your teaching?
   ▪ How do you propose to go about this?
   ▪ Do you fit into your 'desired' model?

Part III

Classroom observation as a means of promoting teacher learning and development

Chapter 7

Classroom observation as a tool for expansive professional learning

Observing practice and the role of critical reflection

Introduction

A considerable body of applied educational research carried out over the last two decades acknowledges that one of the most successful means of improving the quality of student learning outcomes is by investing in effective teacher education and CPD (e.g. Darling-Hammond 2000, 2006; IfL 2010, 2012). Nowadays the notion of the 'reflective practitioner' undergirds any ITT or CPD programme. Teachers are encouraged to critically reflect on what goes on in their classrooms in order to bring about meaningful and sustained change through increasing or shifting awareness in their behaviour. It seems appropriate then to begin the opening section of this chapter by providing the reader with a brief insight into the origins of the reflective practitioner, some of the key factors underpinning the notion of (critical) reflection as well as exploring its practical application through the medium of classroom observation. As part of this discussion, the chapter explores what I refer to as 'expansive approaches to observation' (O'Leary 2012c), with an emphasis on differentiated and peer-based models and their role in promoting teacher learning. The final section includes a range of targeted observation tasks where the focus and structure is varied, enabling observer and observee to maximize the developmental benefits and to use these observations as a springboard for collaborative, professional dialogue and learning.

The role of reflection and criticality in professional learning and development

Reflection is widely regarded as the cornerstone of any programme of professional learning and development of teachers. Dewey (1933) and Schön (1983) are often identified as two of the principal sources associated with the subsequent growth of a reflective approach to professional development. It is over a century ago since Dewey (1904) first took the notion of reflection from the field of philosophy and applied it to pedagogy. One of Dewey's proposals was that teacher education should encourage teachers to develop a critically reflective approach to their teaching rather than simply providing them with training in specific pedagogic techniques and skills. The model proffered by Dewey (1933) represented a fundamental switch from a product to a more process-centred approach. It was also symptomatic of a more scientific approach to development in which the skills of logical reasoning and rational analysis played a central role while intuitive feelings were considered less important.

The starting point for Dewey was the collection of data or 'observed facts' (1933: 104). These data form the raw material upon which reflection is based and from which ideas are then generated. 'Data (facts) and ideas (suggestions, possible solutions) thus form the two indispensable and correlative factors of all reflective activity' (ibid.). One of the key principles stipulated by Dewey was that the practitioner must have 'a genuine situation of experience' (1933: 174) upon which they could reflect since this was likely to lead to more meaningful reflection. Through the notion of reflection, practice could be seen as being more informed. He saw the process of reflection consisting of five overlapping phases, which when viewed as a whole encapsulated an inquiry-based approach to learning about classroom practice:

1.   Identifying the *problem*
2.   Considering the *suggestions* for dealing with the problem
3.   *Hypothesis* building
4.   *Reasoning*
5.   *Testing* i.e. confirming or disproving the hypothesis.

Dewey's five phases were the basis of future models of reflective practice (e.g. Gibbs 1988; Kolb 1984). Schön (1983) built on Dewey's thoughts and although his work was originally targeted at the professional development of the 'practitioner' in general, regardless of their profession, it was not long before his ideas became fully embraced in the educational arena. Following on from Dewey, Schön developed a distinction between what he referred to as 'reflection-in-action' and 'reflection-on-action': the former indicating the practitioner's ability to react and reflect on the spot to an experience and the latter to reflection that takes place after the event. It was thus Schön's belief that it is possible for reflection to occur at the same time as the action itself. This distinction has, however, been the subject of some debate within teaching. It has been argued that teachers rarely have the time or the spare processing capacity to reflect in action as they are often so concerned with the procedure and logistics of the lesson that they are not able to observe processes of learning as they occur. As Shulman (1987) aptly put it, 'practitioners tend to be missing in action rather than lost in thought'. It could also be argued that those teachers who are able to reflect in action may represent a small minority of the profession. In reality, one might be inclined to think that the majority of practising teachers are forced to rely on post-lesson reflection. Thus, as far as novice teachers are concerned, it would seem plausible to suggest that Schön's 'reflection-on-action' has greater relevance.

Since the 1980s the notion of 'reflection-on-action' has increasingly exerted a key influence on the design of ITT and CPD programmes. According to Bartlett (1990: 202), the popularization of a reflective approach to teaching during the 1980s can largely be attributed to the work of Cruickshank (e.g. Cruickshank and Applegate 1981) and Zeichner (e.g. Zeichner and Liston 1987). If this was the case for the 1980s, then Bartlett (1990), Brookfield (1995) and Richards (e.g. 1991, 1998) can certainly be regarded as some of the leading proponents of reflective teaching during the 1990s and Ghaye (2011), Loughran (2002) and Moon (2004) some of the key figures since then. But what exactly does a reflective approach to teaching entail?

Influenced by some of Dewey's early work, Bartlett (1990: 205) developed the notion of what he referred to as 'critical reflective teaching'. He was quick to clarify that the term 'critical' was not to be interpreted in a negative sense, but that it was associated with the adoption of a holistic approach to the way in which teachers view their actions in a broader cultural and social context. According to Bartlett the principal aim of critical reflective teaching was to make the transition from being concerned with instructional techniques or what he referred to as the 'how to' questions, and to concentrate on the more important 'what' and 'why' questions:

> Asking 'what' and 'why' questions gives us a certain power over our teaching. We could claim that the degree of autonomy and responsibility we have in our work as teachers is determined by the level of control that we can exercise over our actions. In reflecting on 'what' and 'why' questions, we begin to exercise control and open up the possibility of transforming our everyday classroom life.

> (ibid.)

In his work, Richards (1991) separated the process of reflection into three simple stages: 1) the event itself i.e. an actual teaching episode; 2) recollection of the event i.e. an account of what happened without explanation or evaluation and 3) review and response to the event i.e. processing at a 'deeper level'. Gibbs' Reflective Cycle (1988) in Figure 7.1 provides a more extended visual illustration of Richards' model.

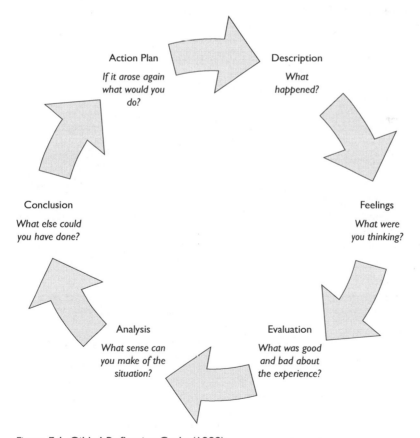

Figure 7.1 Gibbs' Reflective Cycle (1988).

The separation of the teaching act from subsequent reflection upon that act forms the basis of the reflective cycle. For meaningful development to take place, reflection itself should be followed by action; i.e. the implementation of thoughts and ideas emanating from that process of reflection, that, in turn, are reflected upon once they have been put into practice. Thus, within this model, development is seen as a cyclical and iterative process. In paraphrasing the words of Freire (1972), Bartlett (1990) states that 'reflection without action is verbalism: action without reflection is activism – doing things for their own sake' (p. 213).

For Brookfield (1995), what makes critically reflective teaching 'critical' is an under-standing of the concept of power in a wider socio-educational context and recognition of the hegemonic assumptions that influence and shape a teacher's practices:

> Reflection becomes critical when it has two distinctive purposes. The first is to understand how considerations of power undergird, frame and distort educational processes and interactions. The second is to question assumptions and practices that seem to make our teaching lives easier but actually work against our best long-term interests.
>
> (p. 8)

Brookfield draws on Gramsci's concept of 'hegemony' and explains the relevance of its application to the area of critical reflection:

> As proposed by Antonio Gramsci (1978), the term hegemony describes the process whereby ideas, structures, and actions come to be seen by the majority of people as wholly natural, preordained and working for their own good, when in fact they are constructed and transmitted by powerful minority interests to protect the status quo that serves those interests. Hegemonic assumptions about teaching are eagerly embraced by teachers. They seem to represent what's good and true and therefore to be in their own best interests. The dark irony and cruelty of hegemony is that teachers take pride in acting on the very assumptions that work to enslave them.
>
> (Brookfield 1995: 15)

By not situating teaching and learning in its wider socio-political context, teachers can fall foul of what Brookfield (1995) refers to as 'self-laceration'; i.e. they immediately blame themselves when, for example, levels of learner achievement are deemed to be below national benchmarks or when learners resist pedagogic encounters that have been formulated to address their needs.

Brookfield (1995: 29–30) suggests that critically reflective practice takes place when teachers view their practice through four different but interconnecting lenses:

1. personal/'autobiographical' experiences
2. through our students' eyes
3. through colleagues' eyes
4. through the lens of theory/literature.

Viewing their practice through these different lenses enables teachers to unearth some of their assumptions about teaching and learning and provides the stimulus for them to explore 'different perspectives on familiar, taken for granted beliefs and behaviours' (Brookfield 2005: viii). Further discussion in this and the following chapter will explore the first three of Brookfield's lenses in more detail, but for now let me discuss the fourth lens as an example (i.e. the lens of 'theory' or 'literature') of how this can be applied in practice. We have seen in previous chapters how I have drawn on aspects of sociological theories (e.g. from the work of Michel Foucault and Stephen Ball) to make sense of the way in which graded lesson observation has been used in recent years. As an alternative to the hegemonic assumption that the main purpose for the use of observation has been to improve the quality and drive up the standards of teaching and learning, these theories have equipped me with the phenomena and language to be able to challenge such assumptions and offer a very different interpretation of what I and indeed practitioners themselves perceive to be the use and impact of classroom observation. Informed by these theories and literature, I have argued that in reality observation has become normalized as a performative tool of surveillance and control over teachers, which has given rise to a number of detrimental and counterproductive consequences that cannot afford to be ignored by policymakers or practitioners committed to the on-going improvement in the quality of educational provision. This is an example of how the application of one of Brookfield's lenses, in this case theory/literature, can have a powerful impact on the way in which we conceptualize practice.

To sum up then, being critically reflective means a lot more than just thinking about your teaching in the confines of a classroom environment. It involves developing an informed understanding of why you do what you do as a teacher by making your attitudes, assumptions and beliefs explicit in order to identify what it is that you want and/or need to change about yourself, the institutions in which you work and what you/they do to make the educational experience as fulfilling and rewarding as it can possibly be for your learners. An important quality of the critically reflective practitioner is therefore the ability to distance yourself in a controlled and unemotional manner from your actions and those of your learners, and to engage in a process of critical self-reflection and analysis.

Fielding *et al* (2005) contend that in order for teachers to engage with observation as an important tool in their CPD, they must be willing to maintain an open mind when it comes to critically reflecting on their practice and equally be prepared to experiment with new ways of doing things in the classroom. Such willingness to experiment and take risks in one's teaching is fundamental to the CPD of teachers (e.g. IfL 2012); yet, as argued in the following section, opportunities to do so often depend upon the extent to which the teacher's workplace embraces and actively seeks to promote an expansive approach to professional learning amongst its staff.

It cannot be taken for granted that all teachers will naturally develop reflective skills simply as a result of gaining more teaching experience, though the potential rewards can be both exciting and liberating for teachers. When experience is coupled with reflection, it can be a powerful stimulus for professional learning and growth. One of the great attractions of reflection for teachers is thus its potential to transform and improve their classroom practice but once criticality is factored into this, then the teacher is in an even stronger position to develop a greater understanding of how teaching and learning operates within the wider socio-political and educational context. The next section explores the relationship between critical reflection and observation and its role in promoting expansive professional learning.

Classroom observation as a critically reflective tool for expansive professional learning

What do I mean by the term 'expansive professional learning'? For me an expansive learning environment is one in which opportunities for collaborative discussion and wider reflection on professional learning are encouraged and promoted. According to Avis (2003: 316) 'expansive professionalism' is characterized by 'democratic relations that are not undermined by spurious notions of performance management' but instead is something that is constructed collaboratively by means of professional dialogue between colleagues. In relation to classroom observation, my research findings revealed a common core of principles underpinning expansive models across colleges, typically centring on notions of collaboration, trust and professional autonomy (O'Leary 2011). Much of this chapter examines how these principles connect through observation by discussing ungraded, peer-based approaches and their value as a tool for professional learning.

Classroom observation represents a medium through which the process of reflection can be actively nurtured in teachers at all stages of their careers, from pre-service to in-service, NQTs to highly experienced practitioners. Armitage *et al* (2003: 47) argue that 'observation of and by others can be the basis of some of the most useful professional reflection you can undertake in order to improve performance'. Richards (1991) suggested that it is by observing and reflecting on our own teaching that we are able to achieve a higher level of awareness of how we teach. Reflection and classroom observation therefore have close connections in the context of teacher learning and professional development but in order for such learning or development to take place then certain parameters need to be in place.

In drawing on work by Joyce and Showers (2002), Lawson (2011: 5) makes the point that when observation is used as part of a CPD scheme or peer support mechanism then certain conditions need to be established in order for it to be 'conducive to sustained learning'. One of the key factors that he refers to is the use of 'peer coaching' or 'peer observation' (see p. 120 for further discussion of peer observation), which is seen to reduce the levels of stress and tension associated with observation carried out where the power differential is typically reflected by observers occupying senior positions in the institutional hierarchy i.e. teachers being observed by their line managers, though in order for such schemes to work, Lawson argues that there needs to be support for such schemes from senior management.

In my research observees, observers and senior managers across all colleges acknowledged the value of observation as a tool for professional learning. This 'value' was invariably expressed in relation to those models that linked more closely to notions of peer observation discussed in Chapter 3 and on p. 120 than those associated with performance management. In other words, these models seemed to operate according to a set of principles and practices that were characterized by differences in purpose (i.e. emphasis on formative dialogue rather than summative assessment) and in the power differential between observer and observee (i.e. more collaborative and egalitarian as opposed to hierarchical).

Conceptualizing observation as a tool for reciprocal learning has the potential to break down some of the traditional hierarchies and power imbalances associated with the observer–observee relationship, particularly if it is not linked to summative assessment for high stakes purposes i.e. graded lesson observation. In some ways this is reminiscent of Gramsci's call for a more egalitarian teacher–learner relationship based on the premise that 'every teacher is always a pupil and every pupil a teacher' (1971: 350). My research revealed that not only was grading seen as a barrier to encouraging formative dialogue, but by reinforcing the power differential between observer and observee, this also made it more difficult to establish the 'democratic relations' referred to by Avis (2003) above that were considered fundamental to promoting expansive professionalism.

What arguably defines the 'value' associated with peer-based models of observation is the nature of the power–knowledge relationship between observer and observee and the opportunity that the latter has to engage in substantive dialogue as an equal. These are precisely the type of conditions that Avis (2003) and James and Gleeson (2007) argue are essential to foster expansive notions of professionalism. This is in contrast to the performance management model of observation where the 'observer is commonly perceived as possessing greater power' (Cockburn 2005: 384), which can undermine its developmental potential. Boxes 7.1 and 7.2 provide two illuminative mini-case studies of expansive approaches to professional learning through the use of observation from two different institutions.

A differentiated approach to observation

A differentiated approach to observation goes against the grain of most conventional models insomuch as it involves the identification of a specific focus to the observation rather than attempting to carry out a holistic judgement of the teacher's competence and performance via a standardized assessment tool. The focus of the differentiated observation is decided by the observee but it can also be negotiated and/or discussed with the observer (depending on the underlying purpose and context) and can even involve the wider team/ department. The underlying purpose and context is likely to shape the way in which the

---

Box 7.1 Case study A: Suburbia College.

Suburbia College was a small sixth-form college that had moved from a model of observation that was driven by QA goals to one where the focus was on professional development. The grading of observations was removed and other key changes included the make-up of the team of observers i.e. the switch from a small observation team that consisted only of senior managers to a much broader one that constituted approximately a fifth of employees and included teaching staff, heads of faculty, staff from the quality team as well as senior management. The new model also promised a greater emphasis on detailed feedback with a more formalized approach to the way in which areas for development were followed up in the feed forward stage.

When the opinions of staff were canvassed soon after the implementation of the new model of observation, there was an overwhelming consensus among observers and observees that the switch to a non-graded approach was very welcome. Some anxiety was expressed about the workload attached to the new scheme in relation to the formalization of following up areas for development, though it was felt that this might be a price worth paying given that the performative element of grading had been removed and a more collaborative model put in its place.

Box 7.2 Case study B: Middle England College.

Middle England was a medium-sized FE college. Like Suburbia College, its observation policy had been subject to significant revision, although this had taken place over a six-year period. Among some of the most notable changes were: 1) the move away from a top-down, hierarchical team of college observers to a department-led approach; 2) a cultural change in attitudes to seeing observation as a supportive, formative process based on a desire to promote collaboration among colleagues rather than a judgemental process to be feared and 3) a greater sense of ownership and autonomy for teachers in deciding the focus and negotiating which sessions they wished to be observed. In short, the power differential between observer and observee was less marked and seemed to embrace a more collaborative distribution of power in which the observee's voice was regarded as valid as the observer's.

   Middle England's approach to observation seemed to be driven by individual rather than institutional needs. Yet the institution appeared to benefit as well as the individual as there was a continuous 'giving back' and 'sharing of practice' within the college community via an in-house, staff development programme run by staff for staff, along with other outcomes such as the creation of an online repository of useful teaching resources and tips to emerge from college observations.

---

focus is decided. So, for example, in the case of the trainee teacher or NQT whose teaching is being assessed as part of an on-going programme, it may be appropriate for the observer to play a more substantive role in deciding the focus than they otherwise might do if they were observing experienced peers who have identified a specific area of practice that is of particular relevance to their CPD.

   The rationale for a differentiated approach to observation is multi-faceted. Firstly, a differentiated approach is built on the premise that each teacher is likely to have differing strengths and weaknesses in their pedagogic skills and knowledge base in much the same way that any group of learners is likely to differ. Just as the most effective teachers incorporate differentiation into their teaching, so too does it make sense to incorporate it into the way in which teachers' practice is observed. Secondly, as discussed on p. 118, maximizing teacher ownership of the observation process is seen as an important feature of facilitating professional learning that is likely to endure. All teachers have a responsibility for their CPD and they are likely to value this more highly if they feel they are given some ownership of the decision-making process. Thirdly, the collaborative nature of professional learning means that it is not an individual act or the sole responsibility of the teacher but one that involves colleagues working together. So, for example, there may be times when the focus of differentiated observation is driven by wider objectives across a team or department such as a departmental improvement plan. These objectives may stem from a range of sources e.g. self-assessment, inspection reports, appraisal meetings, student evaluations etc. and may be divided into separate strands or themes (e.g. use of formative assessment, use of ICT, behaviour management etc.) to address through observation. In this instance a team/

department of teachers may choose particular themes to focus on, as highlighted in the peer observation scheme discussed on p. 123.

Example protocol for differentiated observation

Notes for the observee

The purpose of this observation is meant to be formative. YOU decide the focus of the observation and what you would like your observer to concentrate on whilst observing. The rationale for this approach is to allow you to choose an aspect of your teaching that you are keen to explore in more depth. This could be something that you are keen to improve, know more about, have some concerns about etc. For instance, you may be interested in studying how you give instructions, how you manage and deal with feedback, your use of a particular resource/form of technology, your methods of assessing learners etc. The important thing is that you choose something that is meaningful and relevant to your development.

Notes for the observer

In keeping with the principles of a collaborative and supportive observation scheme, the most appropriate approach to the recording of data must be one that avoids making judgemental comments about the observed session, as is often associated with those observations that are evaluative in purpose. The purpose of this observation is NOT to evaluate the classroom performance of your colleague, but to stimulate meaningful reflection associated with their chosen aspect(s) of practice.

In your role as the observer you are encouraged to record notes of what you actually observe and these notes should represent a factual record of what occurs during the observation and NOT a subjective interpretation of events (see Table 7.1). These notes are then used to help guide the follow-up discussion between you and your observee as they reflect on the lesson and that particular aspect of their teaching that they have asked you to observe and to keep notes on.

Table 7.1 Form for differentiated observations.

Teacher:	Observer:	Date:
Title:	Level:	Number in Group:
Focus of Observation:		
Field Notes:		

The importance of teacher ownership in classroom observation

Ownership in the context of observation is largely about the devolution of control to the observee, or at least a more balanced distribution between observer and observee in order to allow the latter to take responsibility for their own professional development. Findings from my own research, for example, showed that one of the key strengths of peer observation was the freedom it allowed teachers to set the agenda for the focus of the observation, which resulted in a greater sense of ownership and control over their professional development (O'Leary 2011). These views endorse the argument that if teachers perceive observation as something that 'is done to them', then it is less likely to be successful in achieving meaningful learning outcomes for them. Besides, recent findings from the FE sector reinforce the idea that many practitioners perceive CPD as a management tool that is often unsuitable and/or irrelevant to their needs as it is largely presented as a one-size-fits-all response to the latest government policy/initiative (e.g. IfL 2012).

In discussing the findings from their small-scale study involving HE lecturers participating in a peer observation scheme in Ireland, McMahon *et al* (2007) concluded that their research participants 'were in no doubt that having control over the five key dimensions of choice of observer, focus of observation, form and method of feedback, resultant data flow and the next steps encouraged them to focus on improvement of practice rather than demonstration of existing good practice' (p. 505).

In drawing on earlier work by Lieberman (1986), Middlewood and Cardno (2001) make the distinction between a 'working with' and 'working on' approach to teacher appraisal. They explain what is meant by 'working with' and the rationale for why it is the preferred approach:

> A 'working-with' perspective treats teachers as both partners in their own assessment and active agents of change. This emphasis on shared leadership, horizontal relationships, contextual learning, and reflective decision-making and assessment reinforced the tenets of school restructuring at that time. Such a model when combined with meaningful collaborative involvement and self-directed inquiry, while not perfect, was promising because it recognised that although teachers need guidance and support, they bring considerable expertise to their own development.
>
> (p. 82)

The 'working-with' approach fits well with the philosophy that enhanced understanding and/or knowledge is co-constructed between the observee and observer. It was argued earlier in Chapter 5 that feedback is commonly regarded as the most important part of the observation process. Central to an expansive approach to professional learning through observation is the co-construction of knowledge between observer and observee as part of the feedback or professional dialogue. The emphasis here is on the word 'co-construction' as both have a collaborative and reciprocal role in constructing their personal knowledge and understanding of teaching and learning. This does not mean to say that the two will necessarily share the same interpretation of events observed but that the dialogic process of making sense of those events will be shared in a way that enhances personal meaning. Rather than one person controlling the acquisition and production of knowledge, a shared, dialogic approach necessitates the negotiation of meaning between the two parties, and it is during this negotiation of meaning that enhanced awareness and understanding often emerges.

Feedback is a key element of the observation process and one where the incorporation of the underpinning values of democratic professionalism has the potential to transform the experience of both observer and observee. In their collaborative work, Freire and Shor (1987) explored the notion of 'liberatory dialogue', which for them was an opportunity to use dialogue for *illumination* rather than *manipulation* in the context of the teacher–learner relationship. Unlike conventional conceptualizations of knowledge ownership in the teacher–learner relationship where the teacher is seen as the dominant subject, liberatory dialogue is based on democratic principles and thus the 'object of study' is not seen as the intellectual property of the teacher but rather as a shared asset whose meaning is negotiated and mediated by both parties. This conceptual framework has relevance to the way in which the feedback discussion might be approached during classroom observation.

There are certain parallels between the dominant role of the teacher in the teacher–learner relationship and that of the observer–observee. As we saw in Chapter 5, most evaluation models of observation tend to adopt a top-down, authoritarian approach, where it is the observer who controls the agenda or the 'object of study'. Adopting a dialogical approach, however, offers the potential to provide a balance to the involvement and control of both observer and observee. Let us now see an example of this in practice.

The ITE department in which I work recently introduced a traffic light tracking tool in response to a recommendation made during the previous inspection. This tracking tool was attached to the student teacher's classroom observation booklet, in which all of their observations are recorded throughout the course. Instead of imposing this as a disguised form of grading, several tutors chose to adopt a shared ownership model of evaluation with their student teachers. What this meant in practice was that the observer and observee carried out their own evaluation and self-evaluation of the taught session respectively according to the specified categories of assessment listed on the traffic light grid before meeting to discuss the lesson. Each of these evaluations then formed the basis of the discussion between observee and observer, though it was not always necessary to agree. One of the strengths of such an approach is that it offers a collaborative and discursive way forward for departments and institutions to engage with assessment criteria.

Another variation on a 'working with' model of observation is one that is based on collaborative question setting. As with the differentiated model discussed previously, the observee identifies a particular area of practice that they wish to focus on and then draws up a list of questions before the observation takes place that they would like the observer to think about. These questions are then shared with the observer before the observation and help to provide a framework for the observer's comments when taking notes during the observation. The observer may also make a list of their own questions during/after the observation and together with the observee's original questions, these help to form the basis of the post-lesson discussion and the feed forward stage.

It is important to emphasize that teacher development starts with the individual teacher. Every teacher needs to recognize that the onus for professional growth is on them, it is their responsibility. This does not mean to say that it is a solitary process, far from it. Colleagues and fellow professionals have an invaluable part to play in helping to guide and support a teacher's professional development, but without the desire and willingness to grow on the part of the individual teacher then the support of others pales into insignificance. As Wade and Hammick (1999: 163) have argued, 'it must be recognised that a self-diagnosed need for learning provides greater motivation to learn than an externally diagnosed requirement'. Or as Stronach *et al* (2002: 132) succinctly put it, 'excellence can only be motivated, it cannot be coerced'. This desire and willingness for professional growth requires teachers to maintain an open attitude to the constructive advice of others in all matters relating to the teaching and learning process and a genuine commitment to engaging in critical reflection of their practice and that of others, as Wragg argued: 'Classroom observation can help teachers understand what is happening in their own classroom and elsewhere, and this is a valuable first step to a collective commitment to working collaboratively to improve teaching' (p. 135).

Equally teachers need to be empowered to have control over their own development. As Bailey *et al* (2001: 5) have remarked:

> People can be subjected to assessment, appraisal and evaluation against their will. But no one can be made to develop. Even if you have to complete a portfolio, you can't be made to develop by doing it. Teachers are too good at faking it. We have to be. We can fake development, and should do so, if someone tries to force us. But we develop as professionals, if, and only if, we choose to.

The desire to engage in critical reflection on one's own teaching in order to further develop pedagogic understanding and subject knowledge is fuelled from within. Typically the best teachers are the ones who are extremely self-critical and constantly striving for improvement in what they do.

Finally, the inclusion of a pre-observation meeting is another important aspect of increasing teacher ownership of the process. With many assessment models of observation, the pre-observation meeting is a rare occurrence. Not only does this provide both observer and observee with an opportunity to discuss the focus of the lesson and for the latter to provide a context and rationale for the lesson's focus, but it also enables them to negotiate a set of shared goals that takes into account the needs of the individual and the institution. It is important that a professional, reflective dialogue between the two remains the key driver for these meetings and that they do not become dominated by discussions about procedural aspects of the observation process. That said, if the observation is to be assessed then one of the issues that might be worth discussing is the assessment criteria and their use. Let us now turn our attention to peer observation.

Peer observation

As was discussed in earlier chapters, peer observation is generally understood to refer to a collaborative and reciprocal model of observation whereby peers observe each other as a means of enhancing their pedagogic practice through reflective dialogue, with a view to feeding forward into their CPD and ultimately leading to improvements in the quality of teaching and learning. Tilstone (1998) uses the term 'partnership observation' instead of peer observation and offers the following definition:

> *Partnership* observation involves two people working collaboratively in order to analyse, and to learn from, the events in a classroom or school. Partners can either be

outside partners (who do not work in the school but have been invited in or who visit the school infrequently) and *inside partners* (staff from within the institution). In both cases, the object of the partnership is to offer 'another pair of friendly eyes' in order to improve the teaching and learning taking place.

(p. 59, emphasis in original)

Tilstone goes on to list what she sees as the key components of any successful partnership, which includes notions such as 'trust, commitment, common understanding and the identification of individual needs' (p. 60). There is an emphasis on reciprocal learning and for both parties to provide mutual support but for this relationship to work then there needs to be an equal sharing of power as discussed previously.

In a study carried out by Hammersley-Fletcher and Orsmond (2005) into peer observation in the HE sector, it was evident that some teaching staff felt uncomfortable about providing critical feedback for their peers but, at the same time, felt that this was part of their role as observers (p. 218). This draws attention to the training and preparation of observers. Most teachers have rarely observed others, or been observed by their peers. In most cases this is something that they might only have experienced (if ever!) as part of an ITT qualification. This lack of experience, coupled with some of the hegemonic assumptions about observation, can lead to a reluctance or uncertainty to undertake their role. Is it to assess or to learn or both? Although many peer observation schemes would contest that the latter is usually the central aim, one might speculate that in practice this is not always the case. As a teacher it can be difficult to watch somebody else teach and not to form opinions about the effectiveness of their performance; it seems to happen almost instinctively. This is not surprising given the history of the use of observation discussed in earlier chapters and how it has become deeply embedded in the psyche of teachers as an evaluative tool. Encouraging teachers to detach evaluation from observation requires a significant cultural shift on an individual, institutional and collective level across the profession.

Brookfield (1995: 83) acknowledges the important role that the lens of peer observation and collegial feedback has to play in stimulating critical reflection on teachers' practice: 'For those of us with egos strong enough to stand it, colleagues' observations of our practice can be one of the most helpful sources of critical insight to which we have access, though again this implies an element of judgement in its use'.

The purpose of many peer observation schemes is essentially developmental. An underlying principle of a developmental model of observation is that it is intended to be supportive rather than evaluative. It recognizes the shortcomings of conventional approaches and tries to counter this by encouraging a culture of collaboration between colleagues. Richards (1998) suggests that teachers should see themselves as 'co-researchers' in peer observation. Fullan and Hargreaves' (1992) findings support the argument that teacher development is more likely to prosper when there is a culture of collaboration amongst teaching staff. Their research concluded that teachers working in an institution in which 'Interactive Professionalism' was the norm were much more likely to develop than those who worked as individuals, thus being denied the opportunity to learn from each other and share new ideas:

Many teachers are effective. Their problem is lack of access to other teachers. Access would mean that they could become even better while sharing their expertise.

Many other teachers are competent but could improve considerably if they were in a more collaborative environment. . . . Interactive professionalism exposes problems of incompetence more naturally and gracefully [than punitive appraisal schemes]. It makes individuals reassess their situation as a continuing commitment.

(Fullan and Hargreaves 1992: 18–19)

The underpinning purposes and outcomes of peer observation can be summarized in Table 7.2.

Table 7.2 Key purposes and outcomes of models of peer observation.

Purposes	*Outcomes*
• To stimulate professional dialogue and critical reflection on practice • To create reciprocal opportunities for the exchange of ideas and/or good practice among colleagues • To develop teachers' knowledge base and skills set • To act as a key learning tool in the development of NQTs • To act as a support mechanism for teachers who are in need of guidance on specific aspects of practice	• The creation of a network or community of critically reflective practitioners • The development of a culture of collaboration and sharing of ideas and resources among practitioners • A team of teachers with updated knowledge and skills • Well-prepared and competent NQTs • Improvement in the classroom competence of practitioners

Peer observation in practice

The format of most peer observations tends to be quite similar. Both teachers meet before the lesson to agree on a specific focus for the observation and to share their thoughts and ideas on that chosen topic. With the aid of some type of record sheet the observer then writes down any information pertaining to the agreed focus during the lesson. Both observer and the observee then meet after the lesson to discuss and reflect upon the data that has been collected.

Cosh (1999) comments that despite the shift in focus from judgement to development/ self-development that peer observation implies, the very process of being observed still makes many teachers feel nervous. The underlying reasons for this have been discussed in some detail so far. And that is that although you may be able to dissuade other colleagues from voicing evaluative opinions on your teaching by adopting such an approach, you cannot prevent somebody from making an implicit judgement. Despite what Cosh maintains, simply encouraging teachers to adjust their mind set and concentrate on their own development by 'reflecting' instead of 'judging' each other's teaching would not appear to represent an entirely convincing solution. It could be argued that the true test of peer observation fundamentally depends upon the relationship between colleagues and the respect and trust they have for one another.

Observer preparation and training is a vital ingredient to any successful observation scheme. In the context of peer-based models of observation, this should start with a discussion between observer and observee as to what their respective roles are expected to entail. Much of this discussion is likely to centre on challenging and transforming traditional conceptions of the observer with a view to agreeing on a re-defined role underpinned by the need to ensure that what they record during the observed lesson reflects the factual description of events rather than their opinions or subjective judgements. This is then shared with the teacher at the end of the observation and they are then encouraged to interpret the information. The key features of such a model can be summarized in the bullet points below:

- factual descriptions rather than opinions;
- the present rather than the past;
- *sharing* rather than *giving* ideas;
- alternatives rather than prescriptive statements;
- the individual's needs and how they can be modified;
- the observer *records* what is happening, *agrees* what has happened, *reflects* (with the teacher) on what has been recorded, and finally *encourages* her to interpret the information.

(taken from Tilstone 1998: 108–110)

An example of a peer observation scheme across institutions

Overview

The Peer Observation Partnership Scheme (POPS) was created among a group of teacher educators working on ITT and INSET programmes across a range of partner institutions. Its primary purpose was to act as a supportive and developmental mechanism through which peers teaching on these programmes could share, compare and discuss their practices, but it was also seen as an opportunity to quality assure teacher education provision across the partnership.

Focus of the observations

All members of the POPS agreed that the general focus for the first cycle of observations and professional dialogues should reflect some of the key areas for improvement identified in the previous Ofsted report for ITE provision.

At the same time, participants wanted the process to be flexible enough to respond to their on-going development needs and those areas of professional interest that emerged during the course of the observation cycle.

How it worked in practice

Peer triads were formed as part of the POPS. Each triad consisted of three teacher educators, all of whom belonged to a different institution in the partnership and thus were not colleagues. Each member of the triad took it in turns to teach a session that was observed by the other two whose task was to compile unstructured field notes. In keeping with the principles of the POPS, it was decided that the most appropriate approach to the recording of data must be one that avoided making judgemental comments about the observed session. The purpose of the POPS was not about evaluating each other's classroom performance, but more about stimulating meaningful reflection and reflexivity of practice as a community of teacher educators. These notes then formed the basis for the observer's further reflections and questions, which sought to explore and develop wider issues of pedagogy as part of the follow-up discussion and not just events that were specific to the observed session. The notes thus provided a platform for a subsequent professional dialogue between the triad following the observation.

At the end of the dialogue both observers submitted a copy of their field notes to the observee, who used them to put together a written reflective account of the experience. This reflection was then shared with the two observers who were invited to respond/add to the account. This exchange took place online, i.e. via email or a blog, and was later discussed face to face. Practically it was often easier to schedule this subsequent sharing of the observee's reflective account at the start of the following observation session of the triad.

Once all three of the team had observed each other and completed the cycle, each member of the team was expected to write up a reflective synopsis of the experience from the perspective of both observer and observee. When writing this synopsis they were asked to consider the benefits/drawbacks of the scheme, compare the experience from the eyes of the observee and observer, along with any suggestions as to how to develop or improve the scheme for subsequent cycles. This work was then shared amongst the partnership in the form of a symposium at the end of the academic year.

HOW MUCH TIME WAS ALLOCATED FOR THE OBSERVATION CYCLE?

Stage 1 – Pre-session discussion: 40 minutes × 3 participants = 120 minutes
Stage 2 – Observation – 60 minutes × 3 participants = 180 minutes
Stage 3 – Post-session discussion: 40 minutes × 3 participants = 120 minutes
Stage 4 – Observee's reflective writing: 60 minutes × 3 = 180 minutes
Stage 5 – End of scheme write-up: 60 minutes × 3 = 180 minutes
Total time = 13 hours × 3 participants = 39 hours

Summary

This chapter has focused on the use of classroom observation in promoting expansive professional learning. It started by discussing critical reflection and its role in teacher development in the context of observation and then moved on to exploring the ways in which peer-based models might be used as a tool for stimulating and channelling collaborative learning. The final section that follows includes a range of targeted observation tasks each with differing foci, enabling the observer and observee to use these as a springboard for collaborative, professional dialogue and learning. The following chapter, Chapter 8, explores three alternative models of observation through three mini-case studies and reflects on what these models can add to our understanding of the teaching and learning process and the professional development of teachers.

Targeted observation tasks

This section contains a range of targeted observation tasks, each of which identifies specific aspects of the teaching and learning process for the observer to focus on. These tasks can be used by all teachers, regardless of subject areas and experience.

Task 1: Analysis of teacher roles

Keep a tally of the different roles that the teacher takes on at different stages of the lesson in the chart below. If there are any additional roles that you think are not included but need to be added then enter them in the spaces at the bottom of the chart. After the lesson, compare and discuss your results with colleagues who have done the same observation activity.

Presenter												
Counsellor												
Supervisor												
Facilitator												
Listener												
Manager												
Motivator												
Coach												
Participant												
Assessor												
Corrector												
Observer												

Take three of the roles that you noted above and describe briefly the classroom activity and/or stage of the lesson that illustrates each one.

1.

....

....

....

....

....

....

2.

....

....

....

....

....

....

3.

....

....

....

....

....

....

Task 2: Observing learning styles

- Identify two learners at the start. Try to write a pen sketch of what kind of learners they are (e.g. passive, talkative, inquisitive, detached etc.).
- Make a note of some of their learning strategies. For example, do they take lots of notes during the lesson? Do they like to ask lots of questions? Do their strategies appear to be effective? Can you suggest ways that they might learn things better?

....

....

....

Choose another three learners. Write their initials below, and a descriptor to suit each one's learning style. Select from the following or make up your own descriptors: *risk-taker, leader, joker, daydreamer, questioner etc.*

Name	Descriptor(s)	Reason for the descriptor
1.		
2.		
3.		

Task 3: Managing resources

Record at least three instances on the chart below when the teacher uses any of the following resources:

- **(interactive) whiteboard, flipchart** (e.g. neatness of writing, use of space)
- **hand-outs** (e.g. worksheet, text)
- **visual aids** (e.g. photos)
- **coursebook**

Were the resources a help to learning or were they superfluous? Could they have been used differently (make a note under '**alternatives**')?

Resource	How it was used	Reason for use

Alternatives

....

....

....

 © Matt O'Leary, *Classroom Observation*, Routledge 2014.

Task 4: Case study of an individual learner

Focus on an individual learner for the duration of the lesson. Make notes on their contribution to/participation in the different lesson stages, overall attention span, interest and motivation in the lesson, academic level, how much talking they do in whole class, group, paired and individual activities. Write down some of the contributions (whole class or in group) that your selected learner makes during the lesson. To what extent are they relevant to the lesson's focus and tasks? What do they tell you about the way in which the learner is interacting with the subject matter? Did the learner appear to enjoy the lesson, or not? How do you know?

....

....

....

....

....

....

....

....

....

....

....

....

....

....

....

....

....

Task 5: 'Storytelling'

After providing a brief overview of the subject area and learner group, imagine that you will be asked to narrate your notes of this observation in the form of a story. Here are some questions/prompts to guide your narrative:

- How does the story begin?
- What is happening as you 'enter' the story? Why do you think this is happening?
- Who are the protagonists in the story? Are there certain characters that stand out more than others? If so, who are they?
- What are the roles of these characters in the story?
- What seems to be the main plot of the story?
- Are there any subplots?
- What impact does the setting have on the characters and the plot?
- Is there a sense of drama to the story?
- Is there anything in the story that has puzzled you?
- Are there any questions you would like the opportunity to be able to ask some of the characters in the story? If so, can you list some example questions and the particular characters to who they would be directed?
- Is there a sense of closure to the story or is it 'to be continued'?
- What are your thoughts on how the story might develop in the future?

....

....

....

....

....

....

....

....

....

....

....

....

....

....

....

Task 6: Analyzing classroom interaction

After providing a brief overview of the subject area and student group, draw the layout of the classroom, including the desks/tables, doors, windows, whiteboard, projector etc as well as the seating positions of the students. Use the following codes for each learner M1, M2, M3 (if male), F1, F2, F3 (if female), T = Teacher and TA = Teaching Assistants.

During a period of approximately 10–15 minutes, make a note of the teacher–learner interactions – verbal and non-verbal (e.g. use of feedback, body language, facial gestures etc.) and reflect on the following questions:

- Are you able to identify any patterns in these interactions?
- How might these patterns be explained?
- Is there a 'clustering' of interaction i.e. does there appear to be more interaction with some learners rather than others?
- If so, what are your thoughts on this? Are other learners aware of this?
- Are there any discernible differences in the interactions between males and females?
- Does the teacher have a particular strategy for the way in which they choose to communicate/interact with their body language/facial expressions?
- Does the layout of the room seem to impact on these interactions? If so, why and how?
- Have you learnt anything from this observation about the significance of non-verbal interaction and/or its impact?

Task 7: Teacher focus: strategies and techniques

This task focuses on the strategies and techniques that the teacher employs throughout the lesson in order to interact and communicate with the learners as well as to achieve the lesson's aims.

Number of learners	Teacher
Observer	Level
Length of Lesson	Date

Apparent Aims of Lesson

What kind of gestures does the teacher use during the lesson? What are they used for and what is the effect on learners?

Comment on the quality and use of the teacher's voice in at different stages of the lesson. Why is it important?

How does the teacher present themselves as a professional through their behaviour and interaction with learners? What effect is achieved?

How effective is the teacher at keeping learners' attention? How do they do this?

What overall atmosphere is there in the class? To what extent is the teacher's *presence* and manner contributing to this?

What does this teacher have that you would like to incorporate into your own teaching?

Task 8: Understanding the lesson and its aims

Underpinning every effective lesson is a lesson plan with a clear set of objectives. Observe a lesson without requesting a copy of the teacher's lesson plan. Based on your observation, see if you can identify the overall aims of the lesson as well as the different stages of the lesson and how these fit together.

Number of learners	Teacher
Observer	Level
Length of Lesson	Date

Apparent Aims of Lesson

Stage Aim	Teacher activity	Learner activity	Resources	Grouping

Stage Aim	Teacher activity	Learner activity	Resources	Grouping

Task 9: Teacher questions

A fundamental skill and/or strategy for all teachers to master is the ability to ask effective and appropriate questions. Teachers ask questions for a whole host of reasons i.e. to challenge and check learners' understanding, elicit their ideas and opinions, stimulate their thinking, assess their progress etc. The table below is divided into four columns: teacher questions, learner responses, purpose and comment. Make a list of at least 15 questions along with the responses (if appropriate). Try to deduce the underlying purpose to each of the questions and include additional comments.

Question	Response	Purpose	Comment

Follow-up questions

Does there seem to be any pattern to the TYPE of questions asked?

Is there any pattern to the purpose of the questions asked?

Are the questions effective in what they seek to achieve?

Are there features of the questioning skills of this teacher you wish to adopt?

Has your awareness of questioning skills changed as a result in any way?

Chapter 8

Moving beyond conventional models of classroom observation

Lesson study, unseen observation and remote mobile video technology as alternative case studies

Introduction

It has been argued in previous chapters that conventional models of classroom observation are limited in their ability to foster substantive teacher development, not to mention the shortcomings associated with their use as a method of assessment. Instead of stimulating an environment that is conducive to teachers' open critical reflection and self-evaluation of their work, the high stakes nature of performance management-driven models of observation often militates against this and leads to the creation of a risk-averse culture of teacher learning and the normalization of practice. Added to this, it has to be said that any model of observation that chooses to focus exclusively on either teacher or learner performance is only ever likely to be able to provide a partial account of the classroom and the intricacies of the teaching and learning process.

With these limitations in mind, this chapter explores some alternatives to conventional models of observation through three separate case studies: 1) lesson study, 2) unseen observation and 3) remote mobile video technology. The rationale for the choice of these three different models is that each offers an alternative lens through which to view teaching and learning and as such has the potential to provide additional insights into the way in which classroom observation might be harnessed as a tool for enhancing teacher awareness and understanding of pedagogic skills and knowledge.

Case study one: lesson study

> Classroom observation research can make a significant contribution to the improvement of teaching competence, especially if teachers and [educational institutions], as a matter of policy, research their own practice and act on their findings.
>
> (Wragg 1999: 108)

The above quote draws attention to the potential of classroom observation as a research tool for investigating and informing teachers' practice. Wragg's vision of how observation might best be employed is based on an action-research model, which underpins the epistemological and methodological essence of our first case study in this chapter: lesson study.

As commented earlier in Chapter 3, lesson study is one of the most recent developments in the use of observation as a form of professional development in the last two decades in the Western world. In Japan, from where it originates, it has been in use for over 100 years, predominantly in an INSET context. On the surface, lesson study appears to incorporate many of the features of models of peer observation previously discussed, though there are some significant differences. One of the defining qualities of lesson study is that it is underpinned by an ethos of teacher collaboration and cooperation. Lieberman (2009) argues that it is considered to help promote genuine collaboration as opposed to a 'sharing' of ideas and/or resources, which, in the UK context, is so often referred to as 'sharing good practice'.

In small working groups, teachers critically discuss and evaluate specific aspects of their subject curriculum and their learners' engagement with it, some of which may have been identified previously in student evaluations, self-evaluation reports etc. In short, as a 'model' or 'process' of professional development, lesson study typically involves a group of teachers collaboratively planning a lesson(s), observing a member of the group teaching the lesson(s), meeting to discuss their observations and reflections on the lesson(s) and cascading what has been learnt about the process of teaching and learning (Lewis *et al* 2006). Figure 8.1 provides an outline of the lesson study cycle in which each stage is summarized.

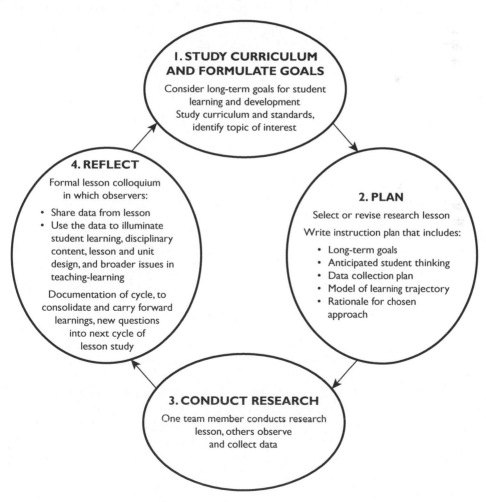

Figure 8.1 Outline of the lesson study cycle (taken from Lewis *et al* 2006: 4).

Prior to the planning and delivery stages, teaching staff meet to discuss the student group and decide upon the key theme(s) on which to base their study; e.g. facilitating learners' independent thinking. During this stage ideas about planning and the subsequent observation(s) are discussed in detail. Upon completion of the planning documentation, the lesson is delivered by one of the members of the group. Meanwhile the remaining group members observe and take detailed notes about the learners' engagement with the topic, their teacher and their peers, as well as their cognitive processing during the lesson; e.g. ways in which they make sense of information, types of questions they ask, ability to complete tasks etc. The data collected during this taught lesson then form the basis for subsequent critical reflection and professional dialogue between the team, which normally takes place on the same day. When the group meet they share their notes and reflections on the lesson, which are used to inform the direction of the discussion. This can result in further refinement and improvement of the taught lesson so that it can be taught and observed again or the selection of a new theme/topic to study and the beginning of another cycle.

It is common practice for a lesson study group to deliver at least two taught lessons. Wang-Iverson (2002) argues that the reason why only two lessons are delivered and observed is because the emphasis is on the 'process' rather than the 'product'. In other words, the lessons act as the platform for extended professional dialogue for teachers to share their interpretations about the specific object of study rather than as an end in themselves.

Lewis *et al* (2006) have argued that one of the defining characteristics of lesson study is the way in which it approaches the observation process. The lesson is seen as a collaborative research context in which to collect data that will provide the platform for classroom-based inquiry:

> The observed lessons, called 'research lessons', are regarded not as an end in themselves but as a window on the larger vision of education shared by the group of teachers, one of whom agrees to teach the lesson while all the others make detailed records of the learning and teaching as it unfolds. These data are shared during a post-lesson colloquium where they are used to reflect on the lesson and on learning and teaching more broadly.
>
> (Lewis *et al* 2006: 3)

Instead of the summative assessment of the teacher's performance being the raison d'être of the lesson, thus leading to a *fetishization* of the one-off observed lesson as I have argued elsewhere (e.g. O'Leary 2012c), lesson study adopts a non-judgemental, analytical approach that concentrates on collecting data about a particular aspect of the curriculum with the ultimate aim of reflecting on how student learning can be further enhanced. Thus the spotlight is not on the individual teacher's competence and performance but on the student experience and the way in which they make sense of the curriculum. Unlike performance-driven models of observation where the observation and the summative grade are an end in themselves, the lesson study model uses observation as a method of data collection whilst avoiding making judgements about individual teachers. The classroom therefore becomes a research site for teachers to study their own subject area and associated pedagogy, while simultaneously understanding more about their learners and their engagement with the curriculum.

Lesson study is designed to promote a collegial approach to observation, enabling teachers to take control of their own development and conceptualize improvement as a shared experience (Lieberman 2009). Wang-Iverson (2002: 2) likens lesson study to a 'bridge' that 'provides an infrastructure for teachers to share and discover best practices in a deliberate and thoughtful manner'. It affords teachers a collaborative platform to engage in professional dialogue about curriculum planning and to share ideas and experiences about student learning.

What distinguishes lesson study from other models of peer observation, for example, is that the planning, teaching and reflection of the lesson occurs within a network of practitioners rather than in isolation. As was touched on in the previous chapter, much CPD activity can be considered irrelevant and unsuitable to the needs of teachers as it is so often driven by an externally motivated agenda to satisfy the latest government directive and as such ends up being something that is 'done to them' rather than responding to their on-going developmental needs. Lesson study offers the potential to redress this imbalance in the 'agency' of the teacher by providing teachers with a platform for exercising greater professional autonomy in setting the agenda themselves and thus making the process more openly democratic. From deciding which aspect(s) of the curriculum/ pedagogy to investigate, to planning and observing the lesson, collecting, discussing and analyzing data during the course of the observation, the process of lesson study actively encourages the development of democratic relations among staff. As there is no hierarchy within the group nor is the process linked to summative assessment, it seems reasonable to assume that staff are likely to be less guarded in what they say, thus making it more conducive to open and honest discussion and debate. In her research, Lieberman (2009) found that lesson study encouraged openness amongst staff and that this helped to expose 'vulnerability' as an issue that affects experienced teachers as much as it does novice teachers. In other words, if experienced teachers are willing to expose their professional souls to NQTs and less experienced colleagues, this leads to the development of what Lieberman calls 'norms of openness' (2009: 89). In turn, this can prompt teachers to take more risks in their teaching as they realize that 'being a teacher means opening their practice to scrutiny, and thinking critically about their lesson plans' (p. 97).

Unlike conventional models of observation where the roles of observer and observee are clearly demarcated in a hierarchical sense (i.e. the observer tends to control the agenda and the decision-making process), lesson study operates on a more democratic basis. Each member of the group's voice is as valid as the next, as no one person is deemed to be in a position of greater authority and/or control than others. In this respect there are certain parallels between the ideology underpinning lesson study as a model of professional development and the ubiquitous 'communities of practice' (Lave and Wenger 1991) so often used to make sense of teacher networks and communities. Both comprise groups that have a shared focus and/or interest and there is an understanding of the 'situatedness' of professional learning.

Wang-Iverson (2002) argues that another indirect benefit of lesson study is the 'pro-fessionalization' of teachers. She contends that learners, parents and the wider education community may take them more seriously if they see them engaging in research in their own classrooms. This is an interesting statement in several respects as it touches at the very heart of the debate about the professionalism and professionalization of teachers explored in Chapter 2. Implicit in Wang-Iverson's comment is the idea that the 'teacher as researcher' is likely to attract more kudos to teachers' status among the wider public. While this is, of course, an unsubstantiated claim, it does raise an important issue regarding the professional autonomy of teachers and the extent to which pedagogy and curriculum development is something that should be based more on a bottom-up approach i.e. where teachers are given the role of active researchers, responsible for investigating their own classrooms, instead of relying on a top-down model that imposes centralized policies written by those who are disconnected from the classroom.

To date lesson study has tended to be used in an INSET context and thus its relevance and potential for use in ITT programmes has been largely unexplored. Some of the ways in which it could be seen to have reciprocal benefit for those involved in such programmes (i.e. not just the student teachers but their university tutors and workplace mentors) might include helping to develop reflective practice, developing a richer, situated understanding of the complexities of teaching whilst on placement, as well as making lesson planning more meaningful and contextualized. If we take the latter as an example, lesson planning is often a solitary process for many student teachers as they are required to compile a detailed plan in preparation for their observed teaching practice. Typically student teachers put together their lesson plans on their own and then show their mentor and/or university tutor a draft copy to get their feedback before producing the final version. One of the advantages of adopting a collaborative approach to lesson planning, as is the case with lesson study, is that all members of the group are privy to each other's thoughts and ideas and are able to comment on and ask questions throughout the planning process. Not only is this helpful in providing a forum for all teachers to verbalize thought processes and decision-making that usually remain in the head of the individual, but discussions can often extend beyond the focus of a single lesson and include more wide-ranging issues that have additional pedagogic benefits for all concerned.

Like many forms of intervention designed to foster professional development, success is dependent on a sustained and coordinated investment in time. Lesson study is no different in this respect. Finding the time to conduct lesson study presents challenges both for teaching staff and managers responsible for timetabling. As the success of lesson study is highly dependent on sustained collaborative work between teams of teaching staff, providing time for them to meet is essential, though not unproblematic. These problems are inevitably exacerbated in large institutions where the task of coordinating staff time-tabling to incorporate an initiative like lesson study both within and across departments can become a logistical nightmare and even impossible in some instances. However, if teaching staff are not formally allocated hours in their timetables to take part in lesson study then this can present a major obstacle to its successful implementation or even getting it off the ground. Liptak (2002: 6) describes how in her school each participant in the lesson study programme was allocated between eighty minutes and two hours per week. She stresses the need to invest time if it is going to be a worthwhile venture but also highlights how senior managers need to view it as a long-term project rather than a short-term fix.

In summary, it would appear then that lesson study has the potential to make a significant contribution to developing understanding and improvement of teaching and learning but with the caveat that organizational elements (e.g. timetabling, administrative support) are carefully considered (Grierson and Gallagher 2009) and further research is needed in order to explore its potential (Lewis *et al* 2006).

If you wish to find out more about lesson study, including a set of practical guide-lines for using it in your institution, along with a list of resources, then the following website: www.rbs.org is a useful starting point. Let us now move on to discussing the second case study: 'unseen observation'.

Case study two: unseen observation

This second case study discusses the model of 'unseen observation'. It starts with a brief explanation of what it is, the key ideas underpinning this model of observation along with some of its potential strengths and limitations. It then moves on to examining its use in practice via a small-scale action research study involving three qualified teachers.

The term 'unseen observation' might seem misleading to some given that it is a model of observation that does not actually involve observing a taught lesson. How does this work you might be thinking? In essence, it is quite similar to existing models of observation, particularly peer observation, but the main difference is that there is no observed lesson. Instead of the observer visiting the class to carry out a 'live observation', the stimulus for the professional dialogue between the observer and the observee is based on the latter's self-analysis and recounting of the lesson itself, as well as a pre-lesson meeting between the two in which the proposed lesson plan is discussed. Figure 8.2 provides an overview of the basic stages of unseen observation as it has been used on an ITT programme on which I taught.

The concept of unseen observation seems to originate in language teacher education and is linked to Rinvolucri (1988), who borrowed the idea himself from the professions of counselling and therapy. The standard practice in these professions is for the counsellor or

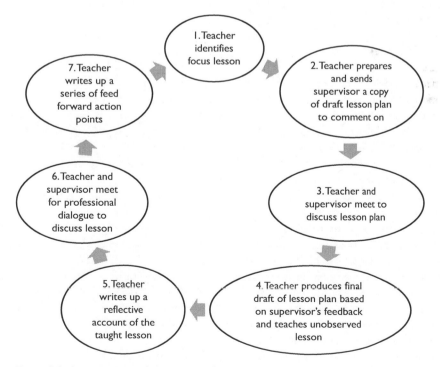

Figure 8.2 An overview of the stages of unseen observation.

therapist to listen to a person's account of a real-life event *after* it has happened as opposed to witnessing it in real time, which, for obvious reasons, cannot happen. How this connects to the role of the 'observer' or the person who is referred to as the 'supervisor' in unseen observation is that they do not actually visit the class to carry out an observation, but instead rely on the teacher's account of the lesson after it has been taught to guide the professional dialogue between the two.

A strong argument for using a counselling approach within teacher education comes from the emphasis that such an approach places on the teacher as an individual. Cogan (1995) argued almost two decades ago that conventional approaches to teacher supervision often fail to address the issue of the teacher as an individual with their own value and belief systems. It was Cogan's belief that teacher development had a lot to learn from the domain of counselling and one maxim that needed to be applied was the importance of treating the teacher as an individual, whose perceptions of their own classroom experience are taken seriously and used as the platform for professional dialogue. Thus in relation to unseen observation it is the teacher's perceptions of the taught lesson that provide the basis for the supervisor's work in their interaction with the teacher. The role of the supervisor in the follow-up dialogue to the lesson is regarded as more supportive and less directive than the conventional observer–observee relationship. One of the repercussions of this is the redistribution of power between supervisor and teacher, with greater autonomy being granted to the teacher than is usually the case in many traditional models of observation. In some ways this reflects Freire and Shor's (1987) 'liberatory dialogue' discussed in the previous chapter.

Equally, Edge's (1992) model of 'cooperative development' shares many of the ideological and ethical features of unseen observation. It too is very influenced by ideas from the practice of counselling (e.g. Egan 1986; Rogers 1983). Although its main aim is to promote self-development, the framework that Edge presents is one that is built on collaboration between colleagues. However, it is recognized that the responsibility for the direction of development should still remain very firmly in the hands of the teacher. It is Edge's belief that teachers are the best judges of what happens inside their own classrooms and what their needs and those of their learners are.

Edge's (1992) model of cooperative development identifies two key roles, which he labels as the 'Speaker' and the 'Understander'; these reflect the roles of the teacher and the supervisor respectively in the model of unseen observation. The Understander is responsible for assisting the Speaker's development by ensuring that they 'make as much space as possible for the Speaker' (p. 8) whilst also maintaining the role of an active listener. It is Edge's belief that by having to communicate their ideas and reflections to the Understander in a spoken form, the Speaker is compelled to make sense of them and in so doing this helps to clarify their beliefs and values in their own minds. Thus, in the context of observation, the post-lesson discussion can be seen to provide the perfect opportunity for teachers to express themselves and to explore their beliefs and ideas.

There are certain parallels between the role of the supervisor in unseen observations and that of the learner-centred teacher. For example, both are guided by a philosophy that seeks to involve the individual more actively in the learning experience, thus increasing their responsibility for their own learning and ultimately leading to a greater sense of professional autonomy. One of the principal beliefs of such an approach would appear to be that it is more meaningful for learners and teachers alike to discover and assess new ideas for themselves rather than having to rely on the prescription of others. In this way, the role of the teacher or supervisor can be seen as 'facilitating' the learning experience rather than directly controlling it.

Undoubtedly, a potential weakness of unseen observation rests on the fact that the supervisor hears only one side of the story and hence is totally reliant on the honesty and accuracy of the teacher's recollection of the lesson. What teachers say they do in a lesson may not necessarily be an accurate reflection of what actually happens. However, in the light of some of the previous discussion concerning the drawbacks of conventional models of observation, there may be a number of distinct benefits to using unseen observation as an alternative approach.

Firstly, post-lesson feedback in conventional models of observation can be an anxious and daunting experience for some teachers, inevitably involving psychological matters such as the teacher's self-esteem, doubts about self-efficacy etc. However, unseen observation avoids some of these sensitive issues since the supervisor is not in the classroom to witness the lesson. As a result, they cannot form an impressionistic judgement. But more importantly, removing the reliance on the observer's subjective interpretation of events provides a platform for building a collaborative trust between the two.

Following on from this, taking into consideration the fact that the role of the supervisor is one of *facilitator* as opposed to *assessor*, the opportunity is there for that awkward power relationship between observer and observee (Wragg 1999) to be redefined in such a way that the two participants start on a more even footing. It is anticipated that as a result of this redistribution of power a more productive and supportive relationship may emerge, which is likely to be conducive to stimulating more candid and meaningful discussion.

Furthermore, Powell (1999) comments on how unseen observation is particularly time effective and easy to schedule since cover does not have to be arranged for one teacher to visit another's class. There are evident financial implications involved here, particularly for institutions with large workforces. In many instances, finance can often be the overriding factor as to whether or not a new initiative or development programme gets off the ground. Undeniably, for most programmes to be effective a significant amount of time needs to be invested by all the relevant stakeholders. On a strategic planning level, this usually implies the inclusion of a number of specifically directed hours in teachers' timetables, which can prove to be costly. Some of these extra costs can be spared with the use of an approach such as unseen observation.

Murdoch (2000) described how unseen observations were offered as an option to teachers with more experience in the large-scale teacher development programme in which he was involved and that they had proven to be an extremely popular alternative to conventional observations. His justification for its popularity can be attributed to two of the advantages discussed above in the light of criticisms of performative approaches to observation i.e. the opportunity to be more adventurous due to the removal of the threat of the loss of face and the power to make one's own decisions, which, in turn, engenders teachers with a sense of confidence in their own capabilities.

Another point made by Powell (1999) is the fact that some issues, e.g. lesson planning, are more receptive to 'honest introspection' than observation. Here he identifies a key factor that underpins its potential success as an alternative model. It is 'honest introspection' that makes or breaks unseen observation and the extent to which teachers are prepared to open themselves up and engage in honest introspection. One could speculate that a teacher's desire to discuss and to openly reflect on their teaching essentially comes from within and cannot be imposed from outside. This is a useful thought to bear in mind as we now move on to examining an example of unseen observation in practice through narrative of the small-scale research project that follows.

Unseen observation research project

I carried out a small-scale, qualitative action research project involving three English to Speakers of Other Languages (ESOL) teachers, each with differing levels of professional experience and qualifications. Teacher A was a NQT in her first teaching post, Teacher B had been teaching for five years and Teacher C had over twenty years' experience. The principal aim of the project was to examine the extent to which unseen observation could be considered a useful form of intervention for promoting active teacher development in an in-service context (O'Leary 2000). My role as 'supervisor' in the project was concerned with heightening and developing the participants' awareness of their pedagogic skills and subject knowledge with a view to them engaging in sustained critical reflection of their practice, which, in turn, could then feed into an improvement in teaching and learning standards in the classroom.

In order to ensure a participant-centred approach to the project, the teachers were allowed to choose the areas of development that they wished to focus on, while I took on the role of supervisor and acted as both an active listener and a facilitator in assisting the professional dialogue. The research design drew on Quirke's model (1996) for using unseen observations, in which he divided the process into five distinct phases:

- Pre-course discussion
- Pre-lesson discussion
- The lesson unseen
- Post-lesson feedback
- End of study interview.

Phase 1: pre-course discussion

The first phase of the project involved a short semi-structured interview with each of the three ESOL teachers who were given the opportunity to discuss their views about language learning, their approach(es) to teaching, the main influences on their teaching and the methodological principles that underpinned these approaches. As Quirke (1996) has highlighted, teachers often have their own theories of language and learning and one of the central aims of unseen observation is to encourage the teacher to engage in a process of reflection and analysis of their theories. Thinking outside of the scope of this project, there is no reason why this approach cannot be adapted to focus on different subject areas.

In order to help the teachers develop their critical reflection in subsequent phases of the project, they were provided with a short checklist (see below) of questions at the end of the first phase to consider whilst planning the lesson and immediately after the completion of the lesson. These questions were designed to act as a guide and stimulus for the teachers' reflection. It is also worth highlighting that it was not my intention to pursue these questions in phase two of the project for reasons discussed below:

- Will/did the students understand this? Are/were my instructions clear and understood?
- Do I need to increase student involvement in this activity?

- Is/was this too difficult for the students?
- Should I try teaching this in a different way?
- Is/was my timing right for this activity?
- Did this activity go as planned?
- Do/did students need more information?
- Do/did I need to improve accuracy on this task?
- Is/was this relevant to the aims of the lesson?
- Is/was this teaching students something that they really need/ed to know?
- Am/was I teaching too much rather than letting the learners work it out for themselves?

(adapted from Richards and Lockhart 1994: 84)

Phase 2: pre-lesson discussion

For each scheduled unseen lesson I met with the teacher for approximately half an hour before the class to discuss their lesson plan. The principal aim of these sessions was for the teacher to provide me with a descriptive outline of the lesson in order to enable me to form a rough mental picture of how the lesson was expected to develop in the classroom and what their anticipated aims and outcomes were. I also expected that the information collected in this discussion would help me to interpret the teacher's description and analysis of the lesson in the post-lesson feedback and serve as a useful reference point for me to explore specific aspects of the lesson with the teacher. We agreed beforehand that the teacher would not be required to submit a written lesson plan as this might lead to undue stress and anxiety on their behalf. It was felt that to do so would affect the very ethos of the study itself and compromise its developmental focus. I therefore recorded the conversations and took notes throughout the meetings. Besides, it was not my intention to interrogate the teachers about the rationale of their lesson plan at this stage as this could potentially have undermined their confidence before the lesson (Phase 3) and created an obstacle to open dialogue in the post-lesson feedback. In short, the main aim of this phase of the project was that of a basic fact-finding mission on my behalf to establish the focus and content of the lesson and what the teacher was hoping to achieve.

Phase 3: the lesson unseen

The lesson takes place, unobserved.

Phase 4: post-lesson feedback

The feedback sessions were programmed to take place an hour after the lessons. It was agreed that this would provide the teacher with enough time for a short break and also to reflect briefly on what had taken place during the lesson before meeting together to discuss it. All three teachers were clearly briefed before the start of the project that the feedback sessions were not intended to be evaluative in any way. It was stressed that the main aim was to assist them in reflecting on their classroom practice and articulating their reasons as to why they acted in the way they did. I also drew attention to the fact that they would be largely responsible for leading and directing the discussion and that my role was as a sounding board and to provide support and encouragement in helping them to make sense of things. It was anticipated that these sessions would be relatively unstructured due to the unpredictability of classroom events, as well as that of the areas of focus selected for discussion and exploration by the teachers themselves.

Phase 5: End of study interviews

The end of study interviews took place two days after the final cycle of phase four of the project had been completed. A standardized interview schedule was used with all three teachers to ensure consistency in the comparability of data. The following questions were therefore asked to all three teachers:

1. What are your thoughts/feelings about the feedback sessions that have taken place over the last eight weeks?
2. Do you feel that you have learnt anything about yourself as a teacher from these sessions? If so, what?
3. What did you like/dislike about the sessions?
4. How did the unseen observation feedback session compare to sessions that you have experienced in the past where the observer has actually observed the lesson?
5. Do you think there have been any changes to your approach to teaching as a result of these sessions?
6. Do you have any more comments that you would like to make regarding your involvement in this project?

Key findings

There is not the scope in this chapter to look at the findings from the study in depth so I have chosen to present a small sample of some of the teachers' comments, along with an overall summary of the key findings and their implications for the future use of unseen observation. The first extract below comes from the end of study interview with Teacher A, who compared the experience of the post-lesson feedback discussion with conventional models of live observation:

> Erm, I don't know, but it makes you feel uneasy having someone watching and scribbling at the same time. It's horrible. That's like when you're in a driving test and they do that as well. It puts you off completely. Your teaching changes because you're completely on edge and your rapport with the students can just go as well so I don't like that but I think this model is much better. It's more worthwhile doing it like this because you get to really think about what you're doing both before and after the class and you don't feel stressed or under pressure.

Teacher A's comment about how the presence of the observer can affect the teacher's confidence and the student–teacher relationship is particularly incisive and links back to the discussion about teacher reactivity on p. 61. In her final comment, she also seemed to suggest that the relaxed atmosphere in which both the pre- and post-lesson sessions were conducted may have facilitated the process of reflection. Interestingly, this final comment also mirrored the beliefs that she expressed in Phase 1 regarding the ideal classroom environment in which to foster learning amongst the ESOL learners with whom she worked.

A noticeable feature of the interviews with Teacher B was the amount of repetition and how much of what she said rarely extended before a descriptive level. For example, when asked to provide a realistic picture of how she felt the lesson had proceeded – usually the first question at the beginning of most post-lesson feedback sessions – she replied, 'I think it went quite well' on all four occasions. Yet, at the same time, no explanation or justification was offered as to why the lesson had been a success even when prompted to do so. Evidence was scarce of the teacher engaging in a process of critical reflection on her practice. There was a distinct absence of the crucial 'what' and 'why' questions referred to by Bartlett (1990) in the previous chapter. It was somewhat surprising that a teacher with over four years' experience should display such a limited sense of critical self-awareness. However, one could argue that Teacher B, even after such a short period in the profession, was starting to show signs of ritualistic, unanalyzed behaviour. This theory was further reinforced by the comments she made in the first phase of the study regarding the absence of change in her pedagogic practice and her subject knowledge since her completion of her ITT course almost five years ago.

Despite not having experienced or witnessed what she described as a 'counselling based approach' to teacher development before, Teacher C confessed that she had always maintained a certain degree of scepticism about such approaches. However, during the end of study interview she expressed her surprise at how much she had actually enjoyed the experience and how useful she had found it to be. She contextualized her interpretation of the potential benefits of the approach by citing a concrete example from one of the feedback sessions that had taken place in phase 3:

> Well, just taking an example from the most recent session. I was having problems with organizing groups, with classroom dynamics and changing partners and having someone sitting there to talk about it with helped. I'd say something and you'd comment on that and take me a step further. I was forced to think it through because you were there listening and I arrived at a solution there with you that I probably wouldn't have bothered to come up with on my own and I certainly wouldn't have thought it through in that way. I think that is the main benefit. . . . It just pushes you to think things through. And also to have somebody to ask about things is really good because you weren't simply passive. You did respond when I asked *you* a question.

Teacher C's comments illustrated the importance of the role of collaboration in teacher development. Within unseen observation, the supervisor is not simply – as she points out – a passive listener, but someone who works in partnership with the teacher to enable them to heighten their sense of self-awareness and to develop their critically reflective skills.

In her response to question four (i.e. comparing unseen with conventional models of observation), it was interesting to note that she raised the issue of high and low inference skills and observer subjectivity as discussed in Chapter 4:

> Well, this way is a whole lot more pleasant because, as I was saying to you yesterday, you know, the person who's doing the feedback doesn't have to have seen every tiny, silly, embarrassing mistake the teacher makes in the classroom. And you don't have to tell them about it and so you're free to concentrate on maybe more higher level things.

Because one thing that can be annoying to any teacher at any stage of their career is if somebody focuses on a little thing in the lesson that just happens to be the bee in their bonnet and doesn't take a global view that can make people feel very, very defensive and very closed because, you know, you think, well, they picked on that because it's *their* thing and I don't think it's very important.

As Teacher C suggests, one of the advantages of unseen observation is that it enables the teacher to dispense with what they might regard as insignificant issues when it comes to feedback and thus to focus on the more meaningful aspects of their teaching, as it is the 'observee' rather than the 'observer' that controls the focus and direction of the dialogue. Besides, as we saw in Chapter 3 when discussing Peel's (2005) autobiographical study of peer observation in HE, using observation as a stimulus for reflecting on wider pedagogic/ curriculum issues can be more beneficial than discussion centring solely on the observed lesson itself.

Given the modest scale of this project, it is impossible to draw generalizable conclusions about the effectiveness of unseen observation as an alternative intervention in teacher development. It is also important to recognize that meaningful and lasting change in teacher behaviour is likely to be a slow process which takes place over a sustained period of time. Such change is therefore difficult to pinpoint in a study like this. However, the findings certainly throw up a number of interesting areas for further exploration.

In short, one of the key findings to emerge was that successful teacher development seemed dependent on the heightening of the teacher's sense of self-awareness and their ability to engage in a systematic process of critical reflection on their practice. The data analysis of the recorded dialogues with two of the teachers involved in the study both affirmed the usefulness of unseen observation as a stimulus for critical reflection. One could speculate that this might create the appropriate conditions under which teachers can ultimately begin to take more ownership of their own development, aided by the guidance of their supervisor whose responsibility it would be to equip them with the necessary enabling skills in order to do so.

There also appeared to be a certain amount of evidence available from the recorded sessions to support Edge's (1992) view that the process of communicating our thoughts to others orally can lead to the clarification and deeper understanding of these thoughts. Once again, the role of the supervisor in facilitating this process would seem to be important. The findings from this study would tend to suggest that certain key skills are required if the supervisor is to play an effective role in guiding the discussion. One might assume that such skills are comparable to those required by a counsellor. However, the exact nature of these skills and how one might go about training supervisors to employ them raises an interesting area for further research.

The findings from Teacher B provided an interesting contrast with those of the other two teachers. They suggested that if a teacher manifests a certain resistance to reflecting and talking openly about their teaching, this could threaten to invalidate the effectiveness of an intervention like unseen observation. This brings to mind the old saying of 'you can lead a horse to water but you can't make it drink'. Admittedly some teachers may be more predisposed to engage in critical reflection on their practice than others, but the less willing a teacher is to take the lead and set the agenda during feedback, the more dominant a role is played by the supervisor, thus defeating one of the primary objectives of a model like unseen observation.

Finally, it would appear that the scope for future research into the application of unseen observation in teacher development is potentially very wide. In the first instance, it would be interesting to chart its effects in a sustained longitudinal study with a larger group of teachers. Added to this, although this particular study focused on its application in the context of language teaching, there is no reason why it could not be adapted to incorporate other subject areas across the curriculum.

Case study three: remote mobile video technology

The use of video to study and record lessons has been a feature of classroom observation for several decades, but the use of remote mobile video technology is a relatively recent innovation in teacher development and assessment and as such represents a growing area of research (Calandra *et al* 2008). Recent advances in technology have meant that lessons can now be observed remotely, synchronously and asynchronously, across digital networks (Dyke *et al* 2008). Web 2.0 technology has given rise to a new range of applications and possibilities for the use of video in classrooms that combines aspects of video conferencing, video streaming, computer controlled cameras, wireless sound systems etc. Subject to the appropriate resources being in place, this means that teachers are able to observe and interact with each other in classrooms all around the world. Potentially, this has significant repercussions for the way in which observation is used in and across educational institutions now and in the future.

Traditionally, the observation of classroom practice has relied on live, face-to-face visits from observers. This practice is not without its logistical and financial challenges for educational providers such as universities offering ITT programmes that encompass a large network of partner schools, colleges and academies stretching across a wide geographical area. University tutors often spend a lot of time observing student teachers in the classroom in a placement or workplace context. Not only is this expensive in terms of staffing hours, but also the travelling costs associated with such visits. A recent calculation of approximate costs incurred across ITE programmes in my own workplace revealed that just under £450,000 was spent on this activity per academic year. For this reason alone, remote mobile video technology is worth considering as a cost-effective means of supplementing and/or replacing live classroom observation visits. This is what might be viewed as the 'business case' for using such technology for observations, though admittedly the hardware and software costs need to be weighed up alongside this, together with on-going subscription costs. Each set of 'hardware' typically includes a live-view camera, wireless microphone and earpiece. The 'software' tends to be charged on a subscription basis and is often sold in 'packages' by the companies offering these products commercially. Having briefly touched on the 'business case' for the use of such technology, what about the 'pedagogic case'?

In 2007 a group of researchers at the University of Nottingham's School of Education carried out an external evaluation of a project involving the use of remote video technology with 29 PGCE student teachers of science, all of whom were following a teacher education programme at the University of Sussex. One of the principal aims of the evaluation was to 'make judgments about the benefits of the project for student teachers' (Mitchell *et al* 2007). These student teachers were asked to complete questionnaires and participate in interviews as part of the data collection.

There were three key findings to emerge from the evaluation. The first pointed to how these student teachers' preparation for their first teaching placements had benefitted as a result of their exposure via video links to the classrooms of the schools in which they were due to be placed, thus leading to an enhanced familiarity with the classroom environment and the development of a situated awareness and understanding of the application of their subject area and the learners they would be working with.

The second revealed how by watching both synchronous and asynchronous lessons via the webcams, these student teachers were exposed to contextualized examples of how some of the theory they had been taught at university was actually being applied in practice, which in turn made it easier for their university tutors to make explicit some of the theory–practice links by drawing on illustrative examples from these videoed classrooms.

Thirdly, the evaluation brought to light how the use of remote video technology was conducive to the 'unobtrusive observation of student teachers by mentors, university tutors and their peers' (p. 3), which offered the potential for a more effective and constructive feedback session between observer and observee, partly for some of the reasons surrounding observer reactivity discussed in the previous section.

One of the areas explored by Dyke *et al* (2008) in their action research project involving in-service trainee teachers was the extent to which mobile digital video technology could represent a valid replacement for face-to-face observation. They found that trainee teachers were open to the use of the technology as a supplement to face-to-face observation but only once the observers had familiarized themselves with the context of their learning environment and the learners by observing them *in situ* before introducing the use of such technology. This highlights the importance of an established relationship between observer and observee and that the former has a situated understanding of the contexts in which they teach. This is an interesting area worthy of further investigation, particularly in relation to how the technology-mediated experience of remote mobile video technology compares to the face-to-face experience for both trainee and experienced teachers, what the benefits and shortcomings are of both, how the process of teacher development and learning might be advanced by combining the use of these two approaches and if so how they might best be combined.

Dyke *et al*'s (2008) studies also revealed a 'strong correlation in the professional judgements of teaching performances by both online and in-class observers'. In relation to this, Calandra *et al* (2006: 138) have argued that digital recordings 'lend a more unbiased authenticity to reflective dialogue among peers and teacher educators'. This is largely due to the fact that having video evidence of an observed lesson reduces the need to rely on the observer and observee's recall and interpretation of what happened during the lesson as opposed to being able to see and to re-play what actually happened. The video clips can therefore help to inject a sense of objectivity or detachment into the reflective dialogue between observer and observee. Calandra *et al* (2006) further claim that digital video plays an important role in promoting reflection and the development of teacher identity.

Wang and Hartley (2003) have argued that one of the reasons why digital video technology is a valuable resource is because recordings can be viewed repeatedly, edited, annotated etc. One such interactive use of video technology that can be used for a range of different purposes with classroom observation, particularly on ITE and CPD programmes, is what is sometimes referred to as the 'interrupted story'. This is when a clip from a recorded observation is played and the group are then given multiple choices to either speculate what happened next or to choose a particular course of action and to discuss the consequences of their chosen course of action. For example, the clip may show a behaviour management incident involving a learner or group of learners. After pausing/stopping the clip, the group of teachers is asked to make a particular choice e.g. to ignore the behaviour, to confront the learner(s) about their behaviour, to ask them to leave the classroom etc. One of the advantages of using remote video technology in this way on ITT or CPD programmes could be that there is a greater likelihood of capturing 'real' events in the classroom as learners may not be aware of the presence of the camera in contrast to the presence of an observer and/or someone operating a video camera in the corner of the room.

Let us now move on to discussing some of the distinctive features of state-of-the-art mobile video technology along with its advantages and disadvantages.

Table 8.1 outlines some of the key features and functions of the technology currently available, some of which are worth expanding on in more detail and relating to the classroom context. The first two features listed emphasize the remote access and control of the technology. What this means in practical terms is that the observer is able to visit the class 'virtually' as opposed to physically, and provided both the observer and the observee have

Table 8.1 Summary of the key features and functions of remote mobile digital video technology.

Key feature/function	Description
1. Remote access	• Observer can be anywhere so long as they have access to the Internet • Similar to the concept of a webcam that is linked to a webpage
2. Remote video control	• Observer can remotely control the camera • Camera can be controlled by a mouse with zoom in/out, pan, tilt functions etc
3. Video recording with embedded feedback and commentary	• Observers can record observations that can be embedded with commentary, observation notes and feedback • Lessons can be recorded and the observee can watch them in their own time, accompanied by written and oral comments from the observer inserted at specific points in the recording
4. Two-way dialogue through earpiece and microphone	• Omni-directional microphones that capture high-quality audio in the classroom so teacher and learners can be easily heard • Observer is able to communicate with the observee through an earpiece and microphone which means they are able to offer instantaneous feedback and advice
5. Portability	• Many current products are lightweight and portable
6. Unobtrusiveness of camera	• Most modern cameras are relatively inconspicuous and thus less likely to affect the validity and reliability of the observational data than the presence of an observer in the room • Not always possible to know when the camera is recording
7. Storage security	• Many of the current products available offer a high level of security where data are stored on secure servers that are only accessible to authorized users

the necessary equipment, they are able to communicate as though the observer were in the room with the observee. There are several advantages to this. Firstly, it offers a cost saving alternative to the observer having to visit the observee on site. Secondly, as highlighted in point six above, it can help to reduce the intrusive element of the observer's classroom presence and the knock-on effects of this as discussed in Chapter 4. This could prove to be a particularly effective strategy for capturing evidence of, for example, challenging areas like behaviour management in the classroom, which are notoriously difficult to get a reliable insight into when an observer is present, especially if the observer also occupies a senior position in the institution, thus making learners even more wary of their presence. In contrast to this though, some might argue that, in the wrong hands, it could be used as a form of panoptic surveillance with both teachers and learners not knowing when and by whom they are being watched during lessons.

With regards to the video recording and embedded feedback and commentary, one of the technological benefits of this is that it allows classroom data to be recorded in a systematic manner and for the observer to make comments alongside a specific time slot during the observation so that the observee is immediately able to relate the comment to the actual point in the lesson. Recording the data in this way allows the observer and the observee to discuss what actually took place and to reflect on the teacher's strengths as well as identifying areas for improvement in the feedback dialogue. It also provides the observer with the opportunity to concentrate on observing what is going on in the classroom rather than having to compile a large collection of documentation/paperwork as part of a trail of evidence. In other words, it frees up the observer and observee to interact.

Another advantage of this type of video technology is its capacity to be used as a coaching tool. In the case of synchronous recordings, the earpiece allows the observee to be coached discretely and to receive instantaneous advice and guidance from their remote observer that they can apply in the lesson in real time.

As recordings can be stored remotely on a server for an unlimited time, it does not take long before a repository of recorded lessons is built up. These recordings can then be used as illustrative examples of particular aspects of practice, both good and bad. In the ITT context, for example, the teacher educator or trainer might want to exploit them as a means of training student teachers how to observe classes effectively so that they are able to maximize the time they spend observing others on teaching practice, which often forms a precursor to beginning their own teaching on many teacher education programmes. Here the teacher educator or trainer is able to draw on contextualized, recorded classroom events as illustrative examples of different forms of practice. Similarly, specific aspects of pedagogic skills or knowledge can be focused on with a view to sharing good practice and/ or modelling practice for others. Other uses might include using the technology as a platform for standardization exercises between observers e.g. between teacher educators and workplace/subject mentors whether this be based on synchronous or asynchronous recordings.

Finally, in a recent report into professional development in schools, Ofsted (2010) acknowledged that one of the most effective means of sharing good practice and teacher expertise was by encouraging the development of collaborative learning communities and that the most successful schools made great efforts to establish such communities of collaborative learning among their staff. This links closely to the concept of 'Communities of Practice', a term most often associated with the work of Wenger (1998), who sees learning as an inherently social and collective activity in which the 'community' is joined by a shared interest. In the context of this discussion, the 'shared interest' is that of teachers developing their professional skills and knowledge to improve the educational experience of their learners. Digital technology has increasingly become a driving force behind the establishment of such communities, particularly in the domain of social networking so extending this to the context of professional learning communities through the use of emerging technology would seem a natural progression.

Summary

This chapter has explored three alternative models of classroom observation via three separate case studies. Each model offers new ways of working with the medium of observation and as such has the potential to offer additional insights into how it can be used to further our understanding of teaching and learning and ultimately improve the learner experience. Like all forms of intervention, if any of these models are to have a tangible impact on teachers' professional learning and development then there needs to be an adequate investment of time on the part of employers for teachers to engage in this activity. Equally important though is for staff to be empowered with appropriate levels of professional autonomy and trust to engage with such forms of intervention in ways that allow them to expand their existing knowledge and skills base.

Discussion topics/tasks

1. *Alternative models of classroom observation*
   You have been asked to participate in a focus group at your workplace, the aim of which is to canvass the views of staff regarding alternative models of classroom observation to those currently in use. Make a list of your suggestions and talk them through with a colleague.
2. *Alternative models of observation feedback*
   You have been asked to participate in a focus group at your workplace, the aim of which is to canvass the views of staff regarding alternative models of observation feedback to those currently in use. Make a list of your suggestions and talk them through with a colleague.
3. *Alternative models in action*
   Depending on resources available in your workplace, choose one of the three alternative models of observation discussed in this chapter and carry out a small-scale project within your department. You may decide to choose particular issues/aspects of practice to focus on.

Chapter 9

Conclusion

This book has sought to provide the reader with a situated and critically informed insight into how classroom observation is used in the English education system. From establishing the backdrop to its emergence, to exploring its use as a method of assessment and as a vehicle for professional learning and development, it has attempted to explain the role of observation in the professional lives of practitioners. It has been argued throughout the book that although observation is a multi-purpose mechanism, in recent decades it has come to be viewed rather narrowly by policymakers and employers as an assessment tool for monitoring and measuring teacher performance. There is little evidence in current government policy to suggest that this emphasis is likely to change at any point in the near future, despite a growing bank of research arguing that such performative approaches have reached the threshold of their capacity in bringing about meaningful and sustained improvements in the quality of teaching and learning. So, where do we go from here then? I would argue that it is important to challenge the hegemony of performative models of classroom observation and this starts with engaging practitioners in debate by getting them to question current practices and critically reflect on their use and impact.

For example, is the current practice of graded lesson observation still fit for purpose? Why do we insist on assessing the performance of teachers against this arbitrary Ofsted 4-point scale? As other researchers have argued, 'there is no published research which confirms that meaningful grading is possible' (Cope *et al* 2003: 683) and yet it continues to be the dominant and preferred model of most colleges and schools. Other professions such as medicine and law are not subjected to this arbitrary system of measurement. Why therefore should teachers be? What purpose does it serve? Who benefits from such practice? Doctors, for example, are either deemed 'fit to practise' or not. Why cannot the same rules apply to teachers? Whilst there are and always will be differences of opinion across the relevant stakeholder groups in education as to what constitutes a 'good' or 'outstanding' teacher, it would seem a much more realistic and achievable target to establish a consensus and consistency about judgements relating to 'fitness to practise' and whether a teacher is deemed competent or not. This would in no way mean settling for mediocrity or represent a threat to the 'pursuit of excellence' as neoliberal policymakers might argue, but would be an acceptance that teaching is not an exact science and that even the most 'outstanding' teachers are not and cannot be outstanding in every lesson they teach.

There is little doubt that teachers value observation as an important tool for developing their pedagogic and subject specific knowledge and skills. Conscientious and committed teachers continuously look for ways in which to improve their professional practice. In my work as a teacher educator and educational researcher one of the things that I repeatedly encounter among teachers is their enthusiasm to learn from and share best practice with each other. In spite of the need to comply with national standards and performance indicators that by their very nature have a tendency to encourage a culture of individualism and isolation among the profession, teachers crave opportunities for collegial support and professional collaboration. We have seen through some of the examples discussed in this book (e.g. peer observation, lesson study etc.) that there are feasible alternatives to current hegemonized models of observation that have an important role to play in developing cultures of professional learning. But if these alternatives are to make a meaningful contribution then there needs to be a clear commitment on the part of all those involved to create and encourage the necessary conditions for them to be able to succeed.

So, what might the future hold as far as the continued use of classroom observation is concerned and what needs to be done to change the status quo? The issue of how best to make use of a mechanism like classroom observation is of course dependent upon important factors such as context and purpose. Yet surely what transcends even these is the desire to encourage teachers to be the best that they can possibly be and in turn to encourage their learners to continuously strive for success. This inevitably raises the question of what it is current approaches to classroom observation are trying to achieve. Is it about improving the quality of teaching and learning as a whole? If it is, then the adoption of a performative model in which teaching skills and attributes are itemized and assessed according to the use of a grading scale seems to do little to contribute to this. Such models of practice divert attention from developing understanding of pedagogy and stimulating meaningful, critical analysis of the process of teaching and learning on the part of both observer and observee. The end result is that observation becomes little more than a box-ticking exercise, devoid of significance and substance for the observer or observee. If, on the other hand, schools and colleges are prepared to accept the limitations of existing hegemonic models and to embrace alternative, evidence-based approaches to observation that are driven by a desire to further practitioners' understanding of the reciprocal relationship between teaching and learning, then perhaps we can make some real headway to achieving the much sought after continuous improvement in the standards and quality of the learners' experience.

An important message to emerge throughout this book has been the need to re-establish professional trust and autonomy for teachers to allow them to take ownership of their professional learning and development rather than having priorities imposed on them by others. What teachers need is more collaboration and less coercion when it comes to interventions in classrooms and a greater trust in their professionalism and professional capabilities to steer change and improvement.

When it comes to assessing and measuring teacher performance, I would argue that whatever systems are used, they need to be informed and shaped by practitioners in the field along with educational research. A 'one-size-fits-all' model of observation clearly does not work. My own research has highlighted how, as a performative instrument, observation has reached its threshold of effectiveness in terms of what it can tell us about the standards of teaching and learning in classrooms and ultimately its ability to improve them. Acknowledging these limitations is an important first step in moving beyond this impasse. The next lies in exploring the alternatives and putting forward the argument for how and why they can contribute to existing knowledge. Peer-based models of observation have been shown to offer the potential to enhance pedagogic understanding and in turn contribute to the on-going process of teacher development. Putting the case forward for such models as a viable replacement to dominant performative models is now the next challenge that lies ahead for teachers if they are to reclaim classroom observation as a tool for empowering their professional learning.

I would like to finish with a quote from Caroline, the vice principal of one of the largest colleges in England, who when asked during a research interview whether she saw a particular model of observation as being more worthwhile than others replied:

> I don't have any empirical evidence for my answer here, but I think if we could get a community of practitioners who actually valued the process of helping and supporting one another and would happily go in and out of each other's lessons and if we had daily conversations between teachers about what's working and what's not and idea sharing happening on an informal basis, not a formal basis, we will have won the battle. And the more formal systems you put in place probably militates against all of that because people then see it as a management driven initiative so we're not there yet but that's where we should be. In my view that would be the best possible environment, community of professionals, self-reflecting, sharing, talking, creatively thinking together and talking about their experiences would be wonderful.

Caroline's vision of a 'community of professionals' collaborating and sharing knowledge and experience on an informal basis offers a credible alternative to current hegemonized models of observation. The extent to which such alternatives could or would sit comfortably alongside managerialist systems of performativity and accountability is questionable. Surely though, as Caroline suggests, the way forward in maximizing the potential of observation as a tool for improving the quality and understanding of teaching and learning lies in the adoption of an enquiry-based approach where teachers are empowered to become active researchers of their classrooms. Until this is acknowledged by the relevant stakeholders, particularly policymakers, then the hegemony of performative lesson observation looks set to continue and with it an impoverished understanding of what makes for effective teaching and learning.

UCU lesson observation checklist – February 2012

UCU lesson observations bargaining checklist

UCU believes strongly that lesson observation procedures must be negotiated between the UCU branch and college management resulting in a formal agreement.

UCU recognises that there is an appropriate place for lesson observations within institutions so long as they are conducted with the right safeguards and procedures in place.

The philosophy and approach underpinning lesson observations schemes must be

- That they are supportive of those being observed
- That it is an opportunity for teaching professionals to receive advice and guidance from fellow professional teachers on their strengths and weaknesses
- To provide material for professional reflection
- To identify areas for CPD and further training and support

Acceptable aims of lesson observation

- To observe actual teaching and learning in order to raise the quality of teaching and learning and so enhance the students' learning experience
- To provide evidence for part of the college's/service's formal appraisal scheme and discussions (not linked to pay)
- To provide evidence for probation and professional formation reports where appropriate
- To provide evidence for appropriate formal procedures such as capability and competence
- To provide a system of identifying, sharing, improving and developing good practice
- To provide evidence for the college self assessment reports
- To provide evidence of teaching and learning during an OFSTED Inspection
- To provide evidence that would encourage staff to reflect on their delivery styles and build on their skills

Issues requiring formal agreement

- Number and frequency – one per year under normal circumstances i.e. not part of capability procedure or probation period etc. No more than three per teaching year.

- Notice period – the amount of notice given by management for the lesson to be observed, seek at least three weeks' notice.
- Window period – should be as small as possible, exact lesson notified in advance is optimal. Window should never be longer than the equivalent period of an OFSTED inspection.
- Selection of lesson – good practice is the line manager and teacher being observed should be involved in selecting lesson to be observed.
- Who observes – observers should be trained teachers, trained in observing. Where peer observation is used a panel of observers should be used from which those being observed can choose.
- Purpose – the purpose of the observation should be clear and agreed.
- Feedback – immediate brief verbal followed up with more detailed and written.
- Outcomes – should be agreed, observed also able make notes on records of observation.
- Grades – where grading is used there should be agreement on what grades result in action being required. UCU opposes compulsory action resulting from satisfactory or grade 3 observations.
- Appeal – there should be a right of appeal when observations are not carried out according to agreed procedures or where staff are unhappy with the outcomes.

Criteria for semi-structured observation report form

Taken from the University of Wolverhampton's ITE programmes in PCE

Lesson observations – essential and desirable features of classroom practice

Level 1 – Semester 1

To pass a lesson observation at level 1 the entire **ESSENTIAL** features **MUST** be achieved and some of the desirable **MAY** be achieved. Features in the desirable column may be used as the basis for future action planning. A fail will be awarded if one or more features from the essential column is not achieved.

Level 2 – Semester 2

To pass a lesson observation at level 2 (modules stratified at level 2 or 3) **ALL** features in **BOTH** the essential and desirable columns **MUST** be achieved.

It may be possible to meet some of the features through discussion during the feedback session following the observation.

At both levels the Subject Evaluation conducted by the Subject Specialist and Placement Teaching Mentor **MUST** be satisfactorily completed over the observation period.

LLUK/LSIS Standards	Level 1 – (Essential for Semester 1)	Level 2 – (Desirable for Semester 1, Essential for Semester 2)
Preparation and Planning AP1.1 AP4.1 BP2.1 BP2.2 BP2.3 BP2.4 BP3.3 BP5.1 BP5.2 CP1.1 CP1.2 CP2.1 CP3.1 CP3.2 CP3.3 CP3.4 CP3.5 CP4.1 CP4.2 DP1.1 DP1.2 DP1.3 DP2.1 DP2.2 EP1.1 EP1.2 EP1.3 EP2.1 EP2.2 EP2.3 EP2.4 EP3.1 EP3.2 EP4.1	The lesson planner has been used to: • Identify aims and outcomes • Acknowledge prior skills and knowledge • Provide evidence of careful planning • Reference skills development where appropriate • Indicate awareness of additional support where appropriate	The lesson planner has been used to: • Signpost specific aims and outcomes • Specify outcomes for skills development where appropriate • Plan appropriately for differentiation • Integrate an appropriate variety of assessment activities/strategies throughout the session

(Continued)

LLUK/LSIS Standards	Level 1 – (Essential for Semester 1)	Level 2 – (Desirable for Semester 1, Essential for Semester 2)
Learning and Teaching Activity AP6.2 BP1.1 BP1.2 BP1.3 BP2.1 BP2.2 BP2.3 BP2.4 BP2.5 BP3.1 BP3.2 BP3.3 BP5.2 CP2.1 CP3.1 CP3.2 CP3.3 CP3.5 EP1.1 EP1.2 EP1.3 EP4.1	• Students actively engaged in learning process • Evidence of differentiated activities/methods – i.e. not one mode of delivery • Reference made to learning outcomes • Appropriate feedback given (verbal and non-verbal) • Positioning • Communication appropriate to context/student group and subject • Recognition of skills development in assessment activities • Clarity of instructions • Opportunities for assessing learning • Lesson planner followed wisely i.e. flexibility allowed for in responding to learners' spontaneous needs and context • Clear demonstrations and examples given to tasks • Teacher promotes English/Maths/ICT skills where appropriate	• Learning outcomes are referenced and reviewed • Methods used identify and meet the needs of individual learners throughout the session • Effective management of transition points in the session • Active and independent learning is promoted • Skills developed in an integrated process • Effective management of physical environment/space • Focussed learning environment for students throughout the session
Equal Opportunities and Safeguarding	• Students dealt with respectfully • Equality of opportunity for students • Language use appropriate to level/age/background of students • Attempts are made to include all learners • Reference made to appropriate frameworks, such as ECM/ELM agenda	• Communication strategies meet the needs of individual students • Inappropriate comments or behaviour challenged via institution's Equal Opportunities Policy • Inclusion of all learners in all activities • Considered reference made to appropriate frameworks, such as ECM/ELM agenda

LLUK/LSIS Standards	Level 1 – (Essential for Semester 1)	Level 2 – (Desirable for Semester 1, Essential for Semester 2)
Resources BP3.1 BP5.1 BP5.2 CP3.5 DP1.2	• Resources are appropriate to the needs of all students • Variety of resources and activities and reflect diversity of students • Resources recognize topic sensitivity where appropriate • Production quality high and language use is accurate • Resources are current	• Diversity of teaching and learning resources • Production of own resources and/or adaptation of existing resources • Resources enhance teaching and learning
Assessment EP1.1 EP1.2 EP1.3 EP2.1 EP2.2 EP2.3 EP3.1 EP3.2 EP4.1	• Assessment activities are linked to learning outcomes • Appropriate variety of assessment methods used to check and support learning • A contextualized introduction to assessment activities is provided for learners • Assessments used are valid, reliable and fit for purpose • Use made of questioning strategies • Appropriate and sufficient feedback provided to learners	• Self-assessment and peer assessment used in appropriate situations • Students take appropriate responsibility for assessment of their learning • Effective use made of a range of questioning strategies • Assessments challenge all learners • Positive responses are made to learner contributions
Personal Qualities and Professionalism AS1 AS2 AS3 AS4 AS5 AS6 AS7 BS1 BS2 BS3 BS4 BS5 CS1 CS2 CS3 CS4 DS1 DS2 DS3 ES1 ES2 ES3 ES4 ES5 AP1.1 AP6.2 BP1.1 BP1.2 BP1.3 BP2.5	• Positive relationship/rapport established with students • Confident classroom manner • Enthusiasm and interest for subject and students • Knowledge of subject accurate and up to date • High expectations of all students; committed to raising educational achievement • Demonstrates empathy and respect for learners and where appropriate for colleagues • Punctuality and lateness addressed appropriately • The session proceeds with purpose and pace • Inappropriate behaviour/s are challenged promptly and appropriately • Appropriate voice projection • Acts with integrity and consistency • Safeguarding matters and Health and Safety issues are appropriately considered	
Teacher Self-evaluation BP2.6 BP3.4 BP5.2	This section must be completed by the teacher after the observation and should include references to issues raised in feedback with the observer(s)	

Criteria for highly structured observation report form

No.	Performance Indicator	Outstanding	Good	Satisfactory	Unsatisfactory
	Grade	1	2	3	4
1	Introduction, aims and learning outcomes	Comprehensive introduction – aims and outcomes explained, shared and displayed. Learners demonstrate very clear understanding about learning purpose.	Clear aims and outcomes shared with learners at beginning of session. Learners clear about learning purpose.	Brief, general introduction. Learning outcomes basic but realistic in lesson context. Learners generally know what they will be doing.	Little if any introduction. No clear aims and outcomes stated or shared with learner. Learners unsure, confused or do not know what they will be doing.
2	Pace and structure of learning	Pace clearly matches subject and learner level. Activities very well structured and timed to maintain interest and stimulate learning for all learners.	Pace matches subject and learner level. Most activities well timed and structured.	Overall pace promotes some learning and interest. Some activities insufficiently matched to learner/subject level.	Activities lack pace/rigour and do not promote learning. Learners lose interest and concentration at some point. Many learners not stretched or over-challenged or confused or struggling to understand
3	Assessment techniques	Highly effective range of assessment techniques used to check all learners' knowledge/progress throughout. Progress and achievements recorded and evaluated regularly with the learner.	Range of assessment techniques used to enhance and check learning throughout. Learner is involved in the evaluation and recording of achievements.	Assessment used to recapitulate, consolidate and confirm learning but range of techniques limited (e.g. over reliance on questions and observation). Some involvement of learners in recording and evaluation.	Ineffective, insufficient or no assessment of learners' progress and achievements. Learners not involved in evaluation and recording achievements.
4	Learning methods	Excellent range/creative approaches used to maximize learning and involve learners; highly appropriate for subject.	Good range of learning methods used to engage learners and promote learning.	Limited range but tutor makes some effort to vary approach and involve learners.	Too much emphasis on 'chalk and talk'. Insufficient variety and involvement of learners. Learners are passive and disengaged. Tutor makes little (or no) attempt to match teaching methods to subject or learner needs.

(Continued)

No.	Performance Indicator	Outstanding	Good	Satisfactory	Unsatisfactory
	Grade	1	2	3	4
5	Identification and support of individual learning needs/ differentiation	Highly effective identification of individual learning needs through use of learning style analyses plus effective initial and diagnostic assessment techniques. Excellent and clearly explained support provided through differentiated resources and activities – extension work, structured group/individual work and in-class customized support (as appropriate).	Good identification of individual needs plus initial and diagnostic assessment techniques. Good individual support evident through development and use of resources, activities and support in lesson (where appropriate).	Some identification of individual learning needs plus initial and diagnostic assessment techniques. Some individual support evident through development and use of resources, activities and support in lesson (where appropriate).	Insufficient or no identification of individual learning needs. Little evidence of initial assessment. Insufficient or no support of individual learning needs in lesson – resources and activities insufficiently developed or amended to meet different learning needs or levels and/or insufficient support in-class even though clearly needed.
6	Inclusive learning strategies	All teaching and reference materials promote inclusion through highly effective use of diverse examples. Tutor models best practice through use of inclusive language, attitudes and terminology.	All teaching and reference materials support inclusion through effective use of diverse examples. Tutor models good practice through use of inclusive language, attitudes and terminology.	Teaching and reference materials demonstrate knowledge of inclusion through use of some diverse examples. Tutor uses appropriate language, attitudes and terminology.	Little or no knowledge or awareness of inclusive learning principles. Tutor uses inappropriate language, attitudes and terminology.
7	Tutor style and communication skills	Passionate about subject. Outstanding oral presentation skills, which engage learners and promote sustained motivation and concentration. Positive verbal/non-verbal behavior; strong voice, fluent speech patterns, clear eye contact, enthusiastic manner and open body language and expression.	Animated delivery shows a good level of commitment and energy and holds learners' interests. Good presentation skills, which promote motivation and concentration. Tutor demonstrates effective verbal and non-verbal communication skills.	Moderate enthusiasm for subject. Delivery clear but may be lacking in 'sparkle'. Oral presentation skills are satisfactory. Tutor uses generally appropriate verbal and non-verbal skills.	Ineffective or unenthusiastic delivery, which does not engage learners. Some of the tutor's verbal/non-verbal skills are ineffective or inappropriate – eye contact, voice, speech, manner, attitude, body movements etc. Learners are bored, uninterested or disengaged.

8	Tutor knowledge	Very knowledgeable and up-to-date in subject area. Very effective reference to vocational/professional examples (where appropriate).	Clearly knowledgeable in subject area and uses relevant vocational/professional examples to good effect in the lesson.	Generally knowledgeable in subject area but some professional updating would improve interest/quality.	Displays a confused, inaccurate or inadequate grasp of some aspects of subject area.
9	Review/recap/summary of learning	Highly effective review of learning at intervals throughout lesson and very clear (and creative) summary linked to learning aims/objectives and to next lesson.	Good review/recap at points in the lesson and clear summary of learning progress at end of lesson with reference to next.	Some review of learning and brief summary at end of lesson and brief reference to next lesson.	Insufficient or no review of learning and/or insufficient or no summary at end of lesson and little or no reference to next lesson.
10	Achievement	Outstanding standards of work. All learners demonstrating excellent knowledge and skills, which illustrate working well above standard for level and stage of programme.	Good standards of work. Learners using good skills and work at or beyond standard for level and stage.	Satisfactory standard of work. Majority of learners working appropriately for standard and stage of programme.	Unsatisfactory or inadequate standard of work. Level of knowledge and skills demonstrated inappropriate for stage and level of programme.
11	Management of learning	Behaviour and standards professionally and vocationally appropriate and demonstrate high mutual teacher/learner value/respect.	Relationships in the lesson reflect vocational/professional context. Tutor and learners value each other.	Instructions generally clear. Appropriate working relationship overall.	Ineffective management of group/individual activities. Instructions not always clear, tutor cannot impose him/herself, inappropriate noise levels, learners not always listening or responding.
12	Learning involvement and response	All learners actively involved and engaged. Highly motivated/interested. Ask and answer questions well. High levels of cooperation, interaction and learners use/take initiative in learning and take responsibility where appropriate.	Good involvement and engagement of learners. Good level of interest and attention. Some examples of effective cooperation, interaction and initiative.	Satisfactory involvement and engagement of learners. Stay on task for majority of lesson. Answer questions; do what has to be done and nothing more.	Insufficient or no involvement or engagement of learners. Learners told what to do and when to do it. Relatively passive. Limited concentration and interest. Some learners bored and showing it.

(Continued)

No.	Performance Indicator	Outstanding	Good	Satisfactory	Unsatisfactory
	Grade	1	2	3	4
13	Attendance and punctuality	Learners display commitment to learning through excellent record of attendance and punctuality (90%+ attendance and exemplary punctuality).	Good attendance and punctuality records (85% attendance and all/nearly all learners on time).	Satisfactory attendance and punctuality (80% and above attendance and most learners on time).	Unsatisfactory attendance and punctuality (less than 75%) attendance and pattern of low attendance overall. Unsatisfactory punctuality – less than two-thirds present at start of lesson.
14	Skills for Life – basic skills (key skill/functional skill) – identified and cross-referenced	Highly effective identification and cross-referencing of basic skills in lesson plan activities/resources. Shared with learners.	Effective identification and cross-referencing of skills in lesson plan activities/resources. Shared with learners.	Some identification and cross-reference of basic in lesson plan activities/resources. Some sharing with learners.	Insufficient or no identification and cross-referencing of skills in lesson plan activities/resources. Learners not informed or opportunities lost.
15	Learning environment	Professional learning environment, wholly relevant, fit for purpose, accessible and excellently and safely equipped.	Good accommodation, fit for purpose, well laid out and resourced, accessible and safely equipped.	Satisfactory accommodation, fairly basic but safe. Does not hinder learning.	Inadequate for learning purposes and/or unsafe. Hinders learning.
16	Health and Safety	Highly effective group/individual management. Clear directions and health and safety stressed throughout.	Good management of group activities. Clear instructions and good emphasis on health and safety.	Satisfactory management of group. Health and safety appropriate.	Ineffective management of group/individual activities. Ineffective or inadequate management of health and safety.

17	Scheme of Work	Comprehensive scheme includes course aims/objectives and sequenced teaching and learning activities, methods, resources and planned assessment. Detailed information which provides excellent insight into planned learning and progress.	Good scheme, which clearly records sequenced teaching and learning activities, methods, resources and planned assessment. Provides a very clear insight into planned structure of learning and progress.	Brief scheme lacking in some detail, but sufficient information to gauge planned outline of teaching and learning activities, resources and assessment.	Very brief or no scheme of work available. Little more than a list of topics. Cursory.
18	Lesson Plan	Highly detailed – timing, structure, resources and method. Excellent range of activities planned to meet different learning style/needs. Excellent links to scheme.	Good, clear structure – identifies resources, and activities linked to different learning styles/needs. Clear contextual links to scheme.	Acceptable outline of teaching method, learner activity and achievement. Some links to scheme of work evident.	Sketchy with minimum detail. Insufficient teaching and learning activities or little relationship to scheme of work.

Please use this as a handy checklist of what we hope to see in lessons

Take note of learner comments

Planning	Quality of Learning/ Delivery of Session
Lesson Plan/Scheme of Work	Students focused and committed
Professionally produced hand-outs and use of learning resources	Differentiated activities and teaching strategies
Probing Targeted Q&A	All learners actively engaged and participative
Stretching, challenging extension activities	Learners aware of what to do
Embedded Skills for Life	Learners' use of ILT – embedded into session
Written feedback promotes improvement	Good attendance and punctuality
Teacher use of ILT effective	Recap of previous and links to future tasks
Equality & Diversity clearly addressed	Health & Safety appropriately monitored
High expectations of all students	Work skills/employability clearly identified
Clear evidence of tracking progress	Homework and other assessments set/collected & marked
Stimulating and challenging session for all students	Effective additional learning support
The learning environment stimulates and inspires the learners	Variety of teaching methods and pace suited to session
Clear targets and outcomes defined and shared	Individual learner reviews/ assessment and feedback Learning clearly assessed and checked
Being healthy – e.g. promoting student self-esteem, encouraging and supporting individuals	Staying Safe – e.g. identifying/ managing risks. Awareness of discrimination and bullying. All students wearing ID
Enjoying and achieving – support disaffected learners, monitoring attendance, behaviour, academic and personal development	Making a Positive Contribution – e.g. understand rights, responsibilities, opinions and views of others

© Matt O'Leary, *Classroom Observation*, Routledge 2014.

Economic Well Being – developing team working and self-confidence. Encouraging work experience

Personalised learning identifies learning styles, extension tasks, level of experience

Learning Assistants included in planning

Learning Assistant deployed appropriately

Observation Grades

1 = Outstanding	All students demonstrate high standard of learning. Individuals fully differentiated on tasks and activities. Inspired, stretched, challenged and supported over and above expected level of performance, to meet individual learning outcomes. High standard of students' work.
2 = Good	All students demonstrate learning. Individuals motivated and working well above expected level of performance. Good differentiation of tasks to meet individual needs and learning outcomes. Good standard of student work.
3 = Satisfactory	Most students demonstrate learning. Evidence of planning but insufficient differentiation. Well executed lesson. Lesson has clear objectives and learners know what is expected of them. Learners working productively expected level. Majority of students' work satisfactory.
4 = Unsatisfactory	Little learning takes place. Standard of student work unsatisfactory. Inadequately planned, differentiated and executed lesson. Aims not met or at appropriate level for course.

Midshire College observation report form

Observee	Observer
....	....
FT/Fractional/VT	Date
....	....
Faculty	Location
....	....
School	Subject Sector Area
....	....

Course	No of learners of register
....	....
Course Code	
....	
Module/Unit	No of learners in session
....	....
Mode FT/PT/Other	Age range of learners
	Pre 16 16–18 19 WBL
....	
Time	
....	

Details of Learning Support:

| |
| |
| |
| |

Signature Observee   ....

Date   ....

Signature Observer   ....

Date   ....

Signature of audit observer (if appropriate)

....

Date   ....

In the following section, please provide observations under the following headings:
- Learning
- Planning and Preparation
- Teaching and Learning methods
- Attention to individual needs
- Managing the learning process
- Assessment and feedback
- Learning resources and environment
- Attainment

Key Strengths	Evidence
Key Areas for Improvement	Evidence

Functional skills comments:

```



```

Health & Safety, Safer Learner and Safeguarding comments:

```



```

Every Learner Matters comments (*Be healthy, Stay safe, Enjoy & achieve, Make a positive contribution, Achieve economic well-being*):

```



```

Equality and Diversity comments:

```



```

Summary of session:

```



```

Recommendations:

```



```

Grade (Teaching, Learning and Attainment)

Outstanding

Good

Satisfactory

Inadequate

(Subject to Moderation)

Indicative observation criteria for Midshire College

Assessment criteria	Outstanding Grade 1	Good Grade 2	Satisfactory Grade 3	Inadequate Grade 4
Learning **– engagement and participation of learners** **– successful completion of tasks and activities** **– enjoyment of learning**	Learners display commitment to learning; they all complete set tasks correctly and participate with enthusiasm; they demonstrate that they have enjoyed the lesson; all learners actively involved and engaged; they are highly motivated and interested; they ask and answer questions very well; high levels of co-operation; learners take responsibility where appropriate.	Learners respond well to questions, are engaged and pay attention; good involvement and engagement of learners; good level of interest and concentration; some examples of effective co-operation, interaction and initiative.	Learners are co-operative but not enthusiastic; some complete tasks as expected but some fail to do so; satisfactory involvement and engagement of learners; learners stay on task for majority of lesson; they answer questions; they do what has to be done and nothing more.	Learners lack engagement in the lesson and are not responsive; insufficient or no involvement or engagement of learners; learners told what to do and do it reluctantly; mostly passive. Learners have limited concentration and interest; some learners bored and showing it.
Planning and preparation **– scheme of work and lesson plan** **– preparation for the lesson** **– introduction, aims and objectives**	Comprehensive scheme of work; detailed lesson plan with timing, structure, methods, resources, assessment and differentiation; careful preparation of highly appropriate learning materials; comprehensive introduction with aims and objectives explained, and displayed; learners demonstrate clear understanding of purpose.	Good scheme of work and lesson plan; good preparation for the lesson; clear aims and objectives shared with learners at beginning of session; learners clear about learning purpose.	Brief scheme of work lacking in some detail; adequate lesson plan; satisfactory preparation; brief introduction with objectives stated by the teacher; learning aims and objectives basic but realistic in lesson context; learners generally know what they will be doing and why.	Very brief or no scheme of work available; sketchy or no lesson plan; poor preparation with inappropriate, poorly designed or out of date materials; little if any introduction; no clear aims and objectives stated or shared with learners; learners unsure, confused or do not know what they will be doing or why.
Teaching and learning methods **– teacher's subject knowledge** **– teaching methods and activities**	Teachers have high levels of subject and vocational expertise; excellent range and creative approaches used to maximise learning and involve learners; highly appropriate for subject; highly effective	Teachers have good levels of subject and vocational expertise; good range of learning methods used to engage learners and promote learning; effective identification and cross-referencing of key/basic skills in lesson plan	Teachers have a sound knowledge of the curriculum and course requirements; appropriate range of methods and teacher makes some effort to vary approach and involve learners; some	Command of the subject is inadequate; too much emphasis on 'chalk and talk'; insufficient active learning with learners passive and disengaged; insufficient or no identification and cross-referencing of key/basic

– effectiveness of support workers **– clarity of explanations and instructions** **– class, group, pair and individual learning** **– appropriate pace and purposeful ethos** **– Skills for Life [key & basic skills]** **– review and recap of learning**	identification and cross-referencing of key/basic skills in lesson plan activities/resources. Key skills evidence used very effectively in portfolios and preparation for national tests; highly effective review of learning at intervals throughout lesson and very clear summary linked to learning objectives.	activities and resources; key skills evidence used effectively in portfolios and preparation for national tests; good review/recap at points in the lesson and clear summary of learning progress at end with reference to next lesson.	identification and cross-referencing of key/basic skills in lesson plan activities and resources; some key skills evidence used in portfolios and preparation for tests; some review of learning and brief summary at end of lesson and brief reference to next lesson.	skills in lesson plan activities and resources; opportunities missed to inform learners about key skills evidence which could be used in portfolios or preparation for national tests; insufficient or no review of learning and/or insufficient or no summary at end.
Attention to individual needs **– learning styles taken into account** **– effectiveness of individual learning plans** **– differentiation to meet all learning needs** **– variety of teaching and learning strategies** **– promotion of equality and diversity** **– responses to additional support needs**	Highly effective identification of individual learning needs through learning styles analyses and use of diagnostic assessment; excellent support provided through differentiated resources and activities; structured group/individual work and in-class customised support (as appropriate).	Good identification of individual learning needs through learning style analyses and use of diagnostic assessment; good individual support evident through development and use of resources, activities and support in lesson (where appropriate).	Some identification of individual learning needs through learning style analyses and diagnostic assessment; some individual support evident through development and use of resources, activities and support in lesson (where appropriate).	Insufficient identification of individual learning needs; little evidence of learning style or diagnostic assessment; resources and activities insufficiently developed or amended to meet different learning needs or levels; insufficient support in-class even though clearly needed.

(Continued)

Assessment criteria	Outstanding Grade 1	Good Grade 2	Satisfactory Grade 3	Inadequate Grade 4
Managing the learning process – prompt start and punctuality of learners – behaviour of learners – encouragement for independent learning – productive working relationships – challenge and inspiration	Learners have excellent record of attendance (90%+) and exemplary punctuality; highly effective group/individual management; very clear directions; behaviour and vocationally standards professionally and vocationally appropriate; high mutual teacher/learner value and respect; teaching promotes independent research and productive use of learners' time.	Learners have good attendance records (85%+) and almost all learners are on time; good management of group activities; clear instructions; relationships reflect vocational/ professional context; teacher and learners clearly value and respect each other; teaching encourages some independent learning and mostly good use of learners' time.	Satisfactory attendance (80%+) and most learners are on time; satisfactory management of groups and individuals; instructions generally clear; appropriate working relationships overall; teachers encourage learners to work effectively on their own, but a few learners remain too dependent on the teacher; behaviour is satisfactory	Unsatisfactory attendance (less than 80%); unsatisfactory punctuality (less than 70% on time); ineffective management of group/individual activities; instructions not always clear; teacher cannot impose his/herself; some lack of respect shown; much teaching fails to capture learners' interest, and activities are not matched to learners' needs to provide suitable challenge; rules for behaviour are not complied with.
Assessment and feedback – regular checks on learning and progress – schedule for assessments – correction of errors and feedback to learners – assessment criteria and marking of work – monitoring & recording of individual progress	Assessment is rigorous and well organised; outcomes are effectively used for planning future learning; highly effective and clearly focused questioning skills used to check all learners' knowledge and progress; frequent correction of any errors and feedback on work.	Assessment is well organised; outcomes are used for planning future learning; good questioning used to enhance learning and check progress; correction of errors and feedback on areas for improvement. Good records of progress are maintained.	Assessment is adequate for teachers to monitor learners' progress and plan their lessons and training; learners know what to do to improve; questions used to recapitulate, consolidate and confirm learning but some opportunities missed; most errors corrected and some feedback.	Assessment is inadequate and some learners do not know how to improve; ineffective, insufficient or no questioning of learners' knowledge or progress; errors in learners' written and oral responses are not corrected and little feedback is given on areas for improvement.

Learning resources and environment
– availability and use of equipment
– teaching accommodation
– health and safety issues
– learning environment

Learning resources including ILT are used very well by teachers and learners; this promotes effective learning; excellent range and high quality (creative) materials clearly presented and well used; health and safety issues stressed throughout; professional learning environment, wholly relevant, fit for purpose, excellent accessibility and safely equipped. (Practical sessions have a session risk assessment, working brief, information and instruction is comprehensive and proportional to the risk. It is unlikely that a theory class will require a written risk assessment. Supervision requirements for the session are comprehensive and reflect activity.)	Learning resources including ILT are used well by teachers and learners to promote learning; good range of materials and resources are effectively used to support session content; good emphasis on health and safety issues; good accommodation, fit for purpose, well-laid out and resourced, accessible and safely equipped. (Risk assessment, working brief, information and instruction thorough. Supervision of the session is good, reflecting activities and the ability/age of the learners.)	Learning resources including ILT support independent study and complement classroom teaching; satisfactory resources and learning materials support learning but some less satisfactory worksheets etc; satisfactory attention to health and safety; satisfactory accommodation, fairly basic but safe, does not hinder learning. (Risk assessment, working brief, information and instruction in place but lacks in detail in some areas. Supervision of the session is in place and is adequate.)	Learning resources including ILT are not used effectively; insufficient or inadequate level of resources to support learning; ineffective or inadequate attention to health and safety; environment has unsatisfactory noise, temperature, interruptions; this inhibits learning. (Risk assessment, working brief, information and instruction are not in place and/or lack direction and/or are out of date. Supervision of the session is insufficient for the activity type or there is none.)

(Continued)

Assessment criteria	Outstanding Grade 1	Good Grade 2	Satisfactory Grade 3	Inadequate Grade 4
Attainment **– standards of** **work produced** **during the** **lesson** **– progress** **towards agreed** **learning targets** **– distance** **travelled**	Work produced by learners is excellent; they are all making very good progress towards their targets. All learners demonstrate excellent knowledge and skills, working above standard for level and stage of programme; learners' progress is considerably better than might be expected.	Learners produce good work in class; most are making tangible progress towards their learning targets; most complete tasks within set times; learners using good skills and working at and beyond standard for level and stage of programme; learners respond well to the challenges set for them.	Work produced is satisfactory; many learners are making progress but a few are not. Majority of learners working appropriately for standard and stage of programme; most learners are likely to achieve their qualification.	Many learners produce work of an unsatisfactory standard; few show tangible progress towards their targets; a few complete tasks successfully but many do not; level of knowledge and skills is inappropriate for stage and level of programme; some learners unlikely to achieve qualification.

Ofsted inspectors' observation checklist

The content of this checklist is taken from Ofsted's guidance for inspectors on judging the quality of teaching and the use of assessment to support learning. Observations and judgements should be recorded separately, using examples wherever possible.

Quality of learning	✓
– What are different groups and individual pupils *actually* learning as opposed to *doing*?	
– Are pupils consolidating previous skills/knowledge or learning something new?	
– Can all pupils make the links between previous/new learning?	
– Can pupils talk about what they are learning, as opposed to simply describing what they are doing?	
– Do they consistently produce work of a good standard?	
– Are pupils working independently? Are they self-reliant – do they make the most of the choices they are given or do they find it difficult to make choices? To what extent do pupils take responsibility for their own learning?	
– How well do pupils collaborate with others? Do they ask questions, of each other, of the teacher or other adults, about what they are learning?	
– Are pupils creative, do they show initiative?	
– How well do pupils follow routines/expectations?	

Enjoyment of learning and attitudes	✓
– Are pupils engaged, working hard, making a good effort, applying themselves, concentrating and productive?	
– Are pupils developing habits of good learning?	
– Are pupils happy with their work? Are they proud of it?	
– Are pupils interested in their work and in what they are learning? Or are they easily distracted?	
– How smooth is the transition from teacher input to group work? Do pupils settle to work easily?	

Assessment to support learning	✓
– Are there any significant differences in the learning of different groups of pupils, or of any individuals?	
– Are pupils involved in assessing their own learning and progress?	
– Do pupils know what they are learning and why?	
– Do pupils have targets and do they understand what they mean/what to do to achieve them?	

Pupils' progress	✓
– Are different groups making the same/different progress?	
– What new skills and knowledge are pupils gaining?	
– How well are pupils developing ideas and increasing their understanding?	
– Are pupils making gains at a good rate in lessons and over time as shown in their work and the school's records?	
– How are weak/good literacy, numeracy and ICT skills affecting pupils' progress?	

The quality of provision	✓
– Are staff using assessment for learning strategies to enable them to differentiate effectively?	
– Are activities pitched at the right level to challenge pupils of different abilities?	
– How well does marking identify strengths and diagnose next steps to improvement?	
– How good is the dialogue and oral feedback? Are teachers alert to pupils' lack of understanding during lessons?	
– How effectively do staff use questioning to gauge pupils' understanding? Are expectations of behaviour sufficiently high?	
– Are teachers alert to the social, emotional, and learning, needs of individuals?	
– What impact are any support staff having?	
– Are resources sufficient? Are they well matched to needs to support learning?	

Taken from: http://www.tes.co.uk/ResourceDetail.aspx?storyCode=6038827 Accessed 16 September 2012.

References

Adshead, L., White, P. T. and Stephenson, A. (2006) Introducing peer observation of teaching to GP teachers: a questionnaire study. *Medical Teacher*, 28, 68–73.

Ainley, P. and Bailey, B. (1997) *The Business of Learning – Staff and Student Experiences of Further Education in the 1990s*. London: Cassell.

Armitage, A., Byrant, R., Dunnill, R., Hammersley, M., Hayes, D., Hudson, A. and Lawless, S. (2003) *Teaching and Training in Post-compulsory Education* (2nd edn). Buckingham: OUP.

Association of Teachers and Lecturers (ATL) (2008) *ATL Advice – Classroom Observation*. Available online at: http://www.atl.org.uk/Images/ADV19%20classroom%20observation.pdf. Accessed 23/3/2010.

Avis, J. (1996) 'The enemy within: quality and managerialism in education', in J. Avis, M. Bloomer, G. Esland, D. Gleeson and D. Hodgkinson (eds), *Knowledge and Nationhood*. London: Cassell, pp. 105–120.

Avis, J. (2003) Re-thinking trust in a performative culture: the case of education. *Journal of Education Policy*, 18(3), 315–332.

Bailey, K. M. (2001) 'Observation', in R. Carter and D. Nunan (eds), *The Cambridge Guide to Teaching English to Speakers of Other Languages*. Cambridge: Cambridge University Press, pp. 114–119.

Bailey, A., Curtis, A. and Nunan, D. (2001) *Pursuing Professional Development: the Self as Source*. Boston, MA: Heinle and Heinle.

Ball, S. J. (2001) 'Performativities and fabrications in the education economy: towards the performative society', in D. Gleeson and C. Husbands (eds), *The Performing School: Managing Teaching and Learning in a Performance Culture*. London: Routledge-Falmer, pp. 210–226.

Ball, S. J. (2003) The teacher's soul and the terrors of performativity. *Journal of Education Policy*, 18(2), 215–228.

Ball, S. J. (2012) *Global Education Inc. New Policy Networks and the Neoliberal Imaginary*. London: Routledge.

Bartlett, L. (1990) 'Teacher development through reflective teaching', in J. C. Richards and D. Nunan (eds), *Second Language Teacher Education*. Cambridge: Cambridge University Press, pp. 202–214.

Bathmaker, A. and Avis, J. (2005) Becoming a lecturer in further education in England: the construction of professional identity and the role of communities of practice. *Journal of Education for Teaching*, 31(1), 47–62.

Bennett, S. and Barp, D. (2008) Peer observation – a case for doing it online. *Teaching in Higher Education*, 13(5), 559–570.

Black, P. (1998) *Testing: Friend or Foe? Theory and Practice of Assessment and Testing*. London: Falmer.

Black, P. and Wiliam, D. (1998) Assessment and classroom learning. *Assessment in Education: Principles, Policy & Practice*, 5(1), 7–78.

Boffey, D. (2012) Lecturers should need a teaching qualification, says NUS president. *The Observer*, 22 April 2012. Available online at: http://www.guardian.co.uk/education/2012/apr/22/liam-burn-nus-academics-lecturers. Accessed 28/7/2012.

Brookfield, S. D. (1995) *Becoming a Critically Reflective Teacher*. San Francisco, CA: Jossey-Bass.

Brookfield, S. D. (2005) *The Power of Critical Theory for Adult Learning and Teaching*. Maidenhead: Open University Press.

Brooks, V. (2012) Marking as judgment. *Research Papers in Education*, 27(1), 63–80.

Brown, J., Collins, S. and Duguid, P. (1989) Situated learning and culture of learning. *Educational Researcher*, 18, 32–42.

Brown, S., Jones, G. and Rawnsley, S. (1993) *Observing Teaching*. SEDA Paper 79. Birmingham: SEDA.

Browne, J. (2010) *Securing a Sustainable Future for Higher Education: An Independent Review of Higher Education Funding & Student Finance*. London: Department for Business, Innovation and Skills (BIS).

Burrows, J. (2008) *Trainee Perceptions of Observation*. Huddersfield: Huddersfield Consortium.

Calandra, B., Brantley-Dias, L. and Dias, M. (2006) Using digital video for professional development: a preservice teacher's experience with reflection. *Journal of Computing in Teacher Education*, 22(4), 137–145.

Calandra, B., Gurvitch, R. and Lund, J. (2008) An exploratory study of digital video editing as a tool for teacher preparation. *Journal of Technology and Teacher Education, 16*(2), 137–153.

Callaghan, J. (1976) 'Towards a national debate', speech given by Prime Minister James Callaghan at Ruskin College, Oxford on 18 October 1976. Available online at: http://education.guardian.co.uk/thegreatdebate/story/0,,574645,00.html. Accessed 10/1/2012.

Campbell, J., Kyriakides, L., Muijs, D. and Robinson, W. (2004) *Assessing Teacher Effectiveness – Developing a Differentiated Model*. London: Routledge-Falmer.

Clarke, J. and Newman, J. (1997) *The Managerial State*. London: Sage Publications.

Cockburn, J. (2005) Perspectives and politics of classroom observation. *Research in Post-Compulsory Education*, 10(3), 373–388.

Coffield, F. (2012a) To grade or not to grade. *Adults Learning*, Summer, 38–39.

Coffield, F. (2012b) Why the McKinsey reports will not improve school systems. *Journal of Education Policy*, 27(1), 131–149.

Coffield, F. and Edward, S. (2009) Rolling out 'good', 'best' and 'excellent' practice. What next? Perfect practice? *British Educational Research Journal*, 35(3), 371–390.

Cogan, D. (1995) Using a counselling approach in teacher supervision. *The Teacher Trainer*, 9(3), 3–6.

Cohen, L., Manion, L. and Morrison, K. (2011) *Research Methods in Education* (7th edn). London: Routledge.

Colley, H., James, D. and Diment, K. (2007) Unbecoming teachers: towards a more dynamic notion of professional participation. *Journal of Education Policy*, 22(2), 173–193.

Cope, P., Bruce, A., McNally, J. and Wilson, G. (2003) Grading the practice of teaching: an unholy union of incompatibles. *Assessment & Evaluation in Higher Education*, 28(6), 673–684.

Cosh, J. (1999) Peer observation: a reflective model. *ELT Journal*, 53(1), 22–27.

Croll, P. (1986) *Systematic Classroom Observation*. London: Falmer.

Cruickshank, D. R. and Applegate, J. H. (1981) Reflective teaching as a strategy for teacher growth. *Educational Leadership*, 38(7), 553–554.

Darling-Hammond, L. (2000) Teacher quality and student achievement: a review of state policy evidence. *Educational Policy Analysis Archives,* 8(1), 430–441. Available online at: http://epaa.asu.edu/ojs/article/view/392. Accessed 12/6/2012.

Darling-Hammond, L. (2006) Constructing 21st-century teacher education. *Journal of Teacher Education*, 57(3), 300–314.

Department for Education and Employment (DfEE) (1999) *The Learning and Skills Council Prospectus: Learning to Succeed*. London: HMSO.

Department for Education and Employment (DfEE) (2001) *Raising Standards in Post-16 Learning: Self-Assessment and Development Plans*. London: HMSO.

Department for Education and Skills (DfES) (2002) *Success for All: Reforming Further Education and Training*. London: DfES.

Department for Education and Skills (DfES) (2004) *Equipping our Teachers for the Future: Reforming Initial Teacher Training for the Learning and Skills Sector*. London: DfES.

Department for Education and Skills (DfES) (2006) *Further Education: Raising Skills, Improving Life Chances*. London: The Stationery Office.

Department for Education (DfE) (2010) *The Importance of Teaching*. Schools White Paper. London: DfE.

Department for Education DfE (2012) Teachers' Standards – May 2012. Available online at: https://www.education.gov.uk/publications/eOrderingDownload/teachers%20standards.pdf. Accessed 13/01/2013.

Dewey, J. (1904) 'The relation of theory to practice in education', in C. A. McMurry (ed.), *Third Yearbook: National Society for the Scientific Study of Education*. Chicago, IL: University of Chicago Press, pp. 9–30.

Dewey, J. (1933) 'How we think', in W. B. Kolesnick (1958) *Mental Discipline in Modern Education*. Madison: University of Wisconsin Press.

Dudley, P. (2007) Lessons for Learning: using lesson study to innovate, develop and transfer pedagogic approaches and metapedagogy. London: TLRP. Available online at: http://www.bera.ac.uk/lesson-study/. Accessed: 4/10/2011.

Dudley, P. (2008) 'Lesson study development in England: practice to policy', paper presented at the World Association of Lesson Studies Annual Conference, Hong Kong, December 2008. Available at: http://www.tlrp-archive.org/tlrp/upload/assets/1231760840_PDWALS08.pdf. Accessed 4/10/2011.

Dyke, M., Harding, A. and Liddon, S. (2008) How can online observation support the assessment and feedback, on classroom performance, to trainee teachers at a distance and in real time? *Journal of Further and Higher Education*, 32(1), 37–46.

Ecclestone, K. (2001) 'I know a 2:1 when I see it': understanding criteria for degree classifications in franchised university programmes. *Journal of Further and Higher Education*, 25, 301–313.

Edge, J. (1992) *Cooperative Development*. Harlow: Longman.

Egan, R. (1986) *The Skilled Helper* (3rd edn). Belmont, CA: Wadsworth.

Ewens, D. and Orr, S. (2002) *Tensions Between Evaluation and Peer Review Models: Lessons from the HE/FE Border*. London: LTSN Generic Centre.

Fawcett, M. (1996) *Learning Through Child Observation*. London: Jessica Kingsley.

Fielding, M., Bragg, S., Craig, J., Cunningham, I., Eraut, M., Gillison, S., Horne, M., Robinson, C. and Thorp, J. (2005) *Factors Influencing the Transfer of Good Practice*. Research Report RR615. London: Department for Education and Skills (DfES).

Finlay, I., Spours, K., Steer, R., Coffield, F., Gregson, M. and Hodgson, A. (2007) 'The heart of what we do': policies on teaching, learning and assessment in the learning and skills sector. *Journal of Vocational Education & Training*, 59(2), 137–153.

Flanders, N. (1970) *Analysing Teacher Behaviour*. Reading, MA: Addison-Wesley.

Foster, P. (1996) *Observing Schools – A Methodological Guide*. London: Paul Chapman Publishing.

Foucault, M. (1977) *Discipline and Punish – The Birth of the Prison*. Harmondsworth: Penguin.

Foucault, M. (1980) *Power/Knowledge – Selected Interviews and Other Writings 1972–1977*. Brighton: The Harvester Press.

Foucault, M. (2002) *Michel Foucault – Power – Essential Works of Foucault 1954–1984*: Vol. 3. J. D. Faubion (Ed.). London: Penguin Books.

Freire, P. (1972) *Pedagogy of the Oppressed*. Harmondsworth: Penguin.

Freire, P. (2005) *Teachers as Cultural Workers – Letters to Those Who Dare Teach.* Cambridge, MA: Westview Press.

Freire, P. and Shor, I. (1987) *A Pedagogy for Liberation – Dialogues on Transforming Education.* London: Macmillan.

Fullan, M. and Hargreaves, A. (1992) *What's Worth Fighting for in Your School.* Buckingham: Open University Press.

Fullerton, H. (2003) 'Observation of teaching', in H. Fry, S. Ketteridge and S. Marshall (Eds), *A Handbook for Teaching and Learning in Higher Education* (2nd edn). London: Kogan-Page.

Further Education National Training Organisation (FENTO) (1999) *National Standards for Teaching and Supporting Learning in Further Education in England and Wales.* London: FENTO.

Gale, T. and Densmore, K. (2003) *Engaging Teachers: Towards a Radical Democratic Agenda for Schooling.* Maidenhead: Open University Press.

Ghaye, T. (2011) *Teaching and Learning Through Reflective Practice: A Practical Guide for Positive Action.* London: Routledge.

Gibbs, G. (1988) *Learning by Doing: A Guide to Teaching and Learning Methods.* Oxford: Further Educational Unit: Oxford Polytechnic.

Gipps, C. (1994) *Beyond Testing: Towards a Theory of Educational Assessment.* London: Falmer Press.

Gleeson, D. (2001) Style and substance in education leadership: FE as a case in point. *Journal of Education Policy,* 16(3), 188–196.

Gleeson, D., Davies, J. and Wheeler, E. (2005) On the making and taking of professionalism in the further education workplace. *British Journal of Sociology of Education,* 26(4), 445–460.

Gosling, D. (2002) *Models of Peer Observation of Teaching.* London: LTSN Generic Centre.

Graham, D. (1987) *In the Light of Torches. Teacher Appraisal, a Further Study.* London: Industrial Society.

Gramsci, A. (1971) *Selections from the Prison Notebooks of Antonio Gramsci* edited and translated by Q. Hoare and G. Nowell Smith. London: Lawrence and Wishart.

Grierson, A. and Gallagher, T. L. (2009) Seeing is believing: creating a catalyst to teacher change through a demonstration classroom initiative. *Professional Development in Education,* 35(4), 567–584.

Grubb, W. N. (2000) Opening classrooms and improving teaching: lessons from school inspections in England. *Teachers College Record,* 102(4), 696–723.

Hammersley-Fletcher, L. and Orsmond, P. (2004) Evaluating our peers: is peer observation a meaningful process? *Studies in Higher Education,* 29(4), 489–503.

Hammersley-Fletcher, L. and Orsmond, P. (2005) Reflecting on reflective practices within peer observation. *Studies in Higher Education,* 30(2), 213–224.

Hardman, J. (2007) *The Use of Teaching Observation in Higher Education: An exploration of the relationship between teacher observation for quality assurance and quality improvement in teaching in higher education, in the light of further education sector experience.* Report produced for Escalate August 2007. Available online at: http://escalate.ac.uk/3311. Accessed 20/1/2010.

Hattie, J. (2003) 'Teachers make a difference: what is the research evidence?', paper presented at the Australian Council for Educational Research Annual Conference on Building Teacher Quality, Melbourne, October.

Hattie, J. (2005) 'What is the nature of evidence that makes a difference in learning', paper presented at the ACER Research Conference: using data to support learning, 7–9 August 2005, Melbourne.

Hay McBer Group (2000) *Research into Teacher Effectiveness: A Model of Teacher Effectiveness.* London: HMSO.

Hodkinson, P., Biesta, G., James, D. and Postlethwaite, K. (2005) *Transforming Learning Cultures in Further Education.* London, TLRP.

Hoyle, E. (1995) 'Changing concepts of a profession', in H. Busher and R. Sarah (Eds.), *The Management of Professionals in Schools.* London: Longman, pp. 59–70.

Hoyle, E. and Wallace, M. (2005) *Educational Leadership: Ambiguity, Professionals and Managerialism.* London: Sage.

Hyland, T and Merrill, B. (2003) *The Changing Face of Further Education – Lifelong Learning, Inclusion and Community Values in Further Education.* London: RoutledgeFalmer.

Institute for Learning (IfL) (2010) *Brilliant Teaching and Training in FE and Skills.* London: Institute for Learning.

Institute for Learning (IfL) (2012) *Leading Learning and Letting Go: Building Expansive Learning Environments in FE.* London: Institute for Learning.

Ingvarson, L (2001) 'Developing standards and assessments for accomplished teachers: a responsibility of the profession', in D. Middlewood and C. E. M. Cardno (eds), *Managing Teacher Appraisal and Performance: A Comparative Approach.* London: Routledge, pp. 160–180.

James, D. and Biesta, G. (eds) (2007) *Improving Learning Cultures in Further Education.* London: Routledge.

James, D. and Gleeson, D. (2007) 'Professionality in FE learning cultures', in D. James and G. Biesta (eds), *Improving Learning Cultures in Further Education.* London: Routledge, pp. 126–140.

Jones, J., Jenkin, M. and Lord, S. (2006) *Developing Effective Teacher Performance.* London: Paul Chapman Publishing.

Joyce, B. and Showers, B. (2002) *Student Achievement Through Staff Development* (3rd edn). London: Longman.

Kincheloe, J. L. (2004) The knowledges of teacher education: developing a critical complex epistemology. *Teacher Education Quarterly,* 31(1), 49–66.

Kolb, D. A. (1984) *Experiential Learning Experience as a Source of Learning and Development.* New Jersey: Prentice Hall.

Lave, J. and Wenger, E. (1991) *Situated Learning – Legitimate Peripheral Participation.* Cambridge: Cambridge University Press.

Lawson, T. (2011) Sustained classroom observation: what does it reveal about changing teaching practices? *Journal of Further and Higher Education.* First published on (iFirst): http://dx.doi.org /10.1080/0309877X.2011.558891.

Lee, J. (2007) Are you being observed? *Times Educational Supplement,* 15 June 2007.

Lewis, C., Perry, R. and Murata, A. (2006) How should research contribute to instructional improvement? The case of lesson study. *Educational Researcher,* 35(3), 3–14.

Lieberman, J. (2009) Reinventing teacher professional norms and identities: the role of lesson study and learning communities. *Professional Development in Education,* 35(1), 83–99.

Lifelong Learning UK (LLUK) (2006) *New Overarching Professional Standards for Teachers, Tutors and Trainers in the Lifelong Learning Sector.* London: LLUK.

Lifelong Learning UK (LLUK) (2007) *Guidance for Awarding Institutions on Teacher Roles and Initial Teaching Qualifications.* London: LLUK.

Lipman, P. (2010) 'Education and the right to the city: the intersection of urban policies, education and poverty', in M. W. Apple, S. J. Ball and L. A. Gandin (eds), *The Routledge International Handbook of the Sociology of Education.* London: Routledge, pp. 241–252.

Liptak, L. (2002) It's a matter of time: scheduling lesson study at Paterson NJ School 2. *Research for Better Schools: Currents,* V(2), 6–7. Available online at: http://www.rbs.org/Special-Topics/ Lesson-Study/Lesson-Study-Conference-2002/Why-Lesson-Study/207/. Accessed 1/2/2013.

Loughran, J. J. (2002) Effective reflective practice in search of meaning in learning about teaching. *Journal of Teacher Education,* 53(1), 33–43.

Lowe, R. (2007) *The Death of Progressive Education: How Teachers Lost Control of the Classroom.* Oxford: Routledge.

Maguire, M. (2010) 'Towards a sociology of the global teacher', in M. W. Apple, S. J. Ball and L. A. Gandin (eds), *The Routledge International Handbook of the Sociology of Education.* London: Routledge, pp. 58–68.

Mahony, P. and Hextall, I. (2000) *Reconstructing Teaching Standards, Performance and Accountability*. London: Routledge.

Marriott, G. (2001) *Observing Teachers at Work*. Oxford: Heinemann.

McKinsey and Company (2007) *How the World's Best Performing School Systems Come Out on Top*. Available at: http://www.mckinsey.com/clientservice/socialsector/resources/pdf/Worlds_School_Systems_Final.pdf. Accessed 10/12/12.

McMahon, T., Barrett, T. and O'Neill, G. (2007) Using observation of teaching to improve quality: finding your way through the muddle of competing conceptions, confusion of practice and mutually exclusive intentions. *Teaching in Higher Education*, 12(4), 499–511.

Metcalfe, C. (1999) Developmental classroom observation as a component of monitoring and evaluating the work of subject departments in secondary schools. *Journal of In-service Education*, 25(3), 447–459.

Middlewood, D. and Cardno, C. (eds) (2001) *Managing Teacher Appraisal and Performance: A Comparative Approach*. London: Routledge Falmer.

Mitchell, N., Hobson, A. and Sorensen, B. (2007) *External Evaluation of the University of Sussex In-School Teacher Education Programme (INSTEP). Final Report to the Gatsby Charitable Foundation (Gatsby Technical Education Projects)*. University of Nottingham, School of Education. Available at: http://www.irisconnect.co.uk/img/stand_alone_files/file/original/instep_final_report-12.pdf. Accessed 12/2/2013.

Montgomery, D. (2002) *Helping Teachers Develop through Classroom Observation* (2nd edn). London: David Fulton Publishers.

Moon, J. (2004) *A Handbook of Reflective and Experiential Learning: Theory and Practice*. London: RoutledgeFalmer.

Moore, A. (2004) *The Good Teacher – Dominant Discourses in Teaching and Teacher Education*. Oxford: Routledge.

Muijs, D. (2008) *Researching Teacher Effectiveness*. Keynote address at School of Education Annual Research Conference, University of Wolverhampton, June 2008.

Muijs, D and Reynolds, D. (2003) Student background and teacher effects on achievement and attainment in mathematics. *Educational Research and Evaluation*, 9(1), 21–35.

Muijs, D. and Reynolds, D. (2005) *Effective Teaching: Evidence and Practice* (2nd edn). London: Sage.

Murdoch, G. (2000) Introducing a teacher-supportive evaluation system. *ELT Journal*, 54(1), 54–64.

Newman, J. (2001) *Modernising Governance: New Labour, Policy and Society*. London: Sage.

National Union of Teachers (NUT) (2006) *A Classroom Observation Protocol: Guidelines for NUT School Representatives*. Available online at: http://www.teachers.org.uk/node/1335. Accessed: 22/1/2010.

National Union of Teachers (NUT) (2007) Classroom observation: no to grading of lessons. *NUT News*, *17*, September 2007. Available online at: http://www.teachers.org.uk/node/6298. Accessed: 22/1/2010.

Ofsted (2003) *The Initial Training of Further Education Teachers: A Survey*. London: Ofsted Publications Centre.

Ofsted (2004a) *Why Colleges Fail*. London: Ofsted Publications Centre.

Ofsted (2004b) *Why Colleges Succeed*. London: Ofsted Publications Centre.

Ofsted (2008a) *How Colleges Improve*. London: Ofsted Publications Centre.

Ofsted (2008b) *A Handbook for Inspecting Colleges*. London: Ofsted Publications Centre.

Ofsted (2010) *Good Professional Development in Schools*. London: Ofsted Publications Centre.

Ofsted (2012a) 'Ofsted announces changes to inspections of schools, further education and skills, and initial teacher education'. Available online at: http://www.ofsted.gov.uk/news/ofsted-announces-changes-inspections-of-schools-further-education-and-skills-and-initial-teacher-edu. Accessed 2/11/2012.

Ofsted (2012b) *The Report of Her Majesty's Chief Inspector of Education, Children's Services and Skills – Schools' Annual Report 2011/12*. Available at: http://www.ofsted.gov.uk/resources/report-of-her-majestys-chief-inspector-of-education-childrens-services-and-skills-schools. Accessed: 04/02/2012.

Ofsted (2012c) *A Good Education for All*. London: Ofsted Publications Centre.

Ofsted (2013) *The Framework for School Inspection*. January 2013, No. 120100. Available at: http://www.ofsted.gov.uk/resources/framework-for-school-inspection. Accessed: 04/02/2012.

O'Leary, M. (2000) *To What Extent can Unseen Observation be Considered a Useful Tool for Promoting Active Teacher Development in an In-service Context?* Unpublished MA dissertation, King's College London, September 2000.

O'Leary, M. (2006) Can inspectors really improve the quality of teaching in the PCE sector? Classroom observations under the microscope. *Research in Post-compulsory Education*, 11(2), 191–198.

O'Leary, M. (2011) *The Role of Lesson Observation in Shaping Professional Identity, Learning and Development in Further Education Colleges in the West Midlands*. Unpublished PhD Thesis, University of Warwick, September 2011.

O'Leary, M. (2012a) Exploring the role of lesson observation in the English education system: a review of methods, models and meannings. *Professional Development on Education*, 38(5), 791–810.

O'Leary, M. (2012b) Surveillance, performativity and normalised practice: the use and impact of graded lesson observations in Further Education Colleges. *Journal of Further and Higher Education*. First published online 28 May 2012 (iFirst), 1–21. Available at: http://www.tandfonline.com/doi/abs/10.1080/0309877X.2012.684036. Accessed 29/5/2012.

O'Leary, M. (2012c) Time to turn worthless lesson observation into a powerful tool for improving teaching and learning. *InTuition/CPD Matters – IfL*, issue 9, Summer, 16–18. Available at: http://www.ifl.ac.uk/__data/assets/pdf_file/0008/27890/InTuition-issue-9-Summer-2012.pdf. Accessed 04/01/2013.

O'Leary, M. and Brooks, V. (forthcoming) Raising the stakes: classroom observation in the further education sector.

Ollin, R. (2009) *The Grading of Teaching Observations: Implications for Teacher Educators in Higher Education Partnerships*. Huddersfield: Huddersfield Consortium.

Peake, G. (2006) *Observation of the Practice of Teaching*. Huddersfield: Huddersfield Consortium.

Peel, D. (2005) Peer observation as a transformatory tool? *Teaching In Higher Education*, 10(4), 489–504.

Perryman, J. (2006) Panoptic performativity and inspection regimes: disciplinary mechanisms and life under special measures. *Journal of Education Policy*, 21(2), 147–161.

Perryman, J. (2009) Inspection and the fabrication of professional and performative processes. *Journal of Education Policy*, 24(5), 611–631.

Pianta, R. C. and Hamre, B. K. (2009) Conceptualization, measurement and improvement of classroom processes: standardised observation can leverage capacity. *Educational Researcher*, 38(2), 109–119.

Pianta, R.C., La Paro, K. and Hamre, B. K. 2008. *Classroom Assessment Scoring System (CLASS)*. Baltimore: Paul H. Brookes.

Powell, G. (1999) How to avoid being the fly on the wall. *The Teacher Trainer*, 13(1), 3–4.

Quirke, P. (1996) Using unseen observations for an In-service Teacher Development Programme. *The Teacher Trainer*, 10(1), 18–20.

Ramsden, P. (1992) *Learning to Teach in Higher Education*. London: Routledge.

Randle, K. and Brady, M. (1997) Managerialism and professionalism in the 'cinderella service'. *Journal of Vocational Education and Training*, 49(1), 121–139.

Ranson, S. (1992) Towards the learning society. *Educational Management and Administration*, 20(2), 68–79.

Richards, J. C. (1991) Towards reflective teaching. *The Teacher Trainer*, 5(3), 4–8.

Richards, J. C. (1998) *Beyond Training*. Cambridge: CUP.

Richards, J. C. and Lockhart, C. (1994) *Reflective Teaching in Second Language Classrooms*. New York: CUP.

Rinvolucri, M. (1988) A role-switching exercise in teacher training. *Modern English Teacher*, Spring.

Roberson, T. J. (1998) 'Classroom observation: issues regarding validity and reliability'. Paper presented at the annual meeting of the Mid-South Education Research Association, 6 November, New Orleans, LA.

Robson, J. (1998) A profession in crisis: status, culture and identity in the further education college. *Journal of Vocational Education and Training*, 50(4), 585–607.

Rogers, C. R. (1983) *Freedom to Learn for the Eighties*. Columbus, OH: Charles E. Merrill.

Rowntree, D. (1987) *Assessing Students: How Shall We Know Them?* London: Kogan-Page.

Sachs, J. (2001) Teacher professional identity: competing discourses, competing outcomes. *Journal of Educational Policy*, 16(2), 149–161.

Sammons, P. (2006) The contribution of International Studies on educational effectiveness: current and future directions. *Educational Research and Evaluation*, 12(6), 583–593.

Sammons, P. (2008) Zero tolerance of failure and New Labour approaches to school improvement in England. *Oxford Review of Education*, 34, 651–664.

Samph, T. (1968) *Observer Effects on Teacher Behavior*. Syracuse, NY: US Department of Health, Education and Welfare.

Satterly, D. (1994) 'Quality in external assessment', in W. Harlen (ed.), *Enhancing Quality in Assessment*. London: Paul Chapman, pp. 53–70.

Schön, D. (1983) *The Reflective Practitioner*. London: Temple Smith.

Scriven, M. (1981) 'Summative teacher evaluation', in J. Millman (ed.), *Handbook of Teaching Evaluation*. London: Sage, pp. 244–271.

Shain, F. and Gleeson, D. (1999) Teachers' work and professionalism in the post incorporated FE sector. *Education and Social Justice*, 1(3), 55–63.

Sharp, S. (2006) *The Grading of Placement in Initial Teacher Education in Scotland*. Available at: http://www.scotedreview.org.uk/pdf/208.pdf. Accessed 17/5/2010.

Sheal, P. (1989) Classroom observation: training the observers. *ELT Journal*, 43(2), 92–103.

Shepherd, J. (2010) Gove's plan to help heads sack teachers anger unions. *The Guardian* 9 January, p. 6.

Shortland, S. (2004) Peer observation: a tool for staff development or compliance? *Journal of Further and Higher Education*, 28(2), 219–228.

Shulman, L. S. (1987) Sounding an alarm: a reply to Sockett. *Harvard Educational Review*, 57(4), pp. 473–482.

Simons, H. and Elliott, J. (eds) (1990) *Rethinking Appraisal and Assessment*. Milton Keynes: Open University Press.

Smith, R. and O'Leary, M. (2013) NPM in an age of austerity: knowledge and experience in further education. *Journal of Educational Administration and History*, 45(3), 244–266.

Stewart, W. (2012) Ofsted challenged to prove its 'integrity'. *Times Educational Supplement* 3 February. No. 4978. Available at: http://www.tes.co.uk/article.aspx?storycode=6172449. Accessed 02/02/2012.

Stigler, J. and Hiebert, J. (1999) *The Teaching Gap: Best Ideas from the World's Teachers for Improving Education in the Classroom*. New York: The Free Press.

Stronach, I., Corbin, B., McNamara, O., Stark. S. and Warne. T. (2002) Towards an uncertain politics of professionalism: teacher and nurse identities in flux. *Journal of Education Policy*, 17(1), 109–138.

Sullivan, P., Mousley, J. and Gervasoni, A. (2000) Caution: classroom under observation. *Asia-Pacific Journal of Teacher Education*, 28(3), 247–261.

Tilstone, C. (1998) *Observing Teaching and Learning – Principles and Practice*. London: David Fulton.

Torrance, H. (2007) Assessment *as* learning? How the use of explicit learning objectives, assessment criteria and feedback in post-secondary education and training can come to dominate learning. *Assessment in Education: Principles, Policy & Practice*, 14(3), 281–294.

University and College Union (UCU) (2009) *Lesson Observation: UCU Guidelines*. Available at: http://www.ucu.org.uk/index.cfm?articleid=2969. Accessed 22/02/2010.

UCU (2012) *Lesson Observation: UCU Principles and Position*. Available at: www.ucu.org.uk/media/pdf/5/1/ucu_lessonobservation_feb12.pdf. Accessed 14/12/12.

Van Tassel-Baska, J., Quek, C. and Feng, A. X. (2007) The development and use of a structured teacher observation scale to assess differentiated best practice (Classroom Observation Scale-Revised). *Roeper Review*, 29(2), 84–93.

Wade, S. and Hammick, M. (1999) Action learning circles: action learning in theory and practice. *Teaching In Higher Education*, 4(2), 163–178.

Wallace, M. and Hoyle, E. (2005) 'Towards effective management of a reformed teaching profession', paper presented at the 4th seminar of the ESRC Teaching and Learning Research Programme thematic seminar series 'Changing Teacher Roles, Identities and Professionalism', King's College London. Available at: http://www.kcl.ac.uk/content/1/c6/01/41/66/paper-wallace.pdf. Accessed 22/09/2010.

Wang, J. and Hartley, K. (2003) Video technology as a support for teacher education reform. *Journal of Technology and Teacher Education*, 11(1), 105–138.

Wang-Iverson, P. (2002) 'What is lesson study?' Research for better schools. *Currents*, V(2), 1–2. Available at: http://www.rbs.org/SiteData/doc/currents_0502/320e53d8a9347dcbe2243a74532a6a41/currents_0502.pdf. Accessed 20/7/2012.

Wenger, E. (1998) *Communities of Practice: Learning, Meaning, and Identity*. Cambridge: Cambridge University Press.

Whitty, G. (2000) Teacher professionalism in new times. *Journal of In-Service Education*, 26(2), 281–295.

Wilcox, B. and Gray, J. (1996) *Inspecting Schools: Holding Schools to Account and Helping Schools to Improve*. Buckingham: Open University Press.

Wilkins, C. (2011) Professionalism and the post-performative teacher: new teachers reflect on autonomy and accountability in the English school system. *Professional Development in Education*, 37(3), 389–409.

Wiliam, D. (1992) Some technical issues in assessment: a user's guide. *British Journal of Curriculum and Assessment*, 2, 11–20.

Williams, M and Watson, A. (2004) Post-lesson debriefing: delayed or immediate? An investigation of student teacher talk. *Journal of Education for Teaching*, 30(2), 85–96.

Wolf, A. (1995) *Competence-Based Assessment*. Buckingham: Open University Press.

Wragg, E. C. (1999) *An Introduction to Classroom Observation* (2nd edn). London: Routledge.

Wragg, E. C., Wikeley, F. J, Wragg, C. M. and Haynes, G. S. (1996) *Teacher Appraisal Observed*. London: Routledge.

Zeichner, K. and Liston, D. (1987) Teaching student teachers to reflect. *Harvard Educational Review*, 57(1), 23–48.

Index

Note: Page numbers in **bold** are for figures, those in *italics* are for tables.